W9-AUC-026

The Randle Report

The Randle Report

UFOs IN THE '90s

Kevin D. Randle

M. EVANS AND COMPANY, INC.
New York

M. Evans and Company, Inc.
216 East 49th Street
New York, New York 10017

Library of Congress Cataloging-in-Publication Data

Randle, Kevin D., 1949–
The Randle report : UFOs in the '90s / Kevin D. Randle.
p. cm.
Includes bibliographical references.
ISBN 0-87131-820-2
1. Unidentified flying objects. I. Title
TL789.R3238 1997
001.942—dc21 96-29946
CIP

Design and composition by *John Reinhardt Book Design*

Manufactured in the United States of America

9 8 7 6 5 4 3 2 1

Acknowledgments

This is always the hardest part of any book because there is always someone deserving who gets overlooked. And, in this book, there were so many who provided assistance, information, photographs, and documents that it would be terrible to forget him or her. So, if you should have been acknowledged and were not, I'm sorry. If you feel you should have been acknowledged and were not, that's my call. You have nothing to complain about.

First, I want to mention the brilliant work of Chris Styles and Doug Ledger. I find it almost impossible to believe that they found a photograph from the Shag Harbour crash. That was a nice piece of detective work. And, of course, thanks for allowing me to report on their work, and their help in finding Wilford Isnor, who took the picture. Thanks to him for graciously allowing me to use his picture.

Thanks also to Jerry Black for his help on the Travis Walton case, and for helping me with introductions in the Gulf Breeze case. Thanks to Rex and Carol Salisberry for allowing me to report on their wonderful investigation of that case. Thanks to Tom Carey for the work he has done in the search for the archaeologists and other witnesses in the Roswell case. Thanks to V. G. Golubic for allowing me to report, first, on the work he has done searching for the nurses. Thanks to Scott Corrales for his help chasing the Chupacabras. Thanks to John Carpenter for kindly allowing me to quote from his taped interviews with those involved with the Brazilian UFO crash. Thanks to Kent Jeffrey for his fine work (bordering on brilliant) in the chase for the truth about the Santilli film. Thanks to Dr. Jack

Kasher for allowing me to report on his work concerning STS-48 and the "ice particles."

I also wanted to thank the J. Allen Hynek Center for UFO Studies, 2457 West Peterson Avenue, Chicago, IL 60659; Fund for UFO Research, PO Box 277, Mt. Rainer, MD 20712, and The UFO Enigma Museum, 6108 S. Main Street, Roswell, NM 88201.

For those who should have been mentioned but weren't, I apologize. I'll try to do better in the future.

Contents

Introduction

The Randle Report—Positive or Negative?

IN *THE UFO CASEBOOK* I predicted that UFO investigations were about to change. I pointed out that we really didn't need to collect more tales of daylight disks or nocturnal lights. After a hundred thousand or half a million such tales had been chronicled, there wasn't much more to be learned from them. We could fill libraries with the accounts, we could analyze the raw data and search for patterns in it, but, in the end, we were left with observations—many times from unskilled observers who were unfamiliar with what was in the sky around them—and little else. UFO research was stagnating from a lack of new and exciting data.

I also predicted that UFO research would find itself in the libraries, looking at old cases, trying to learn if there was something more to them. Were the facts as they had been reported in the various books and magazines as they had been observed by the witnesses? Was there more that could be learned by a reinvestigation of those older, but now classic cases? Was UFO investigation still a worthwhile activity?

The answer here is "Yes!"

And that's what we're going to look at in this book. Those old cases that deserve more attention, and the many new cases that will someday join the ranks of the classics. What we see, in the investigation of these cases, whether it is a reexamination of a classic or a new investigation of a modern case, is an increase in the capability of the investigator. No longer do we have amateurs who have no clue as to how to proceed. Instead, we have talented researchers who are leaving no stone unturned in their quest for the truth.

In the "Alien Autopsy Circus," for example, we see Kent Jeffrey, an airline pilot by trade, who has gone to extremes in his search for information. He is largely responsible for learning the inside details of how military cameramen operated at the end of the 1940s. Given the nature of the autopsy film, this is highly relevant and very persuasive evidence. It allows us to understand why the film is in such dispute, and provides us with the information to develop an informed opinion of the event.

We see the same dedication to research in the Gulf Breeze photographic case. Carol and Rex Salisberry are able to run down some fantastic leads in their attempts to validate the pictures taken by Ed Walters. Again, they have day jobs, but are able to bring a unique investigative insight to their research so that in the end we understand what happened in Gulf Breeze. And we learn some interesting facts about the nature of UFO organizations as they exist today.

The same can be said for Jerry Black. He was interested in the Travis Walton abduction, one of the first to receive widespread publicity. Black's desire for the truth and his beliefs about the case were challenged by Walton and others. Rather than digging in to defend his position, Black charged out in a quest for new information that might shed some light on the case and provide us with the truth.

Or Chris Styles and Doug Ledger, who have been chasing information about a possible UFO crash in the Shag Harbour area of Canada. Although it is a case that took place in October 1967, their research has been conducted over the last few years, in the archives of various governmental agencies. It is a fascinating bit of detective work.

I certainly could go on in this vein. The names of those who provided data has become longer and longer. The list of those who are taking their work as UFO investigators seriously is growing. We see the evidence of the improved research as we study the cases. No longer are the researchers interested in validating their theories; they are interested in learning what the truth is, even when that truth flies in the face of their beliefs. That is something that is important to understanding UFO investigations in the last decade.

There is another point to be made here. I find that this work has become more negative than I intended. I selected the areas of study here because they were the cases that were getting the greatest attention. The Alien Autopsy film, for instance, had been talked about for nearly two years, FOX-TV has shown their special four or five times, and it was a prime discussion on dozens of other television broadcasts in other nations. The Internet, UFO magazines, and UFO conferences were filled with discussions about it. But what was the real story? It was necessary to explore it, even if the results were negative.

Or what about the Gulf Breeze case? Again, it was the subject of a number of books and television shows from tabloid television to respected programs. It, too, was a huge topic of conversation at UFO conventions. It was the subject of several investigations ordered by MUFON (the Mutual UFO Network). It deserved to be examined carefully, even if the results were not those that I wanted to see or pleasing to those supporting the case.

Or what about MJ-12? Here is something that began about a decade ago. Again, there are books on the topic, there are dozens of magazine articles, there are special reports, and there are experts to be interviewed. Are we looking at the "smoking gun" that provides us with the evidence of a government cover-up and alien visitation? Are the documents' disinformation designed to keep the lid down and the cover-up intact? Or are they frauds, designed to promote a belief in extraterrestrial visitation and to bring the spotlight to bear on specific individuals? A complete look at the UFO situation today must contain information about all the MJ-12 documents.

Or what about the Jim Ragsdale story? This is part of the famous Roswell case. Can we really examine the UFO phenomenon today without some word on the Roswell case? This is the granddaddy of them all. It is world famous. It has been written about in this country by a variety of authors, it has been featured on more television shows than Madonna, and it was the subject of one original cable television movie. And, as if that weren't enough, it was a central part of the major blockbusting movie of the summer of 1996, *Independence Day.* It has been featured in "Star Trek: Deep Space Nine," is mentioned frequently in "The X-files," and has turned up in all sorts of arenas including *Penthouse*. It is almost impossible to write a UFO book today without mentioning Roswell.

But Roswell has also become a financial football in which dozens are now involved, each with his or her own agenda. The Jim Ragsdale story seems to illustrate this better than any other. By providing the complete story, rather than the edited and somewhat misleading version that has been published by the International UFO Museum, we learn a few things about the selling of Roswell.

This is not to say that everything you are about to read is negative. Far from it. What we have is the story of the UFO phenomenon today. It is the story of solid investigation, a reliance on fact, and conclusions that are drawn not from wishful thinking, but from the facts as they have been determined. In this light, we have much that is positive in this book. We have much that leads us to conclude that alien visitation is taking place. All we have to do is separate the noise and clutter from the facts as they have been established.

So I make no apologies for the negative aspects reported here. It is the truth as I have been able to learn it. I have attempted to provide all the relevant data; how it was gathered, the sources of that data, and how it can be verified for those who wish to do so themselves. I have tried to paint an honest picture of the UFO phenomenon as it exists today. I have tried to provide all the information that can be found. And I have tried to suggest ways for those who have neither the time nor the resources to venture thousands of miles from home to continue to investigate themselves.

We look at some of the cases that are beginning to break as I complete this work. In Brazil, there seems to be a case of a UFO crash and the recovery of a number of living aliens. In Latin America, there are reports of a strange creature that kills small mammals and sucks their blood. Many researchers have linked the creature to UFOs. And, there is the continuing saga of the Air Force attempts to explain the Roswell case as nothing more than a weather balloon and radar target. Oh, sure, they've changed the name, but it is the same lame answer they provided fifty years ago, and it doesn't work any better today than it did then.

So, yes, there are some negatives in this book, but there are also some positives. This book is the story of UFO investigations today. It is the story of the research that is being conducted today. It is the story of the UFO phenomenon as it exists today and what can be done by researchers who have no personal agenda other than the truth. It demonstrates where we are and what we are doing.

But on a much more positive note, the one which everyone should come away from this work with, is the fact that we have elevated UFO research from the pits it was in to a much higher plain. We, inside the UFO community, without the help of the scientists or the journalists, have taken UFO investigations into a new arena. We might have exposed some of the classic cases as hoaxes, but we have demonstrated that we are in search of the truth, whatever that truth might be. We have done it on our own without any help from the outside, and that is the most positive aspect of UFO research today.

The Randle Report

1 The Shag Harbour UFO Crash

1967

TO DEFINE UFO INVESTIGATIONS of the 1990s, we sometimes look at cases that happened in the 1960s. The Shag Harbour UFO crash is a case that was first reported by the media in 1967 but seems to have been overlooked by UFO researchers. The data available suggested that it was nothing too spectacular, but there was a body of contradictory evidence that intrigued Canadian UFO researchers Chris Styles and Doug Ledger.

According to the thick file provided by Styles, the events began on the night of October 4, 1967, near the small fishing village of Shag Harbour, Nova Scotia. A UFO as large as sixty feet in diameter, by some estimates, seemed to descend on the surface of the water about a half a mile from shore. On it there were four bright lights that flashed in sequence.

As it hit the water, there seemed to be a bright flash and explosion. Several witnesses, thinking that some sort of aircraft might have crashed, called the Royal Canadian Mounted Police at Barrington Passage. Although some talked in terms of an aircraft accident and others mentioned only the bright lights, no one suggested a UFO.

It wasn't long before three officers were at the shoreline. Corporal Victor Werbieki was the officer in charge. Constables Ron O'Brien and Ron Pond were there to assist him. Pond had seen the lights from his cruiser and, later, as the object dived toward the water, he saw a shape behind them. In other words, Pond reported seeing not only the lights, but the fact that he saw those lights attached to a solid object.

Standing on the shore with the Mounties were a number of other witnesses. All of them could see a pale yellow light that floated about a half mile from shore. Through their binoculars, they could see that whatever floated on the surface was creating a foaming, yellow wake as it moved. Because of the location of the object, Coast Guard cutters and local fishing boats were summoned. But the object, whatever it was, disappeared before any of the boats arrived. Those on the fishing boats did see the dense yellow foam, but it had dispersed before Coast Guard Cutter #101 arrived. At three in the morning the search was suspended but was set to resume at dawn.

Styles managed to find Ronnie Newell, the captain of Coast Guard Cutter #101 that evening. He told Styles that he had seen nothing that night.

But Styles was also chasing the log book from the cutter. According to the documentation he received in November 1993, and released to him by the Canadian government, there was no proper log in 1967. The only information they have, according to the government's letter sent to Styles, was a few lines in a notebook at Clark's Harbour. Styles had those records, but noted that the times in them were wrong by as much as fifteen minutes.

A preliminary report was prepared by the Rescue Coordination Center at Halifax for transmittal to Canadian Forces Headquarters in Ottawa. It merely pointed out that something had crashed into the water of Shag Harbour. As the message was headed up the chain of command, that something was described as "no known object." According to Styles, the "Air Desk" which he described as the equivalent to Project Blue Book in the United States, was alerted and ordered the Maritime Command to dispatch a mobile unit.

According to the information available, the HMCS *Granby* was dispatched to Shag Harbour. They apparently searched the area until last light on Sunday, October 8, using divers. When they failed to find anything, the search was called off. Media interest in the case faded.

The case was "investigated" by the Condon Committee, that is, the Air Force–sponsored University of Colorado study commissioned in the late 1960s. It would have seemed that this would be exactly the sort of case that the scientists on the committee would want to investigate. There were multiple witnesses, the possibility of physical evidence, and an opportunity to do the work themselves rather than rely on the investigations conducted by UFO researchers or military officers in the past. It is listed in the *Scientific Study of Unidentified Flying Objects,* which is the final report of the Condon Committee, as case number thirty-four.

Their investigation, according to the report, consisted of telephoning several sources in the Shag Harbour area. They note that they were alerted to the case by Jim Lorenzen, then the international director of the Aerial Phenomena Research Organization (APRO), headquartered in Tucson, Arizona. Based on their telephone investigation, they decided that there was nothing to be accomplished by further work. There was no reason for one of their investigators to travel to Canada.

I want to note something here. In the short, under-two-page report, Dr. Norman E. Levine wrote,

> He [Jim Lorenzen] stated that the original report had come from two teenagers, and that the Navy was searching for wreckage. No aircraft were reported missing in the area. . . . A corporal of the RCMP [apparently Werbieki] stated that the first report had come from five young people, 15–20 yr. old, who while driving near the shore had seen three or four yellow lights in a horizontal pattern comparable in size to a 'fair-sized' aircraft. . . . They observed the light while they drove on about .25 mi., then reported the incident to the RCMP detachment.

This statement makes no mention of Pond's report of the objects or any of the observations made by other adult observers. We are left with the impression that the sighting is based on the reports of a number of young people, the majority of whom are teenagers.

In the report, Levine did write,

> Two officers [O'Brien and Pond] and the corporal had arrived about 15 min. later, in time to see the light on the water. It persisted about

five minutes longer. Ten minutes after it went out, the two officers were at the site in a rowboat; a Coast Guard boat and six fishing boats were on the scene. They found only patches of foam 30–40 yd. wide that the fishermen thought was not normal tide foam. . . .

The site of the presumed impact was in between an island and the mainland, about 200–300 yd. offshore. Apparently no one actually saw anything enter the water [though I must point out that a number of people saw the object descend to the water, which is, essentially, the same thing]. However two young women driving on the island reported that a horizontal pattern of three yellow lights had tilted and descended, and then a yellow light had appeared. . . . The RCMP corporal stated that the light on the water was not on any boat, that Air Search and Rescue had no reports of missing aircraft in the area, and an RCAF radar station nearby reported no Canadian or U.S. air operations in the area at the time, nor any unusual radar object. . . . A search by Navy divers during the days immediately following the sighting disclosed nothing relevant.

Five days later the Naval Maritime Command advised the project [that is, the Condon Committee] that the search had been terminated. The watch officer read a report from the RCMP indicating that at the time in question a 60 ft. object had been seen to explode upon impact with the water. . . . A captain of a fishing boat that had been about 16 mi. from the site of the earlier reports, reported to the project that he and his crew had seen three stationary bright red flashing lights on the water, from sundown until about 11:00 P.M. The ship's radar showed four objects forming a six mile square; the three lights were associated with one of these objects [so now we see that Levine is contradicting himself with radar reports and people seeing the object descend]. At about 11:00 P.M., one of the lights went straight up. The captain had judged that the radar objects were naval vessels and the ascending light a helicopter; he had attached no significance to these observations until he had heard on the radio of the sightings; he then reported the foregoing observations. . . . However, since the position he reported for the objects was about 175 n. mi. from the original site, the two situations do not appear to be related.

No further investigation by the project was considered justifiable, particularly in view of the immediate and thorough search [that had failed to find anything which would suggest that the Condon Committee should be very interested in the case] that had been carried out by the RCMP and the Maritime Command.

But it seems to me that if the Condon Committee was interested in the real events surrounding the UFO phenomenon they would have done more than make a few telephone calls. They would have looked into the reports, noticed the discrepancies, and asked additional questions. But the Condon Committee was designed by the Air Force to end Air Force investigation into UFOs. So, when this case surfaced, they made a few telephone calls, found an excuse not to investigate, and then didn't.

Chris Styles, however, wasn't as convinced as the Condon Committee investigators. According to him, "In the spring of 1993, I decided to reinvestigate the Shag Harbour crash of October 4, 1967." He continued, explaining that his interest was sparked by the rebroadcast of the "Unsolved Mysteries" segment that dealt with the Roswell case. He added, "As compelling as the Roswell segment was, it was not long before my attention focused on a memory I had of a very different kind of UFO crash scenario."

So, once again, as would become common throughout the 1990s, someone decided to reinvestigate a case that had been dormant for over twenty years. There was a hint of something important going on in the past. Because of newspaper clippings and a few official documents, the names of those who had participated in the original event had become easily available to researchers. There was a good starting place for Styles if he wanted to learn anything new.

Styles reported that he was fortunate enough to find some of the divers who were involved in the original search. On Good Friday 1993, Styles conducted the first of his interviews with one of the *Granby* divers. Talking to him, and with the official records that he was able to retrieve later, he was convinced that something important had happened at Shag Harbour in October 1967.

In fact, Styles reported that information he obtained from the Canadian Forces Station Shelburne, which was North America's former coordination center for submarine detection in the Atlantic Ocean and sonar buoy drops from Argus Flights out of the Canadian Forces Base Greenwood, led high-ranking military officers to speculate that a crippled UFO that had hit the water in Shag Harbour was no longer there. In other words, it had traveled, underwater, to a position off Shelburne County's Government Point.

Styles, in his search for information, learned that a small flotilla sat over the submerged UFO for a number of days. There had been talk of some kind of a retrieval operation, but it was postponed when it seemed that a second UFO was there, possibly to repair the first.

After seven days, a Soviet sub entered the picture, violating Canadian territorial waters. Several of the surface vessels turned toward the Soviet intruder. As the maneuvering was being done by the terrestrial vessels above them, the two UFOs also began to move, heading towards the Gulf of Maine. In open water, they surfaced and then leapt into the air to disappear at high speed.

Styles, now completely intrigued by what he refers to as "The Story" wanted to learn more. He reported that he heard The Story from a number of different witnesses including admirals, colonels, cooks, and pilots. With so many telling it, he believed that it had some basis in fact.

Verification of such an extraordinary tale would be valuable. Styles, checking the map, realized that those in the Cape Roseway lighthouse would have had an unobstructed view of any Naval operations that took place off Government Point, and wanted to see their logbooks. On October 25, 1993, he learned, "regretfully those records could not be located . . . further researching would be futile." The letter, according to Styles, was from the office of the Regional Superintendent for the Canadian Coast Guard Service.

The paper trail, as skeptics often tell us, is important. Styles left no stone unturned in his pursuit of that information. In July 1994 he spoke on the telephone with Isabel Campbell who, at that time, was a senior archivist at the Department of National Defence Directorate of History. He asked for the 1967 Annual Stroker's Report, which would note any major target detection made by Canadian Forces radar facilities. In other words, when one avenue for documentation was shut off, Styles quickly developed another.

Within ten minutes, Campbell called him back to tell him that the 1967 Stroker's Report was missing. This, according to Campbell, was strange because it had to be signed out and only members of the staff had access to it. It seemed odd that another of the documents Styles had sought conveniently disappeared.

Two months later, when Styles checked again, he learned that the report had been found, but it contained no mention of any target detections or Rescue Coordination Center inquiries. Styles noted that this was strange because, according to him, "As late as one month after the Shag Harbour crash C.F.S. Barrington's Administrative Officer ran appeals in Nova Scotian newspapers that read 'Military Wants U.F.O.'s Reported.'"

Continuing his research, Styles petitioned and received permission to review the papers of the late Jesuit priest Father Michael Burke-Gaffney, who was a noted astronomer, professor, and UFO investigator for Canada's National Research Council. In those papers, Styles found ten documents that related to UFOs. One of them was an RCMP file of another UFO incident on October 4, 1967, that is, the date of the Shag Harbour crash. This was also part of the Condon Committee report mentioned earlier.

According to Styles, the last sentence reads, "I had never seen anything like it before but it sounds like the thing they are looking for down off Shelburne or Barrington Passage." Styles thought this meant that the men were aware of the search effort off Government Point. He was able to locate Captain Leo Mersey, the master of the fishing vessel mentioned, who confirmed Styles' suspicions.

Another document that Styles located, with the help of UFO researcher Jan Aldrich, who had been researching the files of John Brent Musgrave, was the report that had been sent to APRO and Jim Lorenzen by Musgrave. Normally, such a document, while interesting, might not be of particular significance. However, this report, which gave the names, ranks, and office phone numbers of various members of the Maritime Command, also made reference to USAF activity at the Shag Harbour site hours after the events. It also mentions the identity of a Canadian scientific consultant who was put on standby to receive artifacts. That all suggested that someone believed a real object had fallen into the harbor.

What makes the report interesting is the reference to the U.S. Air Force. Here, according to a report made in 1967, was the suggestion of Air Force interest in a possible UFO crash. We know from other documents available in this country through the Freedom of Information Act, that Project Moon Dust provided the authorization for Air Force personnel to travel outside the United States on missions surrounding the recovery of space debris of foreign manufacture or of unknown origin. The Shag Harbour incident fits those categories. It would seem that Moon Dust might have been the American end of the Shag Harbour UFO crash.

As we saw, in the report sent on to APRO, there was a scientist standing by to receive physical evidence. According to Styles, the *Granby's* divers checked the bottom of the sound with handheld lights. Although a low-tech affair when compared to 1990s equipment, there were rumors that they did find debris. A Shag Harbour fisherman, Donnie Nickerson, said that he watched divers bring up pieces of twisted aluminum-like metal. Of course, the aluminum could have been almost anything and not related to the crash. It has to be noted, as Styles did, that the official reports claimed there were no results from the search efforts.

In his continuing search for information, Styles, in May 1994, was able to interview Lawrence Smith who had a UFO encounter that might be related to the events of October 1967. On November 25, 1970, Smith and his brother Eugene were driving west on Highway 3, heading toward Shag Harbour. As they came over a rise in the highway, Lawrence noticed a small light hovering about two hundred feet in front of them. Before he could say a word, another five lights appeared in formation. The lights were fiery orange and were about 16 inches in diameter. The lowest of the lights seemed to be about eight feet off the highway.

Lawrence slammed on the brakes and the car screeched to a halt. The 8-track tape player quit and (it would be learned later) the tape was ruined. Both men felt strange sensations. After an estimated thirty seconds, all the glowing objects vanished.

Once they got the car moving again, they contacted Constable Ralph Keeping of the Barrington Passage RCMP detachment. Although Keeping drove out to the area of the sighting and searched the highway and the woods, he found nothing unusual. Styles reported that Keeping noticed that both men, the Smith brothers, seemed to have been frightened by the encounter.

The next morning, Keeping was at his desk when Colonel Calvin Rushton called to ask if they had received any UFO sightings the day before. Rushton, when he learned of the Smith encounter, told

Keeping that one of his men, Corporal Timothy Nielson, had seen something very similar. Nielson was about twenty miles from where the Smiths reported their encounter, but it seemed to have taken place about the same time. More importantly, Nielson wasn't alone. He was with his girlfriend and her mother. Rushton requested a meeting with Keeping, as well as a copy of the report, with all witness names attached. That was the last Keeping heard from the colonel. Styles spoke to Rushton in 1995 but he denied any memory of the events surrounding the Smith encounter or his desire to obtain a copy of the Smith report.

Of course, Styles learned that the November 25 sighting was not the only time the Smiths were involved with UFOs. Lawrence Smith was on the *Cape Islander* on October 4, 1967, which was the first boat to reach the last known position of the UFO before it submerged. He saw the yellow foam that so many others had mentioned.

What Styles, as well as Doug Ledger, has discovered is very interesting. He has, through the documentation he found, proved that something unusual happened on the night of October 4, 1967. The documentation, as well as the witness testimony, establishes the reality of the situation. That same documentation also tends to suggest that US Air Force personnel were involved in the search efforts. Of course, there is no official record of that.

While none of this proves that this UFO sighting was of an extraterrestrial craft, it does provide us with some interesting questions. As in the Roswell case in 1947, what could the government be testing that would have to remain secret today? The technology of 1967 is as outdated today as the technology of 1947 would have been twenty years later. There is no reason to keep this case buried if it was some sort of experimental craft or a military aircraft accident.

So, we have the case of something falling into the water, we have two governments interested in it—or three if we count the Soviet sub—and we have denials—no one remembers a thing. Styles underscores this by pointing out that he spoke to a Major Victor Eldridge in 1993. Eldridge denied any knowledge or involvement, even though Eldridge, according to the documentation, was serving at one of the major force's facilities involved in the search, and Eldridge is responsible for a number of newspaper articles asking for help in reporting UFO sightings.

Styles wraps up, however, by writing "if one examines all the evidence on The Shag Harbour Incident, one must conclude that 'something' extraterrestrial in origin was responsible for the strange events." He continues, "Even though the 'nil results' were claimed as the final result to search efforts of agencies such as the RCMP, RCAF, Royal Canadian Navy, and NORAD, none of the aforementioned would drop their conviction that 'something' described as 'no known object' had indeed hovered, then crashed into the ocean. At this point in time, and until further explanation is forthcoming, The Shag Harbour Incident remains the only UFO crash scenario that is supported in that interpretation by available and unrestricted government documentation that is without controversy as to its origin."

2 Travis Walton and Alien Abductions

1975

UFO INVESTIGATION IN THE 1990s is often about alien abduction. The lion's share of reported cases are those of abduction or associated in some fashion with claims of abduction. According to the witnesses, to the researchers, and to the UFO organizations, alien abduction is currently the primary area of research. Hundreds have reported they were abducted, some on a regular basis, while others tell of horrifying experiments on board a flying saucer at the hands of alien creatures.

One of the first such reports to gain national attention was the abduction of Travis Walton in November 1975. It is considered by many to be one of the best such cases because there are independent witnesses who reported they saw Walton hit by a beam of light from a UFO hovering a few feet above the ground near Heber, Arizona. Travis Walton was missing for five days; this is documented. Law enforcement officials conducted a search for Walton. There was Walton's physical condition when he reappeared five days later. And there were the lie-detector tests that Walton and others took in the days that followed the abduction.

According to the original report and Travis Walton himself, the men had been cutting trees on a Forest Service contract in the Apache-Sitgreaves National Forest in November 1975. Walton, along with crew leader Mike Rogers, and fellow workers Allen Dalis, John Goulette, Dwayne Smith, Kenneth Peterson, and Steve Pierce had worked all day thinning the thick undergrowth and stacking the material in accordance with the governmental regulations under which they worked. After the long day, all looked forward to getting home, cleaning up, and relaxing. There was even talk of swimming at an indoor pool in Snowflake, Arizona.

They had climbed into the International Harvester crew cab, and headed toward home when Walton (or possibly Allen Dalis) thought he saw a glow through the trees. Others then saw the light, too, and urged the driver, Rogers, to head toward it. They drove through the trees, along a road that was little more than a track, came out of a pine stand, and had an unobstructed view of the alien craft hovering in front of them. They now knew they were looking at a flying saucer and not the setting sun, the headlights of another car, or a large camp fire.

The craft was later described as luminous, disc shaped, and hovering fifteen to twenty feet above a pile of cut trees, branches, and scrub brush. The craft was about a hundred feet from the truck, about twenty feet in diameter, and maybe eight feet thick. The surface was divided by dark silver vertical lines, longer than they were wide, and into panel-like geometrical forms. A thin band with a protruding ridge circled the middle of the craft. Its milky yellow glow illuminated the ground around it and the trees surrounding the clearing.

Rogers shut off the truck's engine, and as Walton opened the door, someone said, quietly, "That's a UFO." Years later, Walton would write, "I was afraid it would fly away and I would miss the chance of a lifetime to satisfy my curiosity about it. I hurriedly got out of the truck and started toward the hovering ship."

Walton walked forward. He could hear a whine of machinery from inside. The golden glow of the object bathed him in light. Then, according to Walton, "I was startled by a powerful, thunderous swell in the volume of the vibrations from the craft . . . I saw the saucer start wobbling on its axis with a quickening motion . . . I ducked into a crouch, down behind the safety of a nearby log."

Walton didn't see what happened next. He had decided it was time to get away, but a beam reached out toward him as he stood up. He felt a paralyzing blow as he was lifted from his feet and thrown through the air. In his latest book, he wrote, "*I* saw and heard nothing. All I felt was a numbing force of a blow that felt like a high-voltage electrocution." He hit the ground and was still.

Later, he would learn that he had been lifted off the ground, his body arched backward, his arms and legs outstretched. He flew about ten feet and hit the rocky ground on his right shoulder.

His friends in the truck, sure that he had been killed by the flying saucer and the blue beam of light, screamed at Rogers. He started the engine, backed up, turned, and raced toward the track that led from the area. The bouncing of the truck on the rough, nearly invisible road forced Rogers to slow down. He swerved to miss a tree and finally stopped.

Standing outside the truck, the men discussed what to do next. One or two thought Walton was dead, but others thought they should return to look for him. As they climbed back into the truck, Rogers caught a glimpse of something streaking away. He believed that it might have been the golden ship and was impressed with its acceleration. Only he reported seeing the streak of light, but that is unimportant. He was the only one looking in the right direction at the right time to have seen it.

The search failed to find any sign of the now missing Travis Walton. They argued about the location where they had seen the ship. They argued about the location where they had last seen Walton. They argued about what to do next. Badly frightened by the events and by the disappearance of Walton, even the moon now surprised and scared them. Finally they decided their only course was to alert the local authorities.

They telephoned the sheriff's office and told Deputy Chuck Ellison, who responded, that Walton was missing and maybe dead. The deputy called for help and a search was organized later that night. It continued the following day, but failed to find a trace of the missing Walton. Walton's brother Duane said that when he drove into the area the next morning, there were no signs of a search party. He demanded to know what was happening, and, by noon, searchers were again out looking for his brother.

During one of the days of the search, a man in a Forest Service uniform appeared with a geiger counter. According to Walton's latest book, the stranger tested the ground around the supposed abduction site, but never got close to the actual spot where anything happened. More interestingly, however, when he checked the hard hats worn by Walton's fellow workers, he found signs of radioactivity. It is an interesting aberration but of little real importance, especially since no one seems to know who the man was or what he was doing.

During the days Walton was missing, the other members of the crew were given lie-detector tests. According to Walton, apparently all the men passed except Allen Dalis. The examiner, Cy Gilson, suggested that the men were telling the truth about the disappearance of Walton. It seems that the sheriff had believed they had murdered Walton and concocted the flying saucer story as a cover. The polygraph suggested that Rogers and his crew had not killed Walton. It didn't mean that Walton had been abducted, or even that there was a UFO event. The focus had been to determine if Walton had been killed by accident, or murdered by the crew.

According to Walton, among others, each of the men passed this examination, except for Dalis. According to Walton's report on the subject, "After little more than an hour, Allen stormed out of the testing room. He loudly cursed the examiner and slammed the door behind him."

The test results showed that the men were telling the truth. Cy Gilson, in an "unofficial" report to Mike Rogers and the others at the completion of the sessions, said, according to the reconstructed dialogue, "When I started testing you men this morning, I really expected to find that a murder had been committed. After all those hard words this morning, and the way Allen Davis [*sic*] reacted, I was even more sure of foul play. But none of the tests except Allen's showed anything like that."

In the official police report, Case Number 23-75-56, Sheriff's Deputy Ellison wrote, "On Monday, November 10, the six men who were with Walton at the time of his disappearance, were subjected to polygraph tests at their own request, and of the six all of them passed the test with a positive reading. The fifth man [Allen Dalis] was inconclusive on one phase of the test but it was stated that he 'had basically told the truth.'"

During all of this, the searches continued but failed to find a trace of Walton or his body. All were perplexed. No one knew what had happened to Walton until he reappeared five days later, dirty, tired, and slightly confused. He awoke, according to him, cold, along a stretch of highway. Hovering over the highway was a silver disc that suddenly streaked into the sky, disappearing. Walton stood, looked at the highway, and recognized it. He stumbled down the road, found a phone at a gas station, and tried to call his sister for help. He spoke to Grant Neff, his brother-in-law, who at first believed it was another of the many crank calls that had plagued the family after Walton's disappearance had been reported by the media. The voice on the phone had not sounded like Travis.

Neff, finally convinced that the voice at the other end belonged to Walton, drove to Snowflake, Arizona, to find Travis's brother, Duane, at his mother's (Mary Walton Kellett's) house. Neff told them about the telephone call and that he was on his way to Heber.

In Heber, the two men found Walton crouched in the second of the three phone booths at the Exxon service station. He was conscious, but seemed to be dazed and confused. He was shivering in the cold.

After Walton was picked up by Neff and Duane, he said little about what had happened, but told them about the big eyes of creatures he had encountered. The comments were vague and slightly incoherent. Walton said they had stared at him with those big eyes. "They kept looking at me," he said repeatedly. The men didn't immediately understand that Walton was trying to tell them.

Although gone for five days, Walton seemed to think that only a couple of hours had passed. Told he had been missing for five days, he was stunned. At his sister's home, he talked to friends and family about the ordeal briefly, preferring to say as little as possible. He cleaned up in the bathroom and, for some reason, stepped on a scale. He had lost about ten pounds during the five days he had been missing. Almost everyone who writes about the Walton case mentions those lost ten pounds. This is a fact that would become important later.

According to the accounts told then or written now, Walton remembered little about those missing five days, other than seeing the UFO and being struck by the beam of light. His first memory, after being hit by the beam, was to awaken in what he thought was a hospital room. The air seemed wet and heavy and he had some difficulty breathing. All the details of his surroundings didn't register right away. Slowly, he became aware of three small creatures, about five feet tall, dressed in loose-fitting orange jump suits, standing around him.

These creatures, according to Walton, had high, domed heads, large eyes, and tiny noses, mouths, and ears. They were dressed in the standard uniform of a one-piece coveralls. Walton noticed that none of them seemed to have fingernails. He also noticed that their hands all had five fingers. To Walton, the creatures looked frail, with soft, marshmallowy skin.

Walton climbed to his feet and shouted at the creatures. He pushed one of them into another. They seemed to him to be lightweight. He grabbed a cylindrical tube from a shelf, and believing it to be glass, tried to shatter it (like a barroom brawler will attempt to make a weapon of a broken beer bottle). It wouldn't break, but Walton waved it around. The beings keep their distance and finally turned and left through a door behind them.

He walked to the door, which he described as "normal" height and rectangular with rounded corners. He ran from the room and hurried down a corridor until he came to a room on the right. Looking in, he saw that it was round and that he could see the stars through the ceiling. It isn't clear if he was looking outside the craft, or if he was seeing star fields on some kind of equipment. The effect seemed to be one of sitting in a chair in the middle of space. Maybe a better analogy is of sitting in a planetarium as the night sky is projected onto the dome.

In the center of the room was a high-backed, metallic chair. Walton wasn't sure if there was anyone sitting in it because the back was to him. Cautiously, he entered. He sat down and found a lever on the left arm of the chair. When he moved it, the stars seemed to move. When he let go, the lever returned to its original position. The stars stopped rotating and seemed to freeze in the new positions. He manipulated the lever again, but let go, fearing that he would do some real damage to the craft or the equipment. On the other arm were buttons, but Walton didn't experiment with them.

He got out of the chair and examined the wall. The lights came on and the stars faded. He walked back to the chair, and heard some noise. Looking toward the doorway, he discovered a man dressed in blue coveralls. To Walton, the man appeared to be a normal-looking human being wearing a transparent bubble-like helmet. This is one of the first abductee references to human beings working with an alien crew.

Walton tried to ask questions, but the man only smiled back at him. Walton later described the man as about six-two, weighing about two hundred pounds, with long hair that covered his ears.

The man motioned to Walton, and took him by the arm. Together, they walked through the ship, and finally walked out onto what seemed to be a hangar deck. He looked at the craft he'd just exited and thought that it looked like the one he had seen in the forest, only much larger. The hangar deck held another three or four craft.

They crossed the hangar deck and entered another small room where two men and a woman were dressed like Walton's "guide," though they weren't wearing helmets. Because they weren't wearing helmets, Walton thought they might hear his questions. They merely looked at him as the guide crossed the room and exited, leaving Walton with the three beings.

It was at this point that Walton was apparently examined by the aliens. They took him by his arms and guided him to a nearby table. They had gestured for him to climb up on the table but he refused, struggling with them. They forced him onto his back and put an oxygen mask-like device over his mouth and nose. He wanted to tear it from his face, but before he could act, he lost consciousness again.

That was all that he remembered about the missing five days. His next conscious thought was when he awoke along the road with the ship hovering near him. He could see the road and his surroundings reflected in the shiny, metallic surface. His first real thought was to try to obtain some help or get in touch with his family. He walked down the road and, reaching the service station, made the phone call to his brother-in-law.

Because of Walton's physical condition, Duane thought that they should find a doctor to examine Travis. The disappearance, however, had been the focus of media attention for several days. Even self-styled UFO investigators had been calling the family, trying to learn more. The last thing Duane wanted was for his brother to have to put up with a crowd of shouting reporters or UFO researchers who could complicate the case. If they approached a local doctor, the press would surely learn of it. Besides, they probably couldn't do anything until morning and by that time they could be in Phoenix, away from the prying eyes of the press and the media circus they were sure to generate.

When Walton reappeared Duane called Bill Spaulding of the Ground Saucer Watch who had involved himself in the case from the beginning. Spaulding sounded as if he knew what he was doing and had made a number of suggestions about the course of action when, and if, Travis returned. Duane hoped Spaulding could help find a doctor in Phoenix to examine his brother. An appointment was arranged, but the doctor Spaulding found wasn't an M.D., and apparently, according to Coral Lorenzen, wasn't even a Ph.D. At any rate, no physical was performed at that time by that man, though there was some sort of interview conducted. Walton said little while Duane tried to answer the less offensive questions. Timing seems to suggest that the Walton brothers were in the man's office less than an hour.

Coral Lorenzen, of the Tucson-based Aerial Phenomena Research Organization (APRO), also injected herself into the investigation. On the day that Walton reappeared, Lorenzen was able to talk to Duane. She assured Duane that she could provide for a medical examination, suggested it could be conducted at Duane's home in Phoenix, and said she wouldn't alert the press without permission of the brothers. Duane agreed.

Lorenzen, then, through a network of consultants maintained by her organization, arranged for a medical examination that afternoon. The doctors, Joseph Saults and Howard Kandell, arrived on time. They examined Walton and found nothing seriously wrong with him.

Kandell, who wrote the medical report, did say, "There were no bruises or evidence of trauma except for a two-mm red spot in the crease of the right elbow, which was suggestive of a needle puncture . . ."

In what might be a very important clue, but seems to have been overlooked by nearly everyone, Kandell reported, "Urinalysis—volume 560 cc; normal, with good concentration [SpG 1.032]; however, there was no acetate present, which is unusual, considering that any person who is without adequate nutrition for twenty-four to forty-eight hours will break down his own body-fat stores, which should result in ketones [acetones] being excreted into the urine. The absence of ketones in his urine, considering a ten-pound weight loss, is difficult to explain."

While all the maneuvering was taking place to find Walton a doctor for the examination, Jim Lorenzen, International Director of APRO, arranged to inform the *National Enquirer* of the situation. Or, according to some accounts, the *National Enquirer* called Lorenzen, offering money in exchange for APRO's cooperation for an exclusive report. The tabloid newspaper, in the mid-1970s, was extremely interested in UFOs and, in fact, had established a panel of experts to examine whatever evidence was found. In the 1970s, the *Enquirer* was offering a million dollars, in addition to paying for the best case each year, for proof that UFOs were extraterrestrial. According to Lorenzen, the *Enquirer* had the money to pay for research, such as polygraph examinations, that the organization couldn't otherwise afford. Lorenzen agreed to cooperate with the newspaper.

The *Enquirer* arranged for a hotel room for Walton and his brother in Scottsdale. There, they met Dr. James A. Harder, who has a fondness for hypnosis. He soon convinced Travis to undergo hypnotic regression. This was the first time that Walton had told the whole story of what had happened to him. There was little or no difference between what Walton said under hypnosis and what he consciously remembered. He could remember only about two hours out of the missing five days. There wasn't a wild range of detail that might have been expected after Walton's five day absence.

In Scottsdale, the reporters for the *Enquirer* insisted that Walton take a polygraph examination as soon as possible. Sheriff Marlin Gillespie arranged for a polygraph session with Cy Gilson, and all parties agreed that it should be done in private. Unfortunately the press learned of the plans and an angry Duane Walton canceled the test.

But the *Enquirer* reporters still wanted the test done as soon as possible, while Walton was still in Scottsdale and before another publication could get to Walton and get the story. The Lorenzens had learned of another polygraph operator with good credentials living in the Phoenix area. They contacted him.

Coral Lorenzen, writing in *Abducted!*, said, "The operator, John McCarthy, was recommended by an APRO member living in Phoenix who knew only that McCarthy had long experience in the field. Mr. Lorenzen made the initial call to McCarthy to determine his willingness to participate. On his affirmative response Lorenzen turned the phone over to Dr. Harder . . . who discussed at length the agitated state of mind that Travis was in and expressed his doubts concerning Travis's testibility. *McCarthy promised to take this into consideration* [emphasis added] and promised complete confidentiality."

McCarthy met with Walton and spent about two hours with him, telling him about the procedures that would be followed, and reviewing the questions to make sure that they could be answered yes or no. McCarthy completed the tests and was unambiguous in his conclusions. "Gross deception." He also reported then, as he would later, that he believed Walton had resorted to tricks in an attempt to beat the machine.

When Walton flunked this test, the Lorenzens, Walton, and others decided that the test itself was badly flawed. According to Coral Lorenzen, three psychiatrists who had examined Walton on the day he took the test said that the test was meaningless because of Walton's agitated state of mind. She wrote, "When the validity of the test results was overruled by the other experts consulted, there was, of course, no point in requesting its release since it had then become useless information from a scientific standpoint."

What the Lorenzens and others didn't believe to be valuable scientific information was the fact that Walton had taken and failed that first polygraph test. Instead, they arranged for a second, later test to be conducted under their own conditions and by a different operator. This one, they believed, would be more scientifically accurate.

Walton, himself, attempting to alibi this failure, quoted Harder, a civil-engineering instructor and UFO researcher, writing, "Dr. Harder said a polygraph measures stress, not lies per se. The theory behind a lie detector is that people register stressful physiological responses when they lie. He noted that I was still extremely agitated when talking about my experience. He counseled that, if a test was performed, the results not be taken too seriously."

There is a real problem with this assessment. Polygraphs are designed to measure the body's reactions to specific questions. The heart rate, respiration, galvanic response are all measured during a polygraph. Those who are not telling the truth, who are not pathological liars, will respond with elevated heart and respiration rates and increased galvanic response when telling lies. It must be noted, however, that the agitation of the subject is irrelevant to the test. That is why baseline questions are asked. It establishes the responses of a person, no matter how stressed he or she might be. And if he lies under those circumstances, it will be evident to an experienced operator. Harder's comments about the validity of a test run days after Walton had returned are ridiculous. What is important—though Walton, the Lorenzens, and Harder suggest otherwise—is that Walton failed, badly, the first test he was given. It should also be noted that when the test results did not confirm their beliefs, they all conspired to keep the information secret.

Coral Lorenzen went farther, suggesting that the operator, McCarthy, was incompetent and that the test questions were badly worded. She wrote, "Describing this test as meaningless as we have done is really being too kind. It was badly botched by the tester. Sometimes long years of experience can serve to crystallize bad habits."

She would later, as did others, castigate McCarthy for revealing what they believed to be confidential information. When McCarthy reported that it was his conclusion that Walton had failed, the *Enquirer* reporters asked him to wait. They retreated to another room and reappeared minutes later with a hastily typed confidentiality agreement. They misdated it but no one noticed at the time.

I should point out here that I have great respect for both Jim and Coral Lorenzen. Each was more than kind to me during my long affiliation with that organization. Each called me on a number of occasions to ask for assistance in investigations of various UFO sighting cases. Yet, given all that, I find Coral Lorenzen's arguments about the reason for withholding the first test results to be inadequate. It was important information that would have been withheld had other circumstances not conspired to bring it forward.

Although it is unclear because the *National Enquirer* was insisting on an immediate polygraph examination of Walton, it seems that another test was not scheduled until several months later. Dr. Leo Sprinkle of the University of Wyoming in February 1976 was able to travel to Arizona to interview Walton. Sprinkle used hypnotic regression on Walton to gather additional details of the experience.

It was also at this time that another polygraph was arranged. In consultation with Lorenzen and Dr. Harold Cahn, Sprinkle helped polygrapher George J. Pfeifer design the test that Walton would be given. This test would not be without its own controversy.

Walton, who hadn't been in the room when the test questions were drafted, reviewed them with the men before his test; again, normal procedure. Walton then asked for a couple of wording changes and suggested a few additional questions. In his report, Pfeifer wrote that Walton had dictated the questions. Coral Lorenzen said that the dictation was more of a suggestion, a term to which Pfeifer later agreed. Walton said it was more of a discussion of the relevant questions, not outside the normal standards used by other polygraphers.

Walton, according to Pfeifer, passed this examination. It seemed that there was now one test and polygrapher saying that Walton had lied and one test and polygrapher saying that Walton had told the truth. At the moment it seemed to be a wash. Anyone could pick which side he or she wanted and present evidence to support that conclusion.

Or maybe Walton didn't pass this examination either. Pfeifer, for his part, was convinced, and still is convinced that Walton passed this test. However, Pfeifer worked for Tom Ezell and Associates, so naturally, Ezell reviewed the findings. Ezell seemed to think that Walton hadn't passed the test, or at best, had not passed it by much.

Jerry Black, a UFO investigator in Ohio, tracked down both Pfeifer and Ezell and spoke to them. Black thought that Ezell might be trying to keep his organization out of the UFO business. Pfeifer, of course, as the man who had conducted the test, and who had asked the questions, felt that Walton had passed. Ezell, who had merely reviewed the charts and questions, didn't fully agree.

What it boiled down to was that neither of the tests taken by Walton could be considered valid. McCarthy's test might have been given too soon, or there might have been some animosity between McCarthy and Walton as suggested by Walton supporters. Black, who must be considered a disinterested third party, seemed to think, based on his review of the transcripts of the session, that McCarthy didn't like Walton. Maybe he considered the whole thing a hoax and didn't like having his time wasted. Black talked to McCarthy in 1993 and McCarthy said that he still thought Walton was lying, regardless of what anybody else said.

But Pfeifer's test, which Pfeifer said Walton had passed, couldn't be considered any more valid, especially with Ezell reevaluating the results. What is interesting, however, is that in neither test is there a clear indication that Walton was telling the truth. That is a fact that somehow has been overlooked in all the writings that have been done about Walton in the last twenty years.

Another problem arose when it was leaked that Walton had a criminal record. Lorenzen said that Walton himself had supplied the information because he believed that it was necessary to understand the case. He also admitted to using drugs, but all that was in his past and had no relevance to the abduction event.

It didn't help anyone's credibility when Duane was caught in several lies about Walton's background. When Philip Klass, the UFO debunker, asked Duane if Walton had ever been in trouble with the law, Duane denied it. Klass used this to suggest the whole abduction was a hoax.

Coral Lorenzen, wrote in response, "Klass lingers on this lie told by an older brother who is obviously trying to protect his brother from the slings and arrows of individuals, who, like Klass, want to discredit Travis for a deed which was done when he was a young, impressionable man. Klass also leaves out the fact that the two young men who accomplished the check forgery were also aided and abetted by an older man who had a criminal record and who suggested the forgery."

Duane also denied there was an earlier polygraph, as had Jim Lorenzen. Coral wrote that it was Duane's attempt, as it had been Jim's, to protect the confidentiality of that first polygraph. It was suggested that Walton himself had no part in the deceptions perpetrated by the other two men. But it is a relevant fact given all the circumstances.

Coral Lorenzen believed that all the lies had been justified, given the probing nature of some of the questions being asked. The lies and misrepresentations were the result of the pressure from the outside. The real point is that these lies had relatively little to do with the case. Duane told them to protect Walton, should Walton's tale be rejected because of the actions of others.

It should also be noted that the limited criminal activity in Walton's past is irrelevant. These were minor scrapes with the law. They are the sorts of things in which many juveniles find themselves caught up. Walton had stopped using drugs a couple of years earlier. Yes, it must be noted, but little weight should be assigned to it. If these were the only problems with the Walton case, it could be suggested they be ignored completely.

Coral Lorenzen and others have also attacked McCarthy for telling Klass about the failed polygraph. She noted there was the signed agreement that he would not talk about it. She suggested that he had violated the confidentiality of the client, and questioned his integrity.

But in a case that is filled with controversy, even this isn't as cut and dried as it should be. The confidentiality agreement signed by McCarthy was invalid because of the mistyped date. That, however, is a technicality. Ethically, it would seem that McCarthy was obligated to keep the secret.

However, McCarthy didn't violate the agreement. Klass didn't learn of the earlier test from McCarthy. Tom Ezell, who was not a party to the confidentiality agreement, and who didn't know that the *Enquirer* or the Lorenzens would prefer that the information remain hidden, told Klass about McCarthy's interview. McCarthy said nothing about it until Klass called to tell him that Ezell had already informed him.

When Klass called Jim Lorenzen on March 21, 1976, Klass asked if Walton had taken any other polygraph tests, meaning other than that given by Pfeifer. Lorenzen said, "No, never."

Both Jim and Coral Lorenzen believed that Walton had been abducted by aliens. The story he told under hypnotic regression reinforced this attitude. The careful probing by Sprinkle, as well as the second polygraph provided additional proof that convinced the Lorenzens of this version of the truth. Coral Lorenzen wrote, "And so the mystery remains. Where was Travis Walton for five days?"

But Jerry Black, in his reinvestgation, added a few points about the case that should be remembered. First, the Lorenzens did have, at that time, their own agenda. It seemed that they might have been more interested in promoting themselves and their organization into the national spotlight than they were in learning the truth about UFOs and the Travis Walton case. The *National Enquirer*, reporting on the Walton case, would provide them with national exposure, though certainly not of a very credible nature.

Jim Lorenzen, at the beginning of the Walton case, did seem to bow to the pressures of the reporters from the *Enquirer*. One of those reporters, Jeff Wells, prepared a sixteen-page report suggesting that the Walton story be forgotten. Although the reporters didn't believe that Walton had made up the abduction, they did believe that he had some kind of a psychological experience.

Then Klass attacked the first, failed polygraph examination. Jim Lorenzen would defend his stance and his organization, saying, as he and others would always say, "The results [of the McCarthy polygraph examination] are meaningless."

Jerry Clark, in *High Strangeness*, agreed with Lorenzen's assessment, and wrote, ". . . Probably true, but hardly the point." But Lorenzen's assessment may not have been true at all given the nature of the polygraph. More to the point, it suggested that Lorenzen was being less than candid with the public. While everyone expected the *National Enquirer* to shade the truth, Lorenzen and APRO had been accusing the government for years of just that sort of action, that is, shading the truth. Now they were caught doing it.

But Klass also went off on tangents that had nothing to do with the case. He suggested that Rogers, in serious trouble with his governmental contract, had, with the help of Walton, concocted the story so that Rogers could use the "Act of God" clause to invalidate his contract. Klass seemed to believe that Rogers could recover all the money owed him by the government and not complete the contract because of the UFO sighting.

In reality, the penalties for failure to complete his contract on time weren't particularly severe. Although Rogers didn't complete the contract, it did not adversely affect Rogers's future with the Forest Service. He bid on, and won, a number of contracts after this. Klass's suggestion was ridiculous but it is an explanation he frequently uses. Money is somehow the reason behind more than a few UFO sightings. This suggestion in the Walton case is thinner than most.

But Klass isn't the only one who grabs thin information and runs with it. In writing about Klass, Walton said, "PJK's [Philip J. Klass] ties to military/aerospace sources—as editor of *Aviation Week and Space Technology*; his Washington, D.C., address; his prosecutorial, muckraker approach; and his extensive use of propagandist techniques—have lead people in the UFO community for many years to speculate that he is a paid operative of some covert agency interested in promulgating disinformation about UFOs. As one would expect, whether it's true or not, he's always denied it."

Walton then answers the question himself. "Having heard the theory often, what do I think of it? It's plausible, but so far I see no conclusive proof for or against it. If it is true, conclusive proof probably would be unobtainable . . ."

In the UFO field, one of the standards of success is the allegation of governmental ties. Everyone who has ever written about UFOs, lectured to an audience, or expressed an opinion contrary to the accepted view has been labeled a government agent.

Walton does play on the paranoia in the UFO field. He reports, throughout his book, of mysterious men taking geiger counter readings, mysterious phone calls warning about government cover-ups, and writes, "A retired CIA officer warned the family of possible covert government intervention." All this implies that the tale of abduction must be real because the government wouldn't waste time on an illusion or hoax.

Of course, there is no evidence for any of this. If there is a governmental oversight office with the mission of keeping an eye on UFO researchers, investigators, and witnesses, they have long since given up. Our own paranoia, along with the hoaxes and cranks in the field, have rendered the office's mission obsolete. They just need to leave us alone and let us self-destruct. Walton's message, throughout his new book, seems to have been written with that mission in mind.

In this case, there really is no middle ground. Either Walton was, in fact, abducted, or the case is a hoax. The controversy that surrounds both the polygraph examinations seems to eliminate them as useful tools for anyone. The arguments on both sides make some sense, but the reality is that Walton flunked his first test, and if he passed the second, it wasn't by much. The interpretation of the operators during those tests comes into play when trying to understand it.

Unlike most other abduction cases, there are some other facts. Walton was seen by five others as he approached the object. Each of those men did take a polygraph about the events of November 5, 1975. It must be remembered, however, that the majority of the relevant questions dealt with the disappearance of Walton and whether those men had killed him and hidden the body. Only one dealt with the UFO, "Did you tell the truth about actually seeing a UFO last Wednesday when Travis Walton disappeared?"

Cy Gilson, who administered the tests to the men of Rogers's crew, wrote, ". . . [T]hey each answered 'Yes' to question #4 [outlined above]. The test results were conclusive on Goulette, Smith, Peterson, Rogers, and Pierce. The test results on Dalis were inconclusive."

None of that meant that Walton was abducted, but it was interesting. And, there were the five days when Walton was missing. Where was he for those five days? Jerry Black told me that no one had ever come forward with a credible sighting of Walton during those five days. An older couple did report they had seen Walton hitchhiking during the time he was supposed to be missing. However, that account doesn't seem credible.

So, Walton was missing for five days. That much has been documented. Black, among others, points out that it would be difficult for Walton to have gotten out of that area at night, on foot, without help. No one saw him until he reappeared. That information carries some weight.

On the other side are a couple of points that seem to suggest hoax. For example, after Walton reappeared, the sheriff had a couple of deputies dust the telephones at the service station for fingerprints. They didn't find Walton's. This could, of course, be nothing more than a mistake by the deputies.

Second, there is the lack of any trauma on his body. According to everyone in the truck, Walton was slammed into the rocky ground. There was no sign of abrasion or bruising. It could be suggested here that the ground wasn't as hard as it seemed, that Walton wasn't scraped or bruised, or that he was, but had healed.

Third, and possibly most important, is the lack of ketones in the urine sample. Dr. Kandell wrote, "The absence of ketones in his urine, considering a ten-pound weight loss, is difficult to explain."

A medical doctor I talked to wasn't sure this was particularly significant. He argued that the weight loss was not tied to nutrition. Walton could have lost the weight, but if the alien beings had provided some food in any form, the ketones might not show up. Walton, of course, doesn't say that he was provided anything while missing but he also maintains he was unconscious most of the time. This is an interesting aberration and might be of considerable importance.

To me, the lack of any trauma to the body and the lack of ketones in the urine, suggest physical evidence that is in conflict with the tale being told. Neither, however, is of sufficient importance to be used to rule the case as a hoax.

Jerry Black induced Walton and Rogers to take new polygraph examinations. Allen Dalis, because he had been the only one of the original crew whose earlier test was called into question, also took a new test. Black told me that he hadn't actually been pursuing Dalis. That had been a bonus. He just wanted Walton and Rogers.

Cy Gilson made the new tests. He conducted four. Rogers and Dalis were each given one, and both passed them easily. Walton was given two. One concerned the abduction story and the second was to eliminate the claim that Walton had been taking illegal drugs at the time of the events in 1975. Again, Walton passed these tests.

I asked Black if he was satisfied with the new tests and he said, "I am certainly satisfied. . . . I didn't pussyfoot around on these questions. These questions were right to the point. 'Did you see Travis Walton hit by a beam of light by an object that you perceived to be a UFO? Were you involved in perpetrating a hoax?'"

He also said, "In talking with Cy Gilson numerous times I certainly have the upmost trust in his ability. He's been in the business about twenty-two or twenty-three years. He used the latest equipment. . . . All three of them passed at a very high percentage."

I hate to be the one to throw this back into controversy, but I asked a sheriff's deputy on the San Bernadino Sheriff's Department about polygraphs given twenty years after the event. His opinion was that if you had a story that had been shared with the public during that time, that had been told over and over, in front of television and live audiences, that had been written about in books and made into a film, the test might not be one hundred percent accurate. The tellers of the tale have become so comfortable with that tale that the stress reactions do not manifest themselves.

There is still another point that hasn't been raised in connection with the Walton case. A number of UFO researchers, in private conversations, were told by both friends and family of Walton that he planned the abduction from the very beginning. Klass was both right and wrong when he suggested money as the motive. It had nothing to do with a possible default on Mike Rogers' government contracts. It did, however, relate to the *National Enquirer* offer of five thousand dollars for the best UFO case of the year. Walton planned to win the money, designed a case to win it, and in the end, was awarded the prize for 1976.

Dr. Mark Rodeghier, the scientific director of the J. Allen Hynek Center for UFO Studies, told me that he is bothered by the Walton abduction because it is significantly different from the vast majority of abduction reports received by the Center. Walton was grabbed and missing for five days, but most abductions last an hour or less. He remembers virtually nothing about his time on the craft even under hypnosis, yet the majority of abductees remember their experiences in great detail. The alien beings described by Walton do not match those described by other abductees. That is, his aliens, though looking somewhat like the grays, were not grays.

This, by itself, does not mean the Walton abduction was not real. It only means that it varies from the experiences described by others, and that is a point that should not be overlooked.

There is one final point to be made, and that is the amazing coincidence between the Walton case and the abduction of Barney and Betty Hill in 1961. A movie about that case, *The UFO Incident* was broadcast by NBC to a national audience in late October 1975. Walton said that he didn't see it at that time. Mike Rogers admitted that he began to watch it but quickly lost interest. The coincidence, then, is that about two weeks after that movie was aired, Walton disappeared in his own abduction.

What this all means, simply, is that one of the most famous of the abduction cases is, in my opinion, little more than a hoax. The evidence for its reality is shaky, based on the belief that Walton must have concocted the story only after the UFO sighting. The six men couldn't have been involved in a hoax because none have broken ranks, even when offered money to recant. To me, such arguments aren't persuasive. I want to see facts, and that first failed polygraph speaks volumes. When you remember that George Pfeifer and Tom Ezell disagree over the results of the second test, there seems to be, but one, logical conclusion. There are still many indications the Walton case is little more than a hoax, but it does demonstrate what is wrong with abduction research in the 1990s.

3 MJ-12 Again?

1984

THE THING ABOUT UFO INVESTIGATIONS in the 1990s is that we are never free of any of the past reports. Even when we believe that the stake has been hammered through the heart, that the account is dead and buried, and plausible explanations have been offered, some cases rise from the dead. Such is MJ-12, the alleged government documents that confirm the existence of a top secret oversight committee that was formed right after the recovery of an alien spacecraft outside of Roswell. I had believed that the evidence that MJ-12 was a fraud was overwhelming and that the majority of those inside the UFO community who had studied the case concluded it was a hoax. Yet, even with the majority researchers believing the documents to be fake, a new book has been published suggesting otherwise.

So what is the story on the Operation Majestic-Twelve? Is there anything of value in it or is it just another in the long line of hoaxes that have dotted the UFO landscape?

According to everyone, the MJ-12 documents appeared in 1984 when a mysterious package arrived at the home of film producer and UFO researcher Jaime Shandera on December 11, 1984. It was in a standard, plain brown wrapper, with no return address, but had apparently been mailed from Albuquerque on December 8. Inside was an envelope that contained another envelope that contained a black plastic canister that contained the exposed but undeveloped film. The film, when developed, held the first of the MJ-12 documents: a briefing paper allegedly prepared for then president-elect Dwight Eisenhower and a memo from President Harry Truman "authorizing" the creation of the oversight committee detailed in the briefing.

Please note here, and it is a point that is virtually overlooked in discussions of MJ-12, that the original documents are not available for analysis. In fact, no one knows where they came from or why Shandera of all the "UFO researchers" available was selected, and after all the years of research there has been nothing provided that proves the documents authentic. To most of us, the question of the provenance is one that is most difficult to overcome. Without a solid source available, there is no reason to believe the documents authentic and genuine. To trace their history, we get to Shandera and William Moore and we can go no farther. To the objective researcher, this is extremely worrisome.

Moore and Shandera kept the word of the documents secret, revealing their existence only to Stanton Friedman who would become the leading proponent of MJ-12. In 1988, Timothy Good, a British author who had received copies of the MJ-12 briefing from a source he claimed was CIA but now seems to be Bill Moore, announced he was going to reveal the existence of the documents. Moore and Shandera decided to go forward with what they had and made their own announcement. The world learned of MJ-12 at that time.

It was in the summer of 1988 that I first heard about it. I was shown some of the documents because of my background in the Air Force and in intelligence. It was thought that I might have some insight into the documents that civilians might not have. I looked at the photocopies and saw nothing on them, or in them, that would be suggestive of a hoax. That was, however, a preliminary look, while standing in a hallway of a hotel in Milwaukee with a hundred people buzzing around.

Later, Warren Smith, a man who had been involved in UFO research for twenty-five years or more, told me that in the earlier 1950s, he knew a man directly involved in the Del Rio UFO crash of December 1950, which was mentioned in the MJ-12 briefing. Smith said he worked with a man whose wife had been on a dude ranch in south Texas at the time, and wrote her husband with the details as they unfolded. Smith claimed he knew who the man was and that the letters still existed. Here, if true, would be a wonderful corroboration of MJ-12. Two people in widely separated parts of the country couldn't make up the same details. If Smith could find the man, who had told him of the Del Rio events so long ago, we would have some important verification.

Of course the man never surfaced. I spent a great deal of time and effort trying to run down the lead, calling various newspaper offices, supposed friends of the man, and supposed family members. Nothing ever panned out. And, if the man didn't exist to corroborate Smith's tale, then it did nothing to corroborate MJ-12. Smith didn't tell me of it until after he had read the MJ-12 papers.

This personal anecdote has little to do with the real research into MJ-12. It was a minor disappointment but that was all. I became more skeptical about the documents as I learned more about them, problems with the provenance notwithstanding.

To me, the "smoking gun" that showed the Eisenhower briefing document, that is, the report that told of the recovery of the alien craft and bodies outside of Roswell, was Roscoe Hillenkoetter's rank. Hillenkoetter's rank, as it appears on the document, is wrong. I have tried to explain this to Friedman and others who never served in the military, but it seems to be lost on them. I'll give it one more shot.

First, Friedman argues that he has spoken to a number of former military officers who have told him that a mixed list of names, that is, a list comprised of both military officers and civilian officials, would use the generic term of general or admiral for flag officers, regardless of the number of stars worn on the collar. I'll concede this point only because it doesn't affect my argument.

According to the proponents of MJ-12, that is, Moore, Shandera, and Friedman, Hillenkoetter was the briefing officer and probable author of the the document. In fact, Friedman, in his attempts to validate MJ-12, writes that "At the suggestion of Connecticut lawyer Robert Bletchman, I obtained more than twenty different notes, memos and other writings by Hillenkoetter . . . Bletchman gave these and the briefing to Dr. Roger W. Wescott . . . [who] holds a Ph.D. in linguistics from Princeton, has written more than 40 books on linguistics and anthropology and has lectured at Princeton, Harvard, Oxford and other top schools around the world. . . . Here are his comments on the Hillenkoetter material: 'In my opinion, there is no compelling reason to regard any of these communications as fraudulent or to believe that any of them were written by anyone other than Hillenkoetter himself. This statement holds for the controversial presidential briefing memorandum of November 18, 1952, as well as for the letters, both official and personal.'"

Remember first that Wescott is not a questioned document examiner, but a linguist. He is saying that, in his opinion, as an expert in linguistics, he found nothing in the documents to suggest they weren't written by the men who have been suggested as the authors. That is a very real, but subtle point that must be remembered. An expert in linguistics is not an expert in questioned documents. In a trial, Wescott could testify, if properly credentialed as to his area of expertise, linguistics, but if he began to suggest that the documents were authentic, his expertise as a questioned document examiner would be properly challenged. In other words, that he found nothing in the documents to suggest they weren't authentic is irrelevant.

It goes farther than that. Wescott himself later suggested that he didn't accept the point of view that the documents were authentic. He was taking a somewhat neutral view. This is a fact that Friedman seems to have missed.

Wescott's clarification was published in *IUR*, Vol. 13, No. 4, July/August 1988 and also addressed in *Just Cause* (NEW SERIES), No. 18, December, 1988. Wescott wrote, "Thanks very much for your many lively and provocative letters concerning the Roswell 'crash,' the MJ-12 memorandum, and related matters. . . . First, it's clear that I've stepped into a hornet's nest of controversy. Since I have no strong conviction favoring either rather polarized position in the matter, I may have been a bit rash to become involved, even as a somewhat detached consultant, in what amounts to an adversary procedure. On behalf of those who support the authenticity of the memo, I wrote that I thought its fraudulence unproved. On behalf of its critics, I could equally well have maintained that its authenticity is unproved. Whatever the probabilities of the issue, inconclusiveness seems to me to be of its essence . . ."

So, Wescott wasn't saying in his first letter that the Eisenhower briefing was authentic, only that he, as an expert in linguistics, found nothing to suggest it was faked. On the other hand, he is also saying there is no evidence that it is authentic. In other words, the discussion and inclusion of Wescott's letters are irrelevant and should be ignored. There is better and more compelling evidence found in other arenas.

But the real point here is that Friedman is working very hard to prove that Hillenkoetter is the author of the Eisenhower Briefing paper. Fine, I'll concede that point as well. Hillenkoetter is listed as the briefing officer. We are all in agreement that he wrote the briefing.

Here, however, is where we part company. At the top of the second page, it reads, "BRIEFING OFFICER: ADM. ROSCOE H. HILLENKOETTER (MJ-1)." The point is that Hillenkoetter wasn't an admiral but a rear admiral, which means he wore two stars instead of four. We are talking about a document that, according to all the parties involved in the debate, was created by Hillenkoetter. This is not a question of a mixed list of names, but, a notation at the top of the document. Hillenkoetter, knowing that Eisenhower, one of the handful of men to reach five-star rank, would be seeing this document, would not allow it to go forward with the wrong rank on it.

This is the real, but subtle difference that Friedman refuses to understand. I served as a general's aide and I know exactly how carefully these things are monitored. So, even if he thinks it would be acceptable for the generic ranks to appear on the mixed list, it would not be acceptable for Hillenkoetter to be identified as an admiral at the top of the page where he is identified as the briefing officer.

In fact, if you check the official registry of military officers produced by the various branches of service, those having achieved flag rank (designated as such because generals or admirals have flags that display the number of stars they are authorized to wear) are not listed alphabetically but by date of rank. That is so that each officer knows exactly where he stands in the military pecking order. Once someone is promoted to flag rank, his or her name appears at the bottom of that list.

Or let me try to explain in one other way. Friedman has a Masters of Science degree, or an MS. If I created a list and put him on it, listing his degree as an MA, don't you think he would point it out and correct it? Or more importantly, if he was creating a list and put his own degree on it, don't you think he would get it right?

Finally, it should be noted that I have challenged those believing in MJ-12 to produce a single letter from Hillenkoetter where he got his own rank wrong. Friedman responded, saying that since no one signed the MJ-12 document, the challenge is irrelevant. So, let's change it to any document *created* by Hillenkoetter in which he got his rank wrong. That was why it is so important to understand that the Eisenhower briefing was created by Hillenkoetter. As I say, to me, this was the smoking gun.

But, of course, these were not the only problems that were identified by skeptics. Those other problems, such as the dating format, have been written about before. Simply put, the date as it appears on the Truman memo, which accompanied the Eisenhower briefing was "24 September, 1947." Actual military format would be 24 September 1947.

In both the dating of the documents, and in the dates used in the text, there is also a zero in front of the single digit dates. That is, they are written as "07 July, 1947." This too, violates the dating format in use at the time.

Friedman and Moore have both produced military documents that show the comma in the date where it didn't belong and the zero where it didn't belong. But once again, we have some subtle differences here. The documents often submitted are not the same. They are from the British military which is irrelevant. Or they are from message traffic in which the zero is positional and therefore irrelevant. Or they are documents from NATO which uses a slightly different system, and is filled with military officers from our allies, and are irrelevant.

In other words, it is arguing apples and oranges, but neither seems to be aware of the differences. They just don't address them. Rather, they attack the messenger because they don't understand the differences in the usage.

Joe Nickell (who is now one of the leaders of the Committee for Scientific Investigation of Claims of the Paranormal) and John F. Fischer, in an article prepared for the *International UFO Reporter*, examined Friedman's various responses and wrote, "While Friedman has shown that such a feature, although rare (the anomalous comma), it is not unknown in genuine documents of the period, he has fared less well with another date feature: the use of the zero with the single digit dates—e.g., 'On 07 July, 1947 . . .' Friedman has not been able to show the use of the zero in dates of this type. [His citing of examples in which the representation is digital—and the use of the zero is therefore positional—is essentially irrelevant.] We find that the two anomalous features—the comma and the zero—*when taken together* [Nickell and Fischer's emphasis] are quite distinctive. Neither we nor Friedman have been able to demonstrate the combination in a genuine U.S. government document of the period, let alone any document produced by Hillenkoetter."

What we have here is the report of two researchers who looked to see if the errors in the Eisenhower briefing and the Truman memo were repeated in other documents that have been identified as authentic. They did perform due diligence in their search. They looked at a sufficient number of documents so that they could draw a reasonable conclusion. What they found was that the mistakes in the MJ-12 documents were unique to those documents and that suggests they are fraudulent.

Friedman, in his various responses, doesn't attempt to refute the data. Instead, he suggests that we ignore it because it comes from men associated with CSICOP. But, as we look at the data, if it has been corroborated and verified, there is no reason to reject it. So, what we're left with is information that suggests the mistakes in the MJ-12 document are of sufficient importance to lead us to the conclusion that MJ-12 is a hoax once again and from a different direction.

But these aren't the only problems with them. The Truman memo, attached to the briefing, has been called a special executive order. It seems to function as an executive order, but there is a real problem with it, one that Friedman and other proponents seem to ignore. Instead, he attacks me for what he sees as my failures in providing proper information to inform the reader. He writes, "He [me] does not mention that the date on the memo was typed by two typewriters, and the period after the date points to Van Bush's office as the place where it was typed. In addition, he refers to the order as an *Executive Order* or *EO* at least 15 times, using the initials SCEO only once, which implies that there is no difference between an Executive Order and a Special Classified Executive Order."

This is, however, more of the same useless rhetoric designed to mislead rather than inform. Somehow, the reliance on numbers, the counting of the number of times I use a specific term is supposed to be impressive, yet, in reality, is irrelevant, as are many of the other arguments about MJ-12.

Friedman is outraged that I relied on Nickell, a CSICOP fellow, for information, but seems to have missed the fact that I also relied on Barry Greenwood of Citizens Against UFO Secrecy, who made many of the same arguments as Nickell. In fact, Greenwood, editor of *Just Cause*, wrote, "Page 2 of the Briefing Paper refers to the formation of MJ-12 'by special classified executive order of President Truman on 24 September, 1947 . . . We have checked the Truman Library's listing of executive orders and found that no orders were issued on 9/24. Executive order numbers 9891-9896 were issued respectively on 9/15, two on 9/20, 9/23, 9/30 and 10/2/47, none even closely resembling the MJ-12 subject. There is no gap in the number sequence for these dates so none are missing. Further, the number quoted in Attachment 'A' of the Briefing Paper, #092447 . . . is not an executive order number but the date of President Truman's memo, 9/24/47. Executive orders are not numbered by date but are numbered sequentially, and at the time the numbers were only four digits."

Friedman had a rationalization for this, suggesting that it had only been designated an executive order five years after it was written. In a letter to Nickell, Friedman wrote, "[we] don't have any definition of what is meant by a 'special executive order.'"

Friedman also raises the argument that this was a special classified executive order. It wouldn't be with the unclassified documents. It would require special handling because of its high classification. That seems to be logical thinking on his part.

However, had MJ-12 been a legitimate executive order, it would have fallen into the numerical sequence, even if it was highly classified. A paper, headed, "Congressional Research Service, The Library of Congress on Government Operations, March 17, 1987," states, "During the past 70 years, some 40 confidential or security executive orders have been occasionally issued. These were not published, but they *were accounted for in the numbering system* [emphasis added]."

What this means, quite simply, is that if MJ-12 was legitimate, and highly classified, it would have been in the numbering sequence, but not readily available because of its security classification. The document might not be available, but the number used for it would have been in the sequence of executive orders.

There are a couple more subtle points to be made. Franklin Roosevelt, with Executive Order no. 7298 (February 18, 1936) established the format for executive orders. It specified that such orders must bear a "suitable title for the order," be on paper "approximately 8 x 12 1/2 inches," etc., etc., and that "The authority under which the order or proclamation is promulgated shall be cited in the body thereof."

Truman followed these guidelines until he issued EO no. 10006 establishing his own criterion. It began, "By virtue of the authority vested in the Federal Register Act . . . ," and specified, "The authority under which the order or proclamation is issued shall be cited in the body thereof."

While it can be argued that Truman's EO establishing the format of his executive orders follows, chronologically, that of MJ-12, it must be remembered that he followed Roosevelt's order until he officially changed it. In other words, if Truman had issued the memo establishing MJ-12, it would have followed the format in use at that time. Clearly, it is in violation of the regulations as specified in *Code of Federal Regulations, Title 3—The President, 1943–1948 Compilation* (Washington, D.C.: U.S. Government Printing Office, 1957).

When Friedman argues that highly classified executive orders would not be available to unclassified sources, or to those without the proper clearances, he is correct. However, and this bears repeating because it is an important point, Harold C. Relyea wrote in the *Code of Federal Regulations,* "During the past 70 years, some 40 confidential or security executive orders have been occasionally issued. These were not published, but they were accounted for in the numbering system."

Friedman, however, is now saying, "It is not labelled as a Presidential Executive Order. . . . Would everybody please read the short, Sept. 24, 1947, memo again? It is not labelled executive order. It is not labelled Special Classified Executive Order. It has no number on it. . . . I repeat it is false to say it is listed as Executive Order #. . . . It is false to say it is labelled as SCEO # or anything else."

But there is a real problem here. The Eisenhower briefing had a listing of the attachments, only one of which was forwarded. Attachment A contains, according to the briefing itself, "Special Classified Executive Order #092447."

So, once again we have something that does not match the proper format or regulations that were in force in 1947. It could be suggested, and has been, that this was a unique event so that the paperwork surrounding it would be unique, but that doesn't wash. Even for an event of this magnitude, the simple regulations surrounding the creation of executive orders, or special classified executive orders, would have been followed. They all seem to have been ignored in this case.

The final bit of this rather technical and somewhat tiring argument is that the Truman memo is being cited by Hillenkoetter, according to the document itself, as an executive order. And given his position in the government, both in 1947 and in 1952 when the briefing was allegedly written, he should have known what an executive order was. According to Nickell and Fischer, "Besides, the document seems to function as an EO when it states that 'you are hereby authorized to proceed with all due speed and caution upon your undertaking. . . .'" They continue, writing that a "genuine EO would necessarily cite the authority under which the President was acting. . . ." They conclude, "In short, the document's content, like its format, seems incompatible with authenticity."

What we have, in the Eisenhower briefing and the Truman memo, are documents that do not conform to the styles used in the proper time frames. We find a number of problems, from Hillenkoetter's rank being wrong to the very technical details for issuing an executive order that are wrong. All this is suggestive of mistakes and that the documents are frauds. We could, however, get bogged down in these arguments with Friedman making the counterclaim that this was an extraordinary circumstance that required an extraordinary departure from the norm. Of course, there have been no documents found to support that. It is only speculation.

What we have been searching for here is a "direct link" to the

MJ-12. What we have seen, to this point, are arguments about who might be right and who might be wrong. What none of it does is establish that MJ-12 existed, or exists. We have no direct link into the MJ-12.

For example, Friedman makes much of his research into the secret life of Donald H. Menzel, a Harvard astronomer and an anti-UFO skeptic. Menzel wrote books on the topic, waged a campaign to eradicate UFOs from the lexicon of the average citizen, and wasn't above labeling puzzling cases as hoaxes when he could find no other answer for them. Friedman, when he learned that Menzel was an alleged member of MJ-12 performed the Herculean task of searching Menzel's personal papers for some sort of tie to MJ-12 or proof of its existence.

In articles published in *IUR* and in his recent book, he writes about Menzel's "double life." We learn that Menzel spoke Japanese, that during the Second World War he worked as a Navy cryptologist, that he was on a first-name basis with John F. Kennedy, that he was a consultant to the NSA, and that he narrowly survived a McCarthy-era challenge to his loyalty. Menzel was friends, or at least knew, Dr. Vannevar Bush and Dr. Detlev W. Bronk, who are also named as MJ-12 members.

What Friedman has established is that Menzel moved in some very high circles and that he seemed to be a very intelligent man who didn't believe in UFOs. And all of this is irrelevant because it does nothing to establish a direct link to MJ-12. Menzel could be all of these things, and more, and still not be a member of the mythical MJ-12 committee. None of this does anything to provide a provenance for MJ-12 or to proving that MJ-12 is real.

In fact, almost any scientist who was alive and working during the early 1940s was probably involved in some sort of work for the government. The Second World War sucked in all the resources and personnel that it could. Nearly everyone was involved in the war effort because the biggest threat facing the world at that time were the fanatics in Japan and Germany. Had they won the war, the world would have been a much different place than it is today. To learn that any scientist from that era was doing work for the government, even highly classified work, is not surprising.

But in all the searching that Friedman has done, in all the archives he has visited, in the thousands of documents he has reviewed, he has not found a single shred of evidence that MJ-12 existed. There is no verifying evidence of MJ-12. There are only the dubious documents that are riddled with errors and inconsistencies that Friedman ignores or belittles. And none of that provides the direct link to MJ-12 that is needed.

If, for example, Friedman had found anything in Menzel's files such as a note in Menzel's handwriting, or a memo to Menzel about MJ-12, that would be a direct link and it would move us forward in our search. But none of that was found. Instead we are treated to a listing of the secrets to which Menzel was privy, but nothing about MJ-12. There is no direct link and everything else about Menzel, while interesting, is irrelevant.

What we see here, is that the chain of evidence, if you will, is broken. The last link, from Menzel into MJ-12, does not exist outside the document itself. More importantly, in a point that is often forgotten, the first link doesn't exist either. All the documents, whether we are talking about those Shandera received anonymously in the mail, the Cutler-Twining memo that seems to support MJ-12 but was discovered by Moore and Shandera at the National Archives, or any of the documents that have surfaced since, have no provenance. No governmental agency claims them, no Freedom of Information Act requests can find them, and the authorship is still in dispute. In other words, the first link in the chain is broken as well.

Although Friedman, as the leading proponent of the documents, seems to ignore these problems in relation to MJ-12, he is quick to point them out in other arenas. On the Santilli Autopsy film, which we will discuss at length in another chapter, Friedman told a national radio audience, "What I cannot do . . . is tell you that this film was made by company XYZ. . . . I don't have the genesis of it, but the burden isn't on me to prove what I said."

In other words, Santilli and his crew must prove the film or document authentic and have failed to do so. Friedman must prove MJ-12 authentic and he has failed to do so. More importantly, he clearly understands the difference, but ignores it in the case of MJ-12, suggesting, as he did in his *Final Report on Operation Majestic 12,* that North American courts do not require a defendant prove his or her innocence but that the courts prove the guilt. He suggests that no one has proven the documents fake, implying they must, therefore, be authentic. Of course, in questioned documents research, the burden is on the proponent rather than the skeptic, just as Friedman suggested himself in discussing the Santilli film.

But let's move beyond the constant arguments that boil down to, "Yes, he did," and "No, he didn't." Let's address some other items that seem to put an end to the arguments.

First is the typeface on the typewriter used to write the Truman memo. I spoke to a questioned document expert who had the opportunity in 1989 to examine the MJ-12 documents, or more specifically, the Eisenhower briefing and the Truman memo. He told me, at that time, that the typeface was most consistent with a Smith-Corona P102, which was used on typewriters after 1966. If true, this, by itself, means the Truman memo is a fake since it was supposedly created in 1947.

Moore and Shandera, in their report, mentioned a second expert, whom they do not identify, as saying that he thought the typeface was from a Ransmayer & Rodrian 664, but that had no dates of manufacture. Still another expert said the typeface was from an Underwood UP3A, which was manufactured between 1933 and 1946.

The discussion of typefaces seems to be a wash, except for a couple of facts. First, I have no idea who the two "experts" are who identified typewriters with unspecified manufacture dates or dates that precede the creation of the Truman memo. I do, on the other hand, know who the expert is who said that the type is from a machine manufactured after 1966. He told me, "This is the slam dunk." To him, it proved the memo a fake.

Friedman, in his book, writes about the typeface controversy, "Other examiners disagree with Klass's CIA source about the typewriter used for the rest of the memo."

First, the expert is not CIA and has never been CIA. Friedman has confused one source with another. Suggesting a CIA connection is an attempt to eliminate the criticism about the typeface without having to deal with it. If the man is a CIA source, then clearly, his information must be verified from other sources.

But second, and more importantly, I have spoken to an expert who demanded to know who these experts are. He also points out that he wants to see their report and to understand exactly what their expertise is. Unless they have a complete A to Z strike up of both the upper case and lower case letters, as well as all the symbols and numbers for the typeface of the Underwood UP3A, then their argument is without merit. The man I talked to said repeatedly that he had all the drawings from the Underwood factory for the typestyle Friedman and the others claim it is. He said, "I have samples from typewriters with that typestyle on them that I used to type the text of the memo." In other words, he could make a letter by letter examination of the typestyles and draw an expert's conclusions which is that the typestyle is from a typewriter that didn't exist until after 1960. If Friedman has other experts, he must do better than just suggest it. He must present the evidence and he has yet to do it.

In fact, when I challenged him on this point, he told me, or sent me an e-mail to be precise, that he didn't have the names of the experts. If he is relying on information provided by Moore and Shandera, he should require them, at the very least, to provide a copy of the report. Without any of that data, then we can only conclude that those other experts don't exist.

To make it worse, Friedman is relying on the 1991 *The MJ-12 Documents: An Analytical Report* written by Moore and Shandera to suggest that others do not agree with the statement that the typewriter was made after 1960. However, we are once again treated to a misleading statement. The discussion of the typeface and typewriters, as it appears in Moore's report, mentions the idiosyncratic notations made up by Dr. David Crown. They appear in his article in the *Journal of Police Science and Administration.* But they don't have samples of those typewriters or those typefaces.

What they have done is misrepresent a footnote written by Crown that deals with these various typefaces. When you see the footnote on the page, it becomes apparent that they have completely misrepresented it. What's more, Friedman is aware of this but chooses to ignore it. Instead, we are left with an impressive sounding argument written by Moore and Shandera who claim no expertise in questioned documents. There is no citation of the Crown article by Moore and Shandera in their report, which in and of itself is interesting, but also probably irrelevant. Once again, the argument is ducked without proper response.

The second major problem on the Truman memo was Truman's signature. The signature on the executive order matches, exactly, another Truman signature, this one from a letter dated October 1, 1947. The positioning of the signature on the memo also makes it suspect. Truman habitually placed his signature so that the stroke on the "T" touched the bottom of the text. On the disputed EO that is not the case. (Yes, I continue to call the Truman memo an executive order because that was how it is referenced in the Eisenhower briefing.)

Friedman originally reported that the signature on the October 1 letter matched exactly that on the MJ-12 executive order and believed that it proved the signature authentic rather than demonstrating that it was fraudulent. According to Friedman, "The signature matches that on an October 1947 letter from Truman to (Vannevar) Bush." The exact match, in fact, suggests the document is a hoax.

Moore and Shandera, in their *The MJ-12 Documents: An Analytical Report* write, after measuring the Truman signature, that it isn't an exact match. They suggest it is close, and, according to various handwriting experts, this makes the signature more consistent with authenticity.

The controversy over that memo wasn't ended there. Nickell and Fischer received a copy of *The MJ-12 Documents: An Analytical Report* in 1991. Nickell and Fischer believed, according to an unpublished paper *Further Deception: Moore and Shandera's MJ-12 Report*, ". . . [The Moore and Shandera report] provides lessons in how not to investigate a ufologically related questioned document case. . . . Not only is neither a trained investigator, let alone a document specialist, but both are crashed-saucer zealots and one (Moore) has actually been suspected of having forged the documents."

Then, to make their case, Nickell and Fischer again examine the status of the investigation of the Truman memo. They reinforce their conclusion that the document is "an incompetent" hybrid, and say that "no genuine memo has yet been discovered with such an erroneous mixture of elements." Moore and Shandera dismiss this criticism, according to Nickell and Fischer, "with the cavalier observation that there was 'a wide variety of styles and formats in acceptable use at the time.' "

Nickell and Fischer had also pointed out that the Truman signature had been "placed uncharacteristically low." Moore and Shandera countered by saying, "The problem with this assertion is that those who make it used only letters signed by Truman as the basis for their study." Nickell and Fischer responded, writing, "We did no such thing . . . here Moore and Shandera are guilty of outright misrepresentation . . . we studied typed letters and memos, handwritten notes, engraved thank-you cards, inscriptions and photographs. . . . In every instance where Truman had personally signed the text . . . our observation of close placement applied."

Friedman, however, rejects this argument, pointing out, correctly, that Nickell and Fischer have not reviewed every document signed by Truman. That means, somewhere, there could be another Truman signature that conforms to that on the MJ-12 memo. Of course, their examination was of a representative sample of sufficient size for them to draw a legitimate conclusion. It is now incumbent on the proponents to produce a legitimate Truman document signed in the same manner. The have failed, to this point, to do that.

In the final argument listed in their response, Nickell and Fischer again examine the evidence that the signature on the questioned memo is an exact duplicate of an authentic Truman signature from a letter dated October 1, 1947. They write, ". . . in forensic comparisons in which distortion can be a possibility—e.g., in attempting to match fingerprints, or to link a paint flake to a chipped surface—the Moore-Shandera (actually Maccabee) approach is not used. Instead, experts establish matching by demonstrating that an array of distinctive features in one item is also represented in the other. Using this approach, competent examiners have determined that the two [Truman] signatures do in fact match."

While Moore and Shandera claim to have interviewed "four key questioned document examiners . . . none of these four was willing to allow their [*sic*] name to be publicly used . . ." Friedman contacted another who determined that the Truman memo was a fake. Moore and Shandera "omit any mention of this fact . . . as does Friedman in his own *Final Report on Operation Majestic 12.*

I, in fact, was able to speak to that questioned document examiner at length on August 20, 1996. I asked him specific questions about the Truman signature. To him, this was another "slam dunk." It was a second major problem with the document which shouted fake at him.

Friedman has pointed out that the signature from the memo, when placed over the signature from the October 1 letter, is not an exact match. He then belittles the claim that stretching in the copying process would lead to the differences in the signature. He also notes the careful measuring of the various components in the signature carried out by Moore and Shandera, proving their case. He suggests, because they are not an exact match, a reversal of his earlier opinion, that the signature must be authentic.

The measuring of the signature looks good, looks scientific, and is just so much "eyewash," according to questioned documents experts. In other words, it has no relevance in a discussion of copied signatures, especially since the original document is unavailable and had been originally photographed rather than copied on a Xerox or Minolta or Panasonic.

In fact, I was told that there are appearances on the Truman signature that suggest it had been altered prior to it being applied to the memo. One expert said, "That is a demonstrable, transplanted signature."

He said, "Klass is the one who came up with the prototype signature. And that's an absolute slam dunk. There's no question about it. When you look at the points where it intersects the typing on the original donor memo [that is, the October 1, 1947, letter] for the transplant, you can see that it was retouched on those points on the Majestic-12 memo. So, it's just a perfect fit. The thing was, it wasn't photocopied and it wasn't photographed straight on. . . . The guy who did one of the photographic prints had to tilt the base board to try and get the edges to come out square so whoever did the photography of the pieces of paper was not doing this on a properly set up copy stand. It was done, maybe on a tripod, or it was done hand held. However it was done, the documents were not photographed straight on. . . . There's a slight distortion of the signature but it is not enough to make the difference here. Nowadays you could probably get it to fit properly with computer work but it's not that the signature is an overlay but it's that at those discrete points, and their dumb document examiners talked about the thinning of the stroke at this point. At that particular point, at the exact spot where it touches a typewritten letter and it has to be retouched to get rid of the letter."

In talking to him, I said, "So when Shandera and Moore go to all the trouble to measure the signature . . ."

He broke in to say, "Oh, give me a break. . . . It's just eyewash and what they're doing is looking at the distortions that you get from the photocopying process. . . . We're dealing with photocopies of photocopies of photocopies of the October first donor document signature."

He went on to enumerate other problems with the whole Eisenhower briefing, points that I hadn't thought much about. He said, "And it was just perfect because the whole thing of the twelve pages or however many pages it was. Most of the pages were just blank pages with just five words on them, like Top Secret Memo or Appendix A or something like that. The bulk of the narrative said see this appendix for the metallurgical analysis. See that appendix for the autopsy. Now those particular appendices, in order to make them look credible would require a considerable amount of technical knowledge and vocabulary. There is no question about that. You have to know how to talk the talk to write something about metallurgy or anatomy. And you can just say the metallurgical reports found that this was unlike anything that we've ever seen but then you have to list the most advanced tests that would be available in 1947 but would not be available in 1955 and you have to know too much. And you have to know the lingo of the human anatomy. You have to be a doctor basically to say that this structure is not like that structure. So I can see why nobody would bother to fake those."

He continued, "But a simply bureaucratic memo from somebody who is steeped in bureaucratic lingo from having pored through these archives as I'm sure that all the people involved on both sides of this issue have done. To fake one of those, that's no big deal. . . . To get the right people on there and throw in one or two anti-UFO people just for fun. . . . That's not a problem."

As we finished the discussion, he said, "I want to smoke these people out because, quite frankly, I want to nuke them. These people are going around aiding in the . . . why do you want to do this? I'm somewhat annoyed at these people who say they are document examiners who go out there and support a blatantly bad piece of paper. Shame on them. I want to smoke them out. . . . MJ-12 as a documentary hoax, which is what I take it to be, annoys me. I don't know who the hoaxer is."

As I mentioned, I hadn't thought much about the ease with which a bureaucratic memo could be created but the man was right. And, although I wasn't going to mention the so-called Cutler-Twining memo, it is just the sort of bureaucratic document to which he referred. Easy to fake because there isn't much substance to it. And, just a reference to MJ-12 in such a bureaucratic memo would be sufficient to establish the existence of the committee.

What appeared to be the corroboration for the MJ-12 document was found by Shandera and Moore at the National Archives as they reviewed Record Group 341 which had just been declassified. Located in a dusty box of recently reviewed material was a memo that mentioned a rescheduling of an MJ-12 briefing. It was a memo for General Twining, then Air Force Chief of Staff, from Robert Cutler, the Special Assistant to the President. Dated July 14, 1954, it established the existence of the MJ-12 committee and that the committee was still active in the mid-1950s.

The problem with the memo, though it had been found at the National Archives, and had been found in a box that was among the boxes of recently declassified material, was that it didn't belong there. There was no record of the memo being in that box before it was examined by Shandera and Moore, it hadn't been discovered by the review conducted by Air Force officers as part of the declassification of the other material in the box, and, if it was authentic, it should have been withdrawn from the box for a declassification review by the NSC.

Ed Reese of the Military Reference Branch of the National Archives, in a letter to UFO researcher Robert Todd, reported, "In none of these reviews was the Cutler-Twining memorandum identified as present and requiring any special attention. But the declassification guidelines used by both the Air Force and the National Archives would not have permitted them to declassify National Security Council documents. If discovered in the files during any of these reviews such a documents [*sic*] would have been withdrawn and provided to a National Security Council declassification specialist for final determination. It was never so identified."

The purpose of the review was to ensure that no properly classified material was inadvertently released to researchers, historians, or journalists. Since the Air Force had only a general idea of what was in each of the boxes, and since the reviewers, Air Force intelligence officers, wouldn't have been involved in the creation or the filing of the documents, they had to perform a page-by-page search of everything in each of the boxes. In such a review, the memo would have been found and it would have not been declassified without first having been reviewed by an NSC specialist. In other words, the memo required special handling and there is no indication that it received that special attention.

Like the MJ-12 paper, the Cutler-Twining memo, as it is now called, is flawed. The classification at the top of the memo, "Top Secret Restricted," is a combination of two distinct security classifications and is therefore incorrect. Top secret is the highest, requiring special handling, limited access, and specific safeguards. At the time the memo was allegedly written, restricted information was the lowest classification, requiring much less special handling.

Todd, in his investigation of the memo, contacted the Eisenhower Library and was told that "The classification marking on this memorandum is one that we have never seen on an Eisenhower document. 'Top Secret' and 'Restricted' are two different levels of classification."

Now that the curators at the Eisenhower Library had been alerted to the possibility of a mixed classification and therefore might have found something after Todd's investigation, another check was initiated. Tom Braniger said that there were rumors around the Eisenhower Library that the Cutler-Twining memo had been faked. He again confirmed that no document with such a strange classification, that is, Top Secret Restricted, had been found. He was not familiar with the classification and repeated that the memo was not authentic.

Again, like the MJ-12 paper, Friedman has produced a number of documents that almost match the questioned memo. He found several that had been stamped, "Restricted Security Information, Confidential Restricted Security Information, and Secret Restricted Security Information," but none stamped, "Top Secret Restricted." The problem here is that they weren't classified, for example, "Secret Restricted Security Information," but had been downgraded at some point from Secret to Restricted so that both classifications appeared on the document. That meant that a document originally classified as Secret would be reclassified or downgraded as Restricted at a later date. At no time was it classified as Secret Restricted. The examples do nothing to validate the memo and therefore the memo does nothing to validate MJ-12.

We could take the argument even deeper but there seems to be no reason to do so. The National Archives, where the memo was found, made it clear that their certification of a copied document merely means that it is an accurate copy of a document in their possession and not that the document itself is genuine. To provide the Cutler-Twining memo with that sort of pseudo pedigree might be the reason that it was planted there, and all parties seem to agree that it was planted.

What's interesting in this discussion of the various MJ-12 documents is that Friedman, in attempting to refute this information, has attempted to point people to Moore and Shandera's *The MJ-12 Documents: An Analytical Report.* He wonders why other researchers and interested parties have not used it or referenced it in their work. The reasons may be as simple as the $25.00 price tag and the fact that it was self-published with few people even knowing that it existed.

But the real point comes up in the conclusions which Friedman apparently hasn't read recently. Moore and Shandera have looked at all the documents that they consider somehow related to the MJ-12 controversy and that were available to them when they prepared their report. I'm not going to bother with discussing all of them here because the list is long and many of them are irrelevant to MJ-12. I will provide a listing of their specific conclusions about them.

Of the Aquarius Document, also known as the Aquarius Telex, which was supposed to be a real AFOSI message that contained a one sentence reference to MJ-12, Moore and Shandera write, "The document is a hybrid of real and disinformation." I would say that it is a hybrid of real and misinformation because disinformation implies a governmental hand in its creation. The document, according to them, as well as many other researchers, is a phony.

Of the Eisenhower briefing document, they write, ". . . [W]e give a value of 75% to the likelihood that the document is authentic, and 25% to the possibility that it is a fabrication."

Of the Truman memo, they write, "As for the document as a whole, it is either authentic or a well done and very probably official fabrication. We give a value of 35–40% for the former possibility, and 60–65% for the latter."

Of the Cutler-Twining memo, they write, "All things considered, we conclude a 95%+ probability that the document is genuine, and that it was deliberately planted in the National Archives by person or persons unknown who then systematically undertook to be sure that we would discover it there."

So even Moore and Shandera, two of the leading proponents of MJ-12 have serious doubts about the authenticity of the various MJ-12 documents, concluding that it is more likely that the Truman memo, for example, is a fake than that it is genuine. Someone suggested that he wouldn't believe anything Moore said, so rejected, out of hand, these conclusions drawn by Moore, believing instead that the Truman memo was authentic. Of course, since it was Moore and Shandera who released the information in the first place, doesn't that mean that he couldn't accept the document as authentic because he refused believe anything from Moore? Or was this a simple lapse in his judgment?

There is another, subtle suggestion about the creation of MJ-12. Robert Pratt, a writer and former reporter for the *National Enquirer*, said that he had worked on a novel in 1982 and 1983 with Moore concerning a group like the MJ-12, though the designation, according to Pratt, was "Majik." The book itself was about UFOs and only briefly touched on a secret report labeled Majik with several references to MJ-12.

Pratt said that the writing was done in 1982 or 1983 and that Moore had given him some documents or notes dated 1981. When the MJ-12 documents surfaced, Pratt said that he wasn't surprised because the term sounded familiar to him. He said that Moore had been talking about something like MJ-12 for years. Because of that, Pratt believed that the MJ-12 documents were fraudulent.

What we have then, is a number of documents all being released by the same sources. It was Moore who supplied the Aquarius Telex (though some say that Friedman told them that he had gotten the document first from inside sources), Moore and Shandera who found the Cutler–Twining Memo, Moore and Shandera who received both the MJ-12 briefing paper and the Truman memo establishing the committee. Timothy Good, author of *Above Top Secret,* supposedly received the original briefing document from, according to him, a CIA source (Good now says that he believes the MJ-12 documents are fraudulent). That document, however, seems to have been reproduced on the copying machine used by Moore.

An analysis by Barry Greenwood of both the MJ-12 documents as reproduced in *Above Top Secret* and Bill Moore's self-published magazine *Focus* sheds some light on the origin of the documents. Greenwood writes in *Just Cause* (March 1990) "For purposes of comparison I have chosen pages 1–3 of Moore's copy of the Eisenhower briefing as reproduced from *Focus* for April 30, 1987, Moore's first public release of this document. Also chosen are pages 1–3 of Good's copy of the briefing from his CIA source as reproduced in *Above Top Secret.*"

Greenwood examines the "magic marker" deletions through the security markings on both versions and writes, "while the deletions are not identical there is a marked similarity. . . . Early in the MJ-12 debate Moore had already admitted self-censoring his copy. . . . One sees no significant difference between the Moore and the Good versions in the way the markings were applied."

The important aspect of Greenwood's examination is the "vertical ridges" that appear on both versions of the MJ-12 document. Greenwood explained that "If one compares pages from both versions of the document you will notice a pattern of photocopier 'noise,' i.e. a general dirtiness of the photocopy paper caused by an unclean machine. This noise takes the form of vertical parallel ridges across portions of the copies. As in the case of the magic marker deletions, the pattern is not identical but is very similar. The density and clarity of the noise pattern can vary from copy to copy, depending on the maintenance of the machine, but the same general pattern is there, as can be clearly seen in both copies. . . . [What is] suggested here is that the two versions were copied at different times but on the same machine."

One final bit of evidence was uncovered by Greenwood which he characterized as the "Fingerprint." The fingerprint was two lines at roughly a 30 degree angle to the horizontal bottom of the page appearing between paragraphs 1 and 2. They also appeared on Good's version of the paper, but not in the same location. According to Greenwood, "The mark floats on various copies . . . apparently a flaw in the photocopier roller that becomes imprinted onto various areas of the papers as they pass through the machine." Because of that, Greenwood wrote, "I am forced to believe that both came from the same copy machine at different times."

Greenwood's conclusions are self-evident. He writes, "It is important that the various anomalies cited above are not *absolutely* identical in every way, as far as clarity, position and density are concerned. If they were it could be argued that the *original* document, photographed and sent to Shandera, and allegedly copied and sent to Good by a CIA source, possessed these anomalies. As such each person's version could still be attributed to a government source. This is not the case here."

Greenwood finishes by writing, "The Moore/Shandera copy was received in 1984. Hard copy had to be made from the photographic film, resulting in copies possessing the anomalies particular to the photocopy machine used by them. Timothy Good's copies contain the same kinds of anomalies, meaning that the machine used by Moore/Shandera was the source of Good's copies."

Before we leave the discussion of MJ-12 related documents, there is another that must be mentioned, and that is the newly leaked MJ-12 Operations Manual. I wrote about it in the *International UFO Reporter*, pointing out that it suffers from the same problem as all the other MJ-12 documents. That is, no provenance. It arrived, on an exposed roll of 35 mm film, at the home of Don Berliner. He had it developed and then quietly circulated copies inside the UFO community. According to a letter he sent to the editor of the *IUR*, once he had the developed film in hand, he made several xerox copies and "took a set to the General Accounting Office people who were starting their search for Roswell-related documents for Rep. Steve Schiff. I assumed they would be much better able to determine the bona fides of the document than I, or anyone else in the UFO community."

I must say that I agree with that. In fact, I, too, had turned over information that I felt I could do nothing with, but that they might be able to use. Since the GAO is an investigative arm of the congress, and has the power to go almost anywhere in the government, they seemed like the people to advise.

In their report to Congressman Schiff about their search for documentation in the Roswell case, they attach a letter that deals specifically with MJ-12. Richard Davis, who signed the letter, wrote, "In response to your request, we asked several agencies for their views on the authenticity of the publicly circulated written material referred to as Majestic Twelve. The origin of this material is unknown, but it is purported to represent highly classified government records explaining unidentified flying object recovery procedures and the crash of a disc-shaped aircraft near Roswell. . . ."

He explained that they had contacted a number of government offices about the documents and learned, "These agencies responded to the inquiries by stating that their knowledge of Majestic 12 was limited to the written material submitted to them by nongovernmental persons. These agencies added that they found no records in their files relating to Majestic Twelve. Moreover, the agencies' overall conclusion concerning the authenticity of the Majestic 12 written material was the same—there is no evidence that the Majestic 12 written material constitutes actual documents originally created in the executive branch. According to the Information Security Oversight Office and the Air Force, the Majestic 12 material should not be treated as if it had ever been actually classified by an executive branch agency or government official. We found nothing in our work that contradicts the conclusions reached by these agencies."

Hoping to learn something important, I sent the front page of the Operations Manual to the Eisenhower Library to get their impressions of it. The real mistake, on the cover, seems to be a classification of "Restricted." According to Dr. Herbert L. Pankratz of the Eisenhower Library, "The classification markings on the alleged MJ-12 document are not consistent with federal regulations for the marking of classified materials as of April 1954 [the date on the manual]. The 'Restricted' classification category was terminated by executive order in November 1953 and would not have been used on a document in April 1954. Federal regulations also require that the cover page reflect the highest level of classification for any material in the document. Since 'Top Secret' is a higher category than

'Restricted,' only 'Top Secret' should have appeared on the cover of the document."

In other words, the cover of the document violated the federal regulations in effect in April 1954 when the manual was allegedly published. If the document is authentic, it should conform to those regulations. This document, like all the others, seems to be at variance with the proper regulations. Proponents will claim that these regulations weren't ironclad and that variations do exist. However, documents created at this level would be closely monitored and would adhere to the proper regulations, especially since they had just been changed. The classifications on the manual, like those on the other MJ-12 documents, are wrong and there is no reason for them to be. It smacks of hoax.

Pankratz continued in his letter of February 6, 1995, writing, "In addition, we have no evidence in our files that a security classification referred to as 'MAJIC EYES ONLY' ever existed. Executive Order 10501 was signed by President Eisenhower on November 5, 1953. It set up three classification categories: 'Top Secret,' 'Secret,' and 'Confidential.' A fourth category, 'Restricted Data' (not the same as 'restricted'), was established by the Atomic Energy Act of 1954; and it is used only with regard to nuclear weapons."

Friedman's response to these negative results? His pat phrase, "Absence of evidence isn't evidence of absence."

Except, in science, when due diligence has been performed, absence of evidence is, in fact, evidence of absence. How many times, by how many different people, do we have to be told there is no evidence for the MJ-12? When do we finally sit down and say, "Hey! There is no provenance for any of the documents? None." They cannot be traced back to any official source. That means that the chain of evidence breaks before we get there. The chain of evidence can link us into members of the UFO community and that is it. We cannot follow it back into some government archive or office or bureau.

None of what has been written, found, released, or discussed allows any of us to establish the provenance of MJ-12 or to provide a direct link which would allow us to establish MJ-12 as genuine. In fact, not one of the documents, whether from the original bunch made up of the Eisenhower briefing or the Truman memo or the new ones now appearing, establishes the necessary direct link to MJ-12. These are rumors that have been around for nearly a decade and we are no closer to an answer now than we were then.

The arguments for the authenticity of MJ-12 all fall into the same pit. We have an expert who says that the typeface on the Truman memo was not available until after 1960, and then we have Moore and Shandera, who are quick to point out they are not experts in questioned documents, telling us why the typeface is from an Underwood UP3A. But that is nothing more than their unqualified opinion. They should present their evidence rather than their opinion. Show us the report by these other experts where those claims are made. The man I've talked to said that he wants to meet them. If they will present any sort of report or documentation to prove their points, then he will be glad to stand up to be counted, but not until that time. Besides, all of them, Friedman, Moore, and Shandera, know who it is, they originally sought his advice, they all have spoken to him on several occasions but they choose not to acknowledge his work because, to him, the Truman memo is a provable fake.

There has been nothing, absolutely nothing, that establishes the authenticity of MJ-12. Nothing. All the arguments that have been presented to this point have proved nothing concrete about MJ-12. As Friedman has said in conjunction with the Santilli film, proving that he understands the principle, the burden of proof is on those who make the claims of authenticity, not on those who suggest fraud.

Remember this. When it comes down to MJ-12, there is not a single shred of evidence that the documents are real. Not one. There are no direct links from the government or back again. The chain of evidence is broken at both ends. Until it can be linked one way or the other, the only possible conclusion is that the documents, all of them, are fakes.

4 The Gulf Breeze Photographs

1987

FOR NEARLY A DECADE NOW, we have been treated to spectacular stories of a UFO hovering over the Gulf Breeze area in the Florida panhandle. Photographs have been taken, many of them quite spectacular. Others reported that they, too, have seen the object, some of them producing their own pictures including a couple of videotapes. But those taken over a period of several months by a man originally identified only as "Mr. Ed" were, by far, the best.

On November 11, 1987, Ed Walters, a self-described prominent businessman, was working in his office at home. He thought he saw something glowing behind a thirty-foot pine tree in the front yard. He stepped outside to get a better look and saw a top-shaped craft with a row of dark squares and smaller openings across the midsection. There was a bright, glowing ring around the bottom.

Realizing that this was something very unusual, Walters reached into his office and grabbed an old Polaroid camera. He stepped back out and took a photograph as the craft moved from behind the tree. In all, he would take five pictures as the UFO, about a hundred and fifty feet away, continued to drift in a northeasterly direction.

Out of film, he returned to his office, reloaded the camera, and took the fifth picture. The object was closer, and Walters ran into the street to take additional photographs. Then, according to what he would tell some investigators, he was hit by a blue beam of light that paralyzed him and lifted him off his feet. A computer-like voice that he heard inside his head said, "We will not harm you." Other images, and a female voice filled his head. Suddenly, he fell hard on the pavement, as the blue beam vanished. When he looked, the UFO was gone as well.

Just six days later, Walters visited Duane Cook, editor of the *Gulf Breeze Sentinel.* He showed Cook the pictures, but claimed they had been taken by someone else. Walters gave Cook a letter allegedly written by the anonymous photographer explaining the situation. Two days later, on November 19, 1987, the letter and the pictures were published in the newspaper.

On November 20—as Walters returned home and walked through the door, he heard a humming in his ears. At first he hardly noticed it, but it grew in pitch until it was nearly unbearable. He walked through the house, followed by his wife, Frances, and then went back outside. According to Walters, the hum was the same as the one he heard while trapped in the blue beam. They saw nothing in the sky.

Walters went into his office and sat down. He heard voices in his head, speaking in something that sounded like an African dialect to him. When his wife came in to tell him that she, along with their daughter, were going to a football game, he said nothing about the voices.

After they left, Walters picked up his camera, and walked out the front door. Outside, he said, "I hear you, you bastard." There was a rush of air, and the internal voice said, "Be calm. Step forward."

High overhead, a speck of light fell toward him rapidly. Walters raised the camera but a voice told him, in Spanish, that photographs were prohibited. The female voice told him, "You can't expose them. They won't hurt you. Just a few tests. That's all."

But Walters didn't care. He took a picture of the UFO as it hovered above a power pole. While the voices were still speaking to him, the UFO shot to the right and Walters took a second picture. About that time, the first voice told him to take a step forward so that he could enter the craft. Walters told them they had no right to do what they were doing, and the voice said, "We have the right."

The female voice added, "You must do what they say. They haven't hurt us and we are going back home now."

As the first voice said, "We will come for you now," images of naked women filled his mind. Walters took a third picture. The UFO moved forward and then shot upward, into the sky, vanishing almost instantly.

He next saw the UFO on December 2, when he was awakened by the sound of a baby crying. Although there were no babies in either of the neighbors' houses or his own for that matter, Walters was upset. Then he heard the voices, speaking Spanish, and talking about the crying baby. Accompanied by his wife, Walters, carrying a .32 caliber pistol, checked the house and the yard. Out back, he saw the UFO descending rapidly. It stopped about a hundred feet above the pool, then drifted a short distance before stopping.

Walters retreated to the house to join his wife, who was seeing the craft for the first time. What he would later describe as the "UFO voice" commanded that he "Step forward now."

Once again Walters grabbed his Polaroid camera and took it, along with his pistol, out the door. Near the pool in his backyard, he took another picture, but when the flash went off, he felt exposed. He ran back into the house. From the kitchen, he, along with his wife, saw the UFO vanish. When it was gone, the hum inside his head faded.

Back in bed, Walters said he heard the dog bark once, which he said was unusual. Walters again got up, and carrying both his pistol and camera, walked to the French doors, sure that he would see the UFO once again. Instead, when he opened the curtains he saw, just inches from him, a four-foot humanoid with big black eyes. It was wearing a helmet with a bit of transparent material at eye level that apparently allowed it to see.

Walters, who seemed to have remained calm enough through his other UFO experiences to take multiple photographs of the craft and who disobeyed their commands not to photograph the object, forgot about the camera in his hand. He screamed in surprise, jumped back, and tripped. Walters raised his pistol, thinking he would fire if the creature tried to enter the house, but never thought to take a picture.

Walters finally got to his feet and then struggled with the lock on the door. He put down his pistol and camera. The creature retreated, but was no more than twenty feet away. Walters was sure that he could capture it. But, as he opened the door and attempted to step out, he was again struck by the blue beam. It seemed that his foot was nailed to the floor. As the beam lifted his leg, Walters grabbed at the side of the doorway for balance. Frances grabbed at him and pulled on him. Both saw that the UFO was about fifty feet in the air, above the back yard.

With the UFO hovering over a nearby field, Walters, now free of the blue beam, again grabbed his camera, and shot a picture of the UFO. He didn't manage to photograph the alien being, but had the presence of mind to take still another picture of the craft. He saw the object shoot out another blue beam and Walters believed this was to pick up the creature. Maybe to "beam" it aboard.

Over the next several days, Walters would see the UFO again and again. He would hear the voices from the craft again and again. They called Walters "Zehass" and told him they had come for him. He would take more pictures of the craft as it hovered close to the ground. By December 17, he had taken seventeen photographs of the object. By the end of December, Walters had figured out that videotape would be more impressive than still photographs. On December 28, he made a videotape that ran just over a minute and a half. According to Walters, his wife, son Dan, and daughter all saw the object.

The next encounter happened on January 12, 1988. While driving on a county road, Walters was hit by two blinding flashes of light that left his arms and hands tingling with "pin pricks" but no other feeling. Five hundred feet in front of him hovered the now familiar UFO. Walters tried to stop and make a U-turn, but his hands wouldn't obey. He stopped two hundred feet from the object. Although he couldn't drive, he could pick up his camera and take still another photograph of the UFO.

As the UFO began to drift toward him, Walters abandoned the truck, trying to crawl under it to hide. Before he could escape, he was hit again by those blue beams and his legs went numb. The UFO was visible, even though he was halfway under the truck. Walters took another picture as a voice told him, "You are in no danger. We will not harm you. Come forward." Walters ignored the message.

Five blue beams shot from the craft, leaving five creatures on the ground who began to move toward him. Once again Walters was confronted by alien creatures when he had a camera in hand, but somehow he failed to photograph them. Instead, screaming obscenities, he leaped back into the truck, and drove off. Apparently his hands and legs were working fine by that time.

Over the next month, Walters continued to see UFOs and photograph them. On January 21, he was in communication on a walkie-talkie with Bob Reid who was staked out a block away with a camera. Reid saw the lights that Walters reported, but he identified them as a small aircraft. Walters said that Reid was not looking in the right direction to see the real UFO.

At the end of February, the Mutual UFO Network provided Walters with a special camera that had four lenses to take three-dimensional photographs. The camera produced four negatives for each picture. It should have made it possible to gather a variety of technical information about the object, based on measurements from the negatives. That evening, Walters took more pictures of an object, or at least, took pictures of lights in the distance. Frances thought the object was small and close, but Walters thought it was larger and farther away. None of those pictures matched the spectacular nature of the other photographs.

On March 8, Walters returned to a Polaroid camera, now using a newer model. Again he took a picture of the UFO, this time hovering about 300 feet beyond two pine trees. It was much better than the pictures of distant lights he had taken with the special, sealed camera.

In the middle of March, Walters and his wife discussed whether or not they should go "UFO hunting" with newspaper editor Cook and a reporter, Dari Holston. They drove to a park, where there were several other people who were also UFO spotting. After about two hours, the others announced they were going to leave. Within minutes, Walters heard the internal hum that announced the appearance of the UFO. Walters took a single picture with a "self-referenced stereo" (SRS) camera he had built. Just as the UFO vanished, the others returned, alerted, according to them, by flashes of light. None of them had seen the object that Walters photographed.

Brenda Pollak, the wife of one of the UFO hunters, arrived at the park late, telling all that she had seen a UFO while driving to meet them. Dr. Bruce Maccabee, a Navy physicist who investigated part of the Gulf Breeze case, concluded from the pictures that Walters had been looking southwest, over the shoreline, when he took the photographs. That was the general direction in which Pollak had seen her UFO. Maccabee suggested that it was plausible that Walters had photographed the object Pollak saw, which meant there was independent corroboration for at least one of Walter's UFO sightings.

At the beginning of May, Walters, again alone, was in the park with the SRS camera when he heard the faint hum. This time he shouted, "Here I am! I want you out of my life!" As he attempted to photograph the object yet again there was a blinding flash and Walters lost all sensation except for a feeling that he was falling. About an hour later, he regained consciousness at the edge of the water. This was the last encounter that Walters reported.

Jerry Clark, writing in his massive UFO encyclopedia, reported that "The Walterses' sightings were not occurring in a vacuum. In the six months between November 1987 and May 1988 over 100 persons in the Gulf Breeze area reported UFOs. On November 11, for example, there were seven sightings besides Walters'. In one of these a witness, Jeff Thompson, reported seeing an object with a bluish beam."

Because of the nature of the case, the number of sightings, potential corroborating witnesses, and the existence of the photographs, a number of investigations were launched. Researchers from the J. Allen Hynek Center for UFO Studies, including Robert D. Boyd, were convinced, almost from the beginning, that the case was a hoax. Boyd felt that Walters did not react as someone who had six months of self-proclaimed horrifying experiences would react. In fact, it was noted by Center investigators that the only cases in which a witness claimed repeated encounters with multiple photographs were either known hoaxes or strongly suspected to be hoaxes.

On the other hand, the Mutual UFO Network's investigators, including Don Ware and Charles Fannigan, were convinced that this was one of the best cases to have been reported to date. Bruce Maccabee of the Fund for UFO Research was also convinced, based on his professional examination of the photographs, that Walters was telling the truth and that the pictures showed a real craft from another world.

Jerry Clark, in his UFO encyclopedia, in defense of Walters, wrote, "To begin with, the Walterses' motive was obscure at best. They certainly were not seeking publicity. In fact, they went to some lengths to keep their names from getting out, even though the newspaper editor and a handful of locals knew who they were."

This idea, espoused by so many including Ed Walters, apparently wasn't challenged. On the face of it, though, it is ridiculous. Within days of taking the first photographs, Walters was at the offices of the newspaper with his pictures. Within months, everyone knew who he was. If Walters was serious about keeping away from the publicity, then he shouldn't have gone to the newspaper in the first place. Those who seek no publicity do not volunteer to meet with the members of the media. They keep their mouths shut and their drapes drawn. Clearly, from his actions, regardless of what he said, Walters wanted publicity.

Clark continued, parroting what is the Walters' party line. "Moreover, unlike many hoaxers in UFO history, they seemed to have no financial interest in perpetrating UFO fraud."

Of course, that overlooks the fact that there was a financial reward for the case. According to *Publisher's Weekly*, William Morrow and Company paid $200,000 as an advance for the book about the sightings, and a production company paid an additional $100,000 down against $450,000 for the miniseries rights. In other words, it turns out that there was a huge financial reward because of the sightings and photographs. That first book was followed by a second, which increased the financial rewards.

All of these points are interesting. It can be argued that the financial benefits came about, not because of the hoax or plans for a hoax, but as a result of events that Walters didn't or couldn't control. While the case seemed to be a hoax, there was no real evidence that it was. Some of the top investigators in the UFO community had researched it and concluded that Walters was telling the truth.

But there were other hints. One of the first to suggest that there was more to the Walters case than had been published was Tommy Smith. Around the first of January 1988, Smith told family members that he had seen a UFO and showed them a series of pictures he claimed to have taken. But, about a day later, Smith confessed that the photos were part of a prank that Ed Walters, also known as Ed Hanson to those in the Gulf Breeze area, was playing.

According to an investigation conducted by Carol and Rex Salisberry, Smith told his family that Walters had given him the photos and told him to take them to the *Gulf Breeze Sentinel*. There, he was to claim that he had taken them. He also said that he had seen two UFO models at the Walters' home and that he had seen Ed Walters photograph one of them. According to the report prepared by the Salisberrys, Smith said that Walters' wife, son, and another teenager named Hank Boland were all involved in the hoax.

Smith told family members that he didn't know what to do, but his father, Tom Smith, Sr., asked his law partners and then Gulf Breeze Chief of Police, Jerry Brown, what his son should do. They all decided that the best action, at the moment, was no action. They believed that since many people in Gulf Breeze already knew the pictures were part of a practical joke, the interest in them would die quickly.

Of course, that didn't happen. Interest in the photographs continued to spread with national television audiences having a chance to see them. On June 19, 1988, Gulf Breeze mayor Ed Gray called a press conference. Tommy Smith's account was substantiated by sworn testimony and independent interviews conducted with the principals.

Smith was given a number of tests in an attempt to verify his veracity. According to the Salisberrys, a recording of one of the interviews had been made. It was the opinion of a number of professionals that the recording could be used in a voice stress analysis. In a report dated October 10, 1990, Dale Kelly, in a signed statement for the Gulf Breeze Chief of Police, wrote, "At the request of and under the authority of Chief Jerry Brown of the Gulf Breeze Police Department, I analyzed a tape of a person known only as Chris [Tommy Smith] to me. The subject matter was the taking of photos of 'UFOs' and if the photos were faked. Based on the test results, it is the opinion of this examiner that 'Chris' was telling the truth when he described how he was told how the photos were faked. In answer to all questions put to 'Chris,' in my opinion he was telling the truth."

In a second report dated October 18, 1990, Ed Halford, in a signed statement for the Gulf Breeze Chief of Police, wrote, "I ran a test for the chief of police in Gulf Breeze, Fl., to determine the truthfulness of a statement made by a male identified as 'Chris' [Tommy Smith]. The statement was recorded by Chief Jerry Brown and Mayor Ed Gray of Gulf Breeze, with the permission of 'Chris.'

"In my professional opinion, the answers to all the questions asked of this person were truthful. I used the Mark II Voice Stress Analyzer to arrive at this conclusion.

"I have a degree in criminology, twenty years police experience, and thirteen years with the Mark II Voice Stress Analyzer.

"This test was analyzed by the authority of the Chief of police, Gulf Breeze, Fl."

Both Carol and Rex Salisberry continued their investigations, trying to learn more about the photos and the circumstances around them. Smith told them that Walters had bragged to him and others how he faked UFOs in Costa Rica by using hot-air balloons. According to the report, Smith said that "Walters also expressed his satisfaction on how he was fooling the MUFON investigators and Duane Cook. When Walters showed Tommy and others the video which Mr. Cook had taken on the evening of 24 January 1988, Walters roared with laughter at how he had fooled Cook."

Of course, when Smith's allegations were printed in the Pensacola *News Journal*, there was a response from the UFO community, especially those who believed the photographs to be real and Ed Walters to be truthful. By this time, a model of the UFO had been found, and to many it was the smoking gun proving the case a hoax.

According to the massive report prepared by the Salisberrys, after their intense and exhaustive investigation, Craig Myers, a staff writer for the Pensacola newspaper, told of how the model was accidentally found. Walters had sold the house from which he had repeatedly seen the UFO. Myers, according to a statement in the report, went to interview the new owners on June 4, 1990.

Myers wrote, "Because the Menzers live in the house where Walters reports he had encounters with aliens and photographed UFOs, Myers was curious if the Menzers had ever seen anything unusual.

"During the interview Myers asked if they had ever seen or heard anything unusual, found any darkroom materials, models, etc. The

Menzers said they had found what may be construed as a UFO model, and loaned it to the *News Journal.* During the next several days the model was used in an exhaustive series of photographic experiments."

Farther down in the statement, Myers wrote, "Using the model we were able to recreate photographs very similar to those Ed Walters printed in his book. Walters and his supporters have stated that the photographs are not the same because most of his UFOs had two rows of windows. However, a second row of 'windows' can easily be recreated by drawing them on the lower portion of the model."

In what is an important point, Myers wrote, "On Saturday, June 9, 1990, *News Journal* Managing Editor Ken Fortenberry interviewed Walters in Fortenberry's office. Metro Editor Joedy Isert and reporter Nathan Dominitz witnessed the interview in which Walters denied any knowledge of the UFO model, but refused to take either a lie-detector test or a voice stress analysis conducted by independent experts. Walters did, however, sign a sworn statement denying any knowledge of the model. Walters said the model was obviously 'planted' in his former residence by debunkers, and intimated that the government may have been behind the debunking plan."

All of that would seem to have destroyed the credibility of the photographic case. But the believers in Ed Walters weren't finished. They released their own information that proved the story to be real, and that the evidence found and the testimony gathered by the Salisberrys was all part of a clever plot to destroy it.

According to the Salisberrys, "When Tommy Smith's allegations were printed in the Pensacola *News Journal* and the *Gulf Breeze Sentinel,* a furor of activity ensued among Walters' supporters to initiate damage control. Walt Andrus, International Director of MUFON, and other MUFON officials promptly named Tommy Smith a liar."

In fact, in an article written by Craig Myers and printed in the Pensacola newspaper, Andrus' opinions are reported. "But Andrus also said he was convinced the model found in Walters' former home had absolutely nothing to do with the photos and was planted by determined critics. And he said Smith is 'lying' about being with Walters when he faked UFO photos. . . . Andrus said he also believes Walters' story that Tommy Smith is lying to protect his parents' religious beliefs, which do not allow for UFOs."

To understand what is happening here, let's look at two aspects of Andrus' statement to Myers. First, the idea that Tommy Smith would be lying to police officials about the creation of the photographs because of his parents' religious beliefs is absurd on the face of it. However, the Salisberrys checked this out, as they did all allegations slung by all sides, and learned that the Smiths are members of the Gulf Breeze Episcopalian Church, which does not espouse any stern views regarding UFOs.

Second is the idea that critics, debunkers, or government agents planted the model in the house to discredit Walters and the case. According to the report prepared by Carol Salisberry, Ed Walters had said that the model was uncovered in plain sight for anyone to see should they go into the attic. She wrote, "I agreed that it was important for Rex and me to get first-hand testimony and to see the model for ourselves."

If Walters was right and the model was found in plain sight, then the discovery of it smacked of a set-up. If someone had gone to all the trouble to build a model to hoax the photographs, certainly he would be clever enough to destroy it or hide it so that it wouldn't be easily discovered.

In a handwritten statement dated September 9, 1990, Sara Lee Menzer wrote, "We [Robert & Sara Lee Menzer] moved into the house in Nov. 1989 and purchased a new refrigerator as the one that had been in the house had been taken by the previous owner [Mr. Ed Walters]. The previous refrigerator had had an ice maker, and there was a piece of copper tubing protruding from the wall and the water source—the tubing had been crimped to stop the water flow. Our new refrigerator had an ice maker but with many other things to do at the time we put off connecting the ice maker until 6 March [1990]. In order to install the ice maker the water had to be shut off so that the old tubing could be cut and connected to a new piece of tubing long enough to reach the new refrigerator. Unfamiliar with the construction practice of this region, we did not know that the cut off for the entire house was in the ground in the front yard. . . . Having exhausted other ideas as to where the water cut-off was, my husband went into the attic crawl space by way of the garage and worked his way on the joists to the area over the kitchen and followed the pipes to the point it turned down into the kitchen wall. In order to reach around the pipe, he pushed aside the loose insulation. In doing so, he uncovered the paper model of the UFO. He put the model aside, thinking little of it. He then called Ed Walters and asked where the water shut off was."

So the model, which had been reported by some to have been found in the garage, and claimed by others to have been found in plain sight was neither in the garage nor in plain sight. Had Menzer not been searching for the water cut-off valve, he would have never found the model. If debunkers, critics, or government agents planted the model, they hid it so well that the odds of it being found were extremely low. In fact, I have never crawled around in an attic of any of the homes I have owned. There has never been a reason to do so.

It would seem, with the testimony of Tommy Smith, with the discovery of the model, and the misleading statements made about the case, the only conclusion to be drawn is that the Gulf Breeze photographs and the accompanying story was little more than a hoax. But the supporters had their own side of the events. They insisted that there was a conspiracy to destroy the case. Solid investigation, corroboration from additional witnesses, and the shady background of those suggesting a hoax would prove to believers that there was no hoax.

Carol Salisberry began to investigate the backgrounds of those who were suggesting that Ed Walters was a practical joker and who had faked "ghost" photographs, who delighted in frightening teenagers with scary stories, and who had a reputation for inventing UFO tales.

One of the teenagers who corroborated parts of Tommy Smith's story was Nick Mock. Mock had also made a number of damaging allegations against Ed Walters. Mock said that Walters was a known practical joker, that the "demon" or ghostlike pictures that surfaced during the investigation and suggested double exposure had been taken by Walters with his Polaroid camera, and that Walters had told some of his high-school friends during the summer of 1987 that he was going to pull off the "Ultimate Prank." Asked what it would be, according to Mock, Walters said that they would know when he did it.

If those allegations were true, they certainly damaged the Walters case. Carol Salisberry, who investigated the Mock aspect wrote, "I was initially under the impression that Nick Mock was a juvenile delinquent because of a note on a correspondence (from Walt Andrus to Willy Smith [no relation to Tommy Smith]) I had seen in Don Ware's file. Walt was asking Willy if he wanted to see Mock's criminal record. I had also read an article in the *MUFON Journal*, April 1989, #252 (pages 15–16), written by Bruce Maccabee indicating that N.M., a teenager, 'In late 1987 he began to write nasty, demeaning letters to Ed's son . . . put sugar in the gas tank, and scratched the son's car.' So, I added another question to my list, 'What sort of person was Nick Mock?'"

Salisberry learned, again according to her report, ". . . he [Mock] was unfairly smeared in the beginning stages of the Walters' investigation. We have since discovered that he was not the only person accused of damaging Danny's [Walters] car. One girl testified that he was with her during that particular time period, and could not have done that. He has no criminal record and there is no proof that he did any of the things he was accused of during the course of the investigation: damaging Danny's car, writing hate mail, using drugs, being a bad influence. In retrospect, the personal attack on his character was disproportionate to what he had to say to the investigators in 1988. He had a list of 7 or 8 names of other kids who could tell about went on at the Walters' parties. Prior to our investigations, this was originally documented by Bob Boyd in his investigation."

There was quite a bit of discussion about those parties held at the Walters' house. They involved quite a few teenagers over a period of years, while Danny Walters was in high school. During that time Ed Walters was apparently a band booster, doing what he could to promote the high-school band. So, there was nothing wrong with the Walterses hosting parties for teenagers. They sound like a family who were, or are, very supportive of their children's activities.

However, the tricks played, or the photographs taken, during those parties is illustrative of the mind of Ed Walters. Again, according to the investigation conducted by the Salisberrys, "They said that Tommy [Smith] was aware of Ed's tricks and even was Ed's accomplice in a stunt. . . . In one instance of the stunt being played, a girl's name (obviously preselected) was also made to mysteriously appear on a board when a match was struck. According to several witnesses the girl was so scared by this that she ran from the room in tears. (Ed told Charles Flannigan, Rex, and myself that he had chosen Tommy to be in on the stunt because Tommy was so quiet that no one would suspect him of being an accomplice.)"

Salisberry, attempting to corroborate these parties investigated further and learned, again according to her report, "I asked one young woman if she had ever gone to a party at the Walters' home. Her reply surprised me. 'It was no party; it was a seance! I'm a Christian, and I was offended by what happened there and I never went back again.' She explained that there was a pentagram or star on the floor and that Ed had 3 girls sit in the middle of a circle surrounded by the other guests. Then he read the 23rd Psalm backwards, having the kids recite after him. (Summoning the ghost for the Polaroid pictures of 3 individuals, one of which would be the chosen one. The chosen one would have the ghost in the picture with her.) This girl's brother, who was also present at this party, and some of the others I interviewed verified this. . . . The kids, now all graduated from high school, said that they couldn't figure out how Ed did the pictures or some of his other tricks. Those interviewed considered Ed to be very clever and that he seemed to know a lot of tricks and games. . . . Several of these witnesses who knew Danny . . . said that they thought it was unusual that Danny never spoke about the numerous UFOs that appeared at his house . . ."

Let's stop and take a look at all this. Tommy Smith said that he was asked by Walters to take the UFO photos into the newspaper office. He said that he had seen two models at Walters' home, and he was involved in one of Walters' practical jokes.

Nick Mock was another teenager who said many of the same things. He also talked about the faked ghost pictures and the practical jokes that Walters created.

And we have the testimony of a number of other teenagers who were there when some of the jokes were played or who saw the results of the trick Polaroid pictures. Some were offended by Walters' seances, and others participated in his practical jokes. In other words, there was a great deal of corroboration for the fact that Walters played practical jokes.

But let's look at this aspect of it carefully. There is very good evidence, from a number of people, that Walters used a Polaroid camera in his jokes. He created photographs of ghosts to fool the teenagers at these parties. A Polaroid camera was used to produce evidence that the seance had worked and that there were ghosts in the room. This is all the result of double exposures.

There is one more aspect of this that needs to be examined. During the initial MUFON investigation, Don Ware was given a list of names of the teenagers who had participated in the parties. Ware, according to Carol Salisberry, said that he had enlisted the aid of a teenager to attend a party to find out what went on at them. The names on the list supplied by Mock were not interviewed at any time by MUFON investigators. Ware told Salisberry that those kids had been interviewed by a reporter for the Pensacola newspaper, but there is no record that the interviews ever took place.

Carol Salisberry concluded, "Based on the information given in peer group interviews, it seems that the Walters had a variety of parties and also small group gatherings at their home. The same teens did not always attend the gatherings. All the parties did not involve a mock seance or spooky tricks but there seem to have been several parties in 1986–87 where these things did take place and a ghost photo was taken. Most of the interviewed teens and parents stated that when the UFO pictures first came out in the paper they thought it was just another of Ed's jokes."

All this seems to suggest there are some major problems with the Ed Walters case. But on the other side are a number of lie-detector tests taken by Ed Walters to prove that he was telling the truth. In fact, in the *MUFON UFO Journal* No. 280, August 1991, Ed Walters wrote, "I have taken and passed four lie-detector tests administered by three different examiners, all of whom signed their reports."

Walters, went farther, writing, "The Salisberrys are guilty of quoting only part of the MUFON sponsored PSE [lie detection test]. The complete sentence says, 'The rest of the interview, from the standpoint of being able to say he [Ed Walters] is being truthful about what he saw and what he did, *does not show any reactions to cause this examiner to doubt his answers* [emphasis in original].'"

Walters also wrote, in that letter, "In April 1990, Rex Salisberry told other MUFON Investigators [Bruce Morrision, etc.] that he had seen the 'Gulf Breeze type' UFO. That makes him a witness to the UFO that I photographed. [You figure that one out.] Either he was confused about seeing the UFO then, or he is confused about it being a hoax now."

These would seem to suggest that, like so many other UFO cases, we will not learn the truth. It comes down to who you want to believe. Tommy Smith, Nick Mock, and the teenagers, or Ed Walters who took four lie-detector tests and even had one of the MUFON investigators claiming to have seen the UFO Walters photographed.

Fortunately, there is additional information that will allow us to sort all this out. First, the lie-detector tests seem to indicate that Walters actually took the pictures of a real UFO even though he apparently has a reputation for practical jokes.

What we learn is that Charles Flannigan, one of the original investigators on the case, arranged for a polygraph examination to be given by Hugh Jones. Walters, however, failed to keep the appointment. When asked why, in September 1990, Walters said he had simply forgotten it.

Walters did arrange for two polygraph examinations himself. Walters apparently went to the phone book, looked for the names of polygraphers, and then called two to arrange for tests. Two examinations were arranged and performed on February 18 and 23, 1988. Walters explained the two examinations, writing, "I expected that I would receive the results then. Later I discovered that McLaughlin [the polygrapher] wanted to confer with some of my references and had also wanted to ask the MUFON investigators what particular questions they wanted to have answered."

According to the lengthy report prepared by Carol Salisberry, "During the discussion of the pre-test interview, the examiner states: 'He [Walters] claims to desire no personal gain or remuneration from these sitings [*sic*].' Yet, Charles Flannigan and Donald Ware both admit that they encouraged Walters to keep good notes, as early as December 1987, so that he could write a book. Additionally in January, 1988, Bud [*sic*] Hopkins writes: 'After outlining the salient facts and chronology of the Gulf Breeze sightings Don [Ware] told me he had called me for two reasons. First, he wanted to know if I would speak to Ed Walters, the key witness, and offer him some advice having to do with publishing issues.' The above seems to indicate that Walters was contemplating the writing of a book as a commercial venture as early as January 1988 despite what he supposedly told the polygraphist."

Jerry Black told the Salisberrys that a copy of McLaughlin's report should be evaluated by a disinterested third party. They sent all the information they had to the Florida Polygraph Association. Billy J. Rakes, then the president, wrote back, telling them that an "overall fair and impartial analysis could not be made without the complete data from the exams."

He also noted that McLaughlin had never been a member of the Florida Polygraph Association, nor any professional polygraph association that adheres to standards of practice, principles, and ethical conduct of polygraph examinations.

But more importantly, Rakes echoed a cautionary note that had been raised by Hugh Jones after Walters failed to appear for the first scheduled test. Rakes said that self-sponsored tests are not advisable. Jones had said, "Can one imagine the predicament of the polygraphist in having to tell the client, 'Well, sir, your tests show that you are lying. That will be two hundred dollars, please.' "

The conclusion, then, of the examiners questioned by the Salisberrys, and of the president of the state board, was that self-sponsored examinations mean very little. Couple that to the report written by McLaughlin in which he writes, "With the information that is available to this examiner at this time, it is felt that Mr. Walters truely [*sic*] believes that the photographs and personal sitings [*sic*] he has described are true and factual to the best of his ability," and a good case can be made that none of the tests are valid.

Rakes, in his letter to the Salisberrys wrote, "The paragraph under 'opinion' indicated the examiner based his opinion on his 'feelings' by stating 'it is felt' the examinee answered truthfully. Experts in the field base their conclusions and opinions on careful analysis of the examinee's physiological reactions noted on the polygraphs during the examination."

In other words, the test was not valid. Walters, at best, was ill-informed about the validity of the tests. At worst, he was misrepresenting the situation in an attempt to elevate his flagging reputation.

But that isn't the end of the lie-detector tests. In 1988 Robert Oeschler, a self-promoted UFO expert, submitted two taped interviews to Dektor Counterintelligence & Security, Inc., in Glen Burnie, Maryland, for voice stress analysis. These two tapes are apparently the rest of the basis for Walters' claim of four lie-detector tests. The two administered by McLaughlin and the two voice stress analyses which are not, of course, the same as a polygraph.

The report, which was signed by Michael P. Kradz said, "The way the interviews were done and the type of information discussed does not give the examiner the verbal material necessary for him to be able to say if these individuals are being completely truthful with the interviewer."

So, there aren't actually four lie-detector tests that Walters passed. There are two self-sponsored tests, and two voice stress tests that were inclusive. When Walters wrote, "I have taken and passed four lie-detector tests administered by three different examiners, all of whom signed their reports," he wasn't being strictly accurate. It could be argued that a man whose reputation has been challenged has the right to a little self-promotion, but some of what he said in that same published letter was intentionally misleading.

Remember, Walters wrote about the voice stress tests by Dektor, "The rest of the interview, for what it's worth from the standpoint of being able to say he is being truthful about what he saw and what he did, *does not show any reactions to cause this examiner to doubt his answers* [again, emphasis added by Walters]."

But like so much else in this case, that is not the final word. Walters ended the statement with a period after the word answers. It should have been a comma, because it continued, "but the interview is not covering any specifics, therefore a more general discussion and it appears Ed is enjoying the discussion mainly about photography."

So, Walters, in his attempt to validate his sightings and his photographs, took the portions of the letter that he wanted, quoted only the parts that supported him, and left out the rest. It's not unlike a movie advertisement in which it quotes a reviewer as saying the film is "Stupendous," but neglects to reveal the reviewer had said, "A stupendous bore."

In that same letter, remember, Walters wrote that Rex Salisberry had seen the same type of UFO that Walters had photographed. Walters wrote, "That makes him a witness to the UFO I photographed." A stunning statement, if at all true.

However, in a letter dated August 6, 1991, Rex Salisberry clarified that point. He wrote, "I have never seen, nor have I claimed to have seen, an unidentified flying object which resembled any of the photos shown in Walters' book. I have seen the UFO model which was found in the attic of the Walters' former residence and it does resemble some of the photos in the book."

The confusion, if that is what it was, came about because Salisberry had told reporters for "A Current Affair" that he had seen a dim red glow while attending a Pensacola MUFON meeting and that the red glow did resemble the red glow on a photograph allegedly taken by Walters outside the meeting that night.

In fact, there were lots of sightings of the red glowing UFO around Gulf Breeze and Pensacola during the early 1990s. Hundreds of people saw it, dozens photographed it, and a few even made videotapes. Believers in Ed Walters said that it proved his sightings authentic. The logic seemed to suggest that the hundreds couldn't be in on the hoax.

The problem is that the red UFO was not the same thing that Walters had photographed. There were those, including the Salisberrys, who believed that the red UFO was nothing more than a railroad or emergency flare carried aloft by a balloon. In one piece of video it seems that a burning bit flare is seen to drop away. Believers suggest it is a "scout" ship falling away from the mother.

Bruce Maccabee, in a statement read by Walt Andrus at the MUFON Symposium held in Albuquerque, New Mexico, in July 1992, said that he found such a suggestion—that is, the emergency flare—to be inconsistent with the facts. It is not only illegal to launch such a device, but if the burning material fell on a house, it could start a fire. Of course, when was the last time that someone pulling a practical joke worried about legalities and consequences of their actions?

All the evidence seems to weigh against Walters. He stands alone against a large number of witnesses to his love of jokes, his ability to fake photographs, and his attempts to induce others to join in the jokes. His lie-detector and voice stress tests are meaningless, and his desire for publicity seems to outweigh his caution. All of this makes a great circumstantial case suggesting the story is a hoax, but the die-hard believers are always going to say it doesn't prove it. Find real evidence that the pictures are faked.

The final test of this comes from an examination of the photographs that Ed Walters claimed to have taken over a period of several months. Some had suggested that if one was proven to be a hoax, then it could be claimed that all were a hoax. To me, that seems to be a valid theory. After all, if a man is taking photographs of a real object on a number of occasions, what purpose could be served by faking one? Instead of having twenty such pictures, he has only nineteen, which puts him way ahead of everyone except contactees.

One of the Ed Walters pictures has been proved to be faked. Photograph No. 19, which Walters claims to have taken from his truck, clearly shows the hood of the truck, part of the road, and the UFO. It is a hoax. The photograph itself also shows a darkening sky, a tree line, and some other detail, seen at twilight. Several disinterested photographic analysts have used that picture to prove the point.

We could go through, carefully, the analysis of all the other pictures that Walters took of the UFO. Some of them, under objective analysis, provide us with clues, but all the analysis from various sources leads to indefinite conclusions. Those who believe will continue to believe and those who are skeptical will find no persuasive evidence that the pictures are authentic. The case lives or dies on Photograph No. 19.

Early on in the investigation of the photographs, Bob Boyd tried to warn the MUFON investigator, among others, that there were problems with some of the Ed Walters pictures in general and Photograph No. 19 in particular. On March 7, 1988, he wrote, "The photographic evidence reveals certain inconsistencies which cause suspicion. One example is the state highway 191 B photograph [this is Photograph No. 19, which was taken as the object hovered over the highway] of the object a few feet above the road. The reflection below the object on the pavement does not conform to proper physical features consistent with such reflections."

Although this was a serious defect, Bruce Maccabee, according to the Salisberry study, conducted an investigation. Using a flashlight, Maccabee reported ". . . By holding a flashlight at various heights above the road and about 200 feet away it was determined that no reflection in the hood [of the truck] appeared until the light was seven or more feet above the road. This is because the front of the hood was bent by a collision in the fall of 1986 . . ." Later, Maccabee revised his measurements, suggesting that it should be set at six feet.

More importantly, however, Ray Sanford said that he had examined Photograph No. 19, which had been "light blasted and enhanced for detail as published in Walters' book." He noticed that he could see the reflection of the tree line on the hood and believed that the reflection from the UFO illumination should also be visible. This especially when it is remembered that not only was there a light ring under the UFO, but porthole lights around the center and some sort of light on the top. Even if the light ring was too low to reflect in the hood of the truck, though there is debate about that, those other lights should have been reflected and they were not.

That led to the suggestion that another analysis be performed. The best of the various independent analyses was completed by William G. Hyzer, with an assist from his son, Dr. James B. Hyzer. Their investigation of Photograph No. 19 revealed "There was no UFO present and the photo is a product of multiple exposure techniques."

Hyzer, in his report, ". . . There are three sources of light related to the UFO-like object: 1) the crescent-shaped illuminated dome and dome light at the top of the object, 2) the light from the power ring on the underside of the object and, 3) the light reflected from the surface of the roadway. His photometric analysis of the photograph shows that all three of these sources are brighter than the overcast sky above the tree line and, hence, bright enough to cause a reflection on the hood of the truck."

To put all this in context without resorting to minor detail that is unimportant, it must be said that a number of experiments were performed on the road. The Salisberrys, among others using various light sources, distances, and a truck similar to the one owned by Walters, established an "envelope" of distances, heights above the road, and deflections right or left of the truck. Inside the envelope there would have been a reflection in the truck's hood. According to all the information available, the UFO, as well as the lights on it, fell inside the envelope. In other words, given the location, time of day, and evidence as available on Photograph No. 19 itself, there would have been a light reflection on the hood of the truck if a UFO had been hovering over the road. That there was not was the conclusive evidence that Photograph No. 19 was a double exposure and therefore a hoax.

Hyzer, in his report, wrote, "It is this author's professional opinion that the results of this study are conclusive: if the UFO-like object in photograph number 19 had been real, reflections of luminous sources associated with the dome and dome light at the top of the object would have to be visible in the truck's hood; but they are not."

If that isn't enough to convince most of the UFO believers that they have been taken for a ride by Ed Walters, that the Gulf Breeze case is a hoax, and that the multiple witness sightings used to substantiate the Ed Walters story are the result of flares and balloons, let's add one more bit of data. It is provided by the original statements of Walters, taken right after he supposedly saw the first of the UFOs.

On November 16, 1987, Ed Walters, claiming to be an intermediary, provided the *Gulf Breeze Sentinel* with a statement about the facts surrounding the sighting and photographs. Now, I have no problem with Walters attempting to protect his identity by suggesting he was acting for someone else. But, I do have a problem when others begin to suggest that Walters' original statement was part of the deception and shouldn't be considered too important.

In that first statement, written by "Mr. X," it said, "I was reluctant at first to show them [the photos], but my wife convinced me to show them . . . I had just sat down to dinner . . . before it shot up and disappeared. . . . It was, however, quite a distance away. . . . The markings [windows?] on the upper and lower sections were aligned and equally spaced . . . no beams coming from it. None of that 'Star Wars' stuff; it was just a dull grey-blue thing."

As we have already learned, some of these things do not square with the story that Walters later told, nor would there be any reason to lie about them originally because they would do nothing to identify him as the photographer. They were just details of the story. Remember, Walters said that he was alone in the office, not that he had just sat down to dinner. The object was close, not far away. But the important point here is the claim that there were no beams coming from it.

According to the report prepared by the Salisberrys, the comment about no beams is important because, "Ed specifically denies the object had any beams at all. Yet, when he learned about Mrs. Zammit's sightings [UFO sightings made by another witness about the same time] and her blue beam, the feature was promptly incorporated into both his narrative and his photos. It has been argued that Ed had no way to know about Mrs. Zammit's sightings, as the published version of *The Sentinel* (Nov. 25) had no mention of the blue [beam]. This is true, but it is also true that in the report prepared by Don Ware on 14 Dec. 1987 the characteristics of Ed's objects are listed but no beam, blue or otherwise, is indicated. In this same report, however, Mrs. Zammit's blue beam is mentioned. The report is also signed by Duane Cook, so there is no doubt that he received a copy; since Ed was a daily visitor to *The Sentinel* in those days, it is clear how he learned about the blue beam."

At the expense of seeming to beat a dead horse, the report continued, "An interesting anachronism appears here. As correctly pointed out by Robert Boyd, the blue beam did not make an official appearance until the second MUFON report, dated January 25, 1988, and not until February 25, 1988, in *The Sentinel*, when Ed [said] that 'what was unreported was the UFO shot a blue beam that froze and lifted me from the ground.' But in Ed's photographs, the blue beam had debuted in PHOTO #11, allegedly taken on December 2! There are then two choices: (1) Ed lied when he completed his first MUFON report (as Mr. X) on December 7; or (2) he lied when he dated PHOTO #11 as taken on December 2. Either way, one more untruthfulness has been proven."

The one thing that I have learned during various investigations is that when a witness begins to change his story, it is a very good indication that the story a hoax. When the witness begins to incorporate new elements into the story, in an attempt to provide additional corroboration, such as mentioning a blue beam after others had reported such an event, there is a very good chance that the case is a hoax. This is, and should be, the last item in a long list of items that suggest the photographs taken by, and the story told by Ed Walters is little more than a hoax.

Is it necessary, at this point, to again list the evidence against Ed Walters and the case? Shouldn't one or two of these items be enough to suggest to all of us that the case is a hoax? How many different problems is it necessary to find before all of us become convinced of the truth?

The thing that strikes me here is how UFO investigations in the 1990s has evolved. We have learned how to conduct a detailed and proper investigation as outlined by the considerable work done by Carol and Rex Salisberry, with a great deal of help from Jerry Black. They spoke to dozens of potential witnesses, they cross-checked information, and they used all the tools available to them to learn the truth.

Others, rather than look at that truth, tried to find reasons not to believe it. This also demonstrates an aspect of UFO investigations of the 1990s. When the information flows against you, attack the messenger. Tommy Smith is a liar, though no proof of that is offered. Nick Mock is a liar and a criminal, though the record suggests something else. Photograph No. 19 might be a hoax, but that doesn't mean all the others are hoaxes. Ed Walters might be a practical joker, but that doesn't mean he knew how to take double exposures with his Polaroid camera. That he did take double exposures with that camera to fake "ghost" photos to fool and terrorize teenagers doesn't mean that he faked the UFO photographs.

We could go on, over the evidence against the Gulf Breeze sightings and photographs once again, but is it necessary? It is clear what happened here. Ed Walters, playing a somewhat admitted practical joke, found himself the center of attention, and he loved it. The fact that there was nothing to the sightings meant nothing to him. He grabbed the spotlight as quickly as he could, and has done everything possible to stay in it. But his story, from the very beginning, was a hoax.

5 STS-48: *Discovery* and UFOs

1991

NASA HAS CLAIMED for years that the astronauts do not see UFOs during their missions. Although, recently, several former astronauts, including Gordon Cooper, have said that they have seen UFOs on various occasions, the idea that UFOs are monitoring our space program has been repeatedly rejected. NASA scientists have found nothing and have seen nothing that would suggest otherwise.

Cooper, in 1996, again told the public about his UFO sightings. According to Cooper, in an interview published in *UFO* magazine, he was a major assigned to the flight testing facility at Edwards Air Force Base when three men came into his office. They were photographers who were setting up their equipment to record landings during scheduled flight tests. The men went to Cooper's office with several exposed cans of film, telling Cooper that they had filmed the landing of disc-shaped craft on the desert.

Following regulations at the time, that is, Air Force Regulation 200-2, Cooper notified his superiors, which he believed was USAF Headquarters, and told them of the film. Arrangements were made to transport it immediately to USAF HQ. Cooper remembered that he was told not to make any copies of the footage before it was sent.

Although it seems that we have a second-hand report here, Cooper did see two of the three reels before they were sent to the higher headquarters in Washington, D.C. Cooper said that it was a typical, double-inverted lenticular saucer with three landing gear that landed on the dry lake bed. No physical evidence of the landing, other than the film itself, was found.

Cooper told Robert T. Leach, in *UFO,* that years later he had tried to check on the sighting with Project Blue Book officials, but that he received no response from them.

However, looking at the Air Force regulations in effect at the time, it is possible that the film and the sighting report never made it to Project Blue Book. In Air Force Regulation 200-2 published on August 12, 1954, there was no requirement to report UFO sightings to Blue Book. The regulation required that the 4602d Air Intelligence Service Squadron, at Fort Belvoir, Virginia be alerted. The regulation also required that a report be transmitted to the Air Technical Intelligence Center at Wright-Patterson Air Force Base, the parent unit to Project Blue Book, but no requirement for ATIC to send the report on to Blue Book.

But that wasn't Cooper's only experience with UFOs. As a fighter pilot assigned to the 525th Fighter Bomber Squadron at Neubiberg Air Force Base in Munich, Germany. While flying an F-86, Cooper saw "an armada of flying saucers." He was quoted in Leach's article in *UFO* as saying, "They'd come over in pretty sizable numbers in flights like we would fly in our group formation."

Cooper said that he, as well as others, chased the saucers, but failed to catch them. In fact, they didn't get close enough to see much detail, other than they were metallic and saucer shaped. They were similar to what was seen on the dry lake bed several years later.

Leach asked Cooper why more of the astronauts didn't tell their tales, but it seems that once again, UFO researchers, investigators, and writers are responsible. Cooper pointed out that they didn't want to be caught in sensationalistic stories that bore little, if any, relation to reality. Cooper said that he was quoted as saying that he was a witness to a landing in Florida. Others have found their names attached to sightings that never happened, or to events that were greatly exaggerated. Most of them just prefer to keep quiet about anything they might have seen.

Cooper also said that there were no rules or regulations that prohibited astronauts from talking about what they might have seen in space. At least during the years he was at the space agency there were no such directives. He pointed out that the whole space program is under public scrutiny and it would be difficult, if not impossible, to hide anything. Such was once the case, but the rules are changing.

It was during the flight of STS-48, Space Shuttle *Discovery*, on September 15 and 16, 1991, that something strange was seen. Or to be more accurate, something strange was recorded as it seemed to maneuver near the Shuttle. A review of videotape made by Donald Ratch showed an object traveling near *Discovery* suddenly change course and fly away.

In 1991 NASA had its own cable channel. Called the NASA K-band, or NASA select, it provided live broadcasts of the Shuttle flights. Those with cable systems that carried it could watch the whole flight as it unfolded. Ratch, of Dundalk, Maryland, was recording the flight on the down link monitored by a local community college.

In reviewing the tapes later, Ratch noticed something unusual. There was an anomalous object rising upward from below the Shuttle, traveling in a straight line from left to right and then suddenly changing direction. There seemed, on the tape that I have seen, to be a number of small, dim objects that followed nearly the same path. There is a flash, and the largest and brightest of the objects seemed to triple its speed. Just after that, another object shot upward, relative to the view on the screen, at great speed.

To me, the objects are small and dim. Dr. Jack Kasher, who works at NASA's Marshall Spaceflight Center and is a professor of physics at the University of Nebraska at Omaha, explained that the size of the objects is relative to the distance. Although they look small, if they are several miles from the Shuttle, it would mean that they are large and bright. Distance is the important factor here.

Ratch, when he found the objects on the videotape, sent a copy of the tape to Vincent DiPietro, an engineer at Goddard Space Center. He was impressed with what he saw, and according to Kasher, pulled the original NASA tapes in October 1991. DiPietro showed the tape to members of the Fund for UFO Research, sent a copy on to Kasher and to Harry Jordan, and alerted NASA.

NASA contract employee, noted space writer and former Air Force officer Jim Oberg, as well as other NASA engineers, believes the objects in the tape are nothing more important than ice particles.

Oberg, as well as those others, claims that such debris often is shed by the Shuttle. There was nothing unusual about it.

DiPietro also sent a letter to Representative Beverly Byron, requesting that she look at the STS-48 footage. She, in turn, also contacted NASA. George E. Brown, Chairman of the Committee on Science and Technology, wrote back to Byron, telling her that the objects are probably nothing more than ice crystals caused by a Shuttle water dump. Records show there was such a dump, but it happened minutes after the objects flashed around the Shuttle.

So, once again, we find ourselves in the same position in which we have been during all our recent investigations here. Two groups, both with impressive credentials, who have viewed the same tape have arrived at two separate conclusions. One is convinced it shows nothing more spectacular than ice crystals, a phenomenon well established during the Shuttle flights, and the other is convinced that the tape shows something other than those ice crystals. Can we learn anything more about this case?

There were a number of UFO researchers who studied the tape, and who believed that there was something unusual about it. Jack Kasher was one of these. To Kasher's credit, he was the first to point out that he is a member of the Mutual UFO Network, is their state director for Nebraska, and serves as one of their scientific consultants. He is, by all definitions, a ufologist, but one of the few with a solid scientific background. But he also said that he believed he could look at the data objectively, without his views on UFOs getting in his way. There is no reason to suspect that he was less than honest, or objective, in his analysis of the tape.

In fact, Kasher believes that he had found four proofs that the objects on the tape are not ice crystals. Because of the shifting nature of the camera, as it rotates from showing space until it shows the front of the Shuttle, Kasher knows where the camera was mounted. By examining the tape carefully, he can also postulate, to a fair degree of accuracy, where the objects on the tape are located in relation to the camera and the Shuttle. Finally, because of the documentation available about the Shuttle, he is able to tell where the various thrusters are located. None of this information is in dispute. Anyone examining the tape can, and will, reach the same conclusions as Kasher.

If the objects were ice crystals, they would drift along with the Shuttle, or would continue to "fly" straight unless acted upon by an external force. The source of that force would be a jet of gas from one of the Shuttle's thruster rockets.

Kasher mentioned that there were thirty-eight main strength thruster rockets and six smaller, weaker vernier rockets. Given the location of the larger thruster rockets, they are eliminated as a source of that force. None were in a position to cause the change of direction of the objects witnessed on the tape.

Kasher believes that none of the other six, vernier rockets, given their locations, could be the cause either. He does point out, however, that the jet of hot gases, vented into space, would move in a straight, but expanding line. In other words, that expanding "cloud" of gas could have reached the ice particles, if that's what they were, and caused the sudden change in direction. Kasher doesn't think it happened, but he admits, fairly, that it could have. His first proof then, is the speculation, based on the location of the thrusters, that the gas would not have reached any ice particles. There would be no force to act upon the crystals to change their direction.

The next proof, though Kasher is quick to point out that it isn't one of the four proofs, is based on the motion of the main object seen on the tape. He carefully charted the movement of the objects through the three dimensions of space. Given the nature of the tape, and the data that could be recovered from it, Kasher was able to plot the movement through all three dimensions. The graph revealed that the main object, whatever it was, stopped for a half second before it changed course. Kasher pointed out that the object, moving away from the shuttle, would have had to encounter something blowing in toward the shuttle for it to stop. Since there was nothing out there to act upon an ice crystal, it should keep moving until it is reached by the firing of the thruster.

The second proof, according to Kasher, is even more convincing than the first. He uses an analogy to explain it. If he was holding a dandelion seed out in front of him and blew on it, he could trace the original force back to his mouth. In the vacuum of space, the seed would move in a straight line unless acted upon by another force. His mouth, of course, represents the thruster and the dandelion seed the ice crystals alleged by NASA.

He also points out if he holds out two seeds, blows on them, and then traces the force back, he will have two lines that intersect at his mouth. In other words, the two seeds will move straight away from him. If there were ice crystals in space, then a plot of their motion should lead directly away from the thruster. By backtracking those plots, the lines should intersect at the thruster. On the charts that he has prepared, the lines do not intersect at the thruster. In fact, tracking those lines back shows that they would never meet.

This means, quite clearly, that there was more than one force at work on the alleged ice crystals or that the objects on the tape were not ice crystals. The motion of the objects is not consistent with ice crystals. Kasher points out, repeatedly, that ice crystals would be tumbling as they traveled through space. A close examination of the film doesn't reveal any tumbling by the objects in it. Ice crystals, then, are eliminated by another of Kasher's proofs.

Kasher's third proof is somewhat more complex. He can calculate the speed the main object should have obtained as it was pulled along by the exhaust of the venier rocket, if that is what happened. Kasher pointed out that if the object was big enough, the exhaust gases would have had no affect on it. If it was small enough, as the gases passed it, they would have dragged it along, causing the object to seem to accelerate. Given a certain amount of information that Kasher had, that is, how long the rocket would fire and the speed of the exhaust gases, he could make a series of precise calculations.

If the objects on the tape are ice particles, they would be dragged along with the exhaust. Kasher said they could calculate how fast the ice particles should be traveling based on the ratios and the known speed of the gas from the rocket. That worked out to to be about 8300 feet per second.

Kasher ran the calculations, based on the data and the camera angles, and discovered the speed of the objects worked out to five or six feet per second. That meant the object, if it was an ice particle, was moving far too slowly.

It must be noted that Kasher ran the figures based on the idea that the objects were ice particles. That provided him with a distance from the shuttle and the attitude adjuster rockets for the object. That, coupled with the speed of the exhaust gases, provided a set of figures from which he could calculate the speed, if it was an ice particle.

The fourth proof was based on the distance the exhaust gas had to travel and the reaction of the object to that gas. It is a simple time and distance calculation, so easy that, according to Kasher, he could do it in his head.

Kasher, explaining it, said to assume the flash seen on the tape was the firing of the rocket, and since it takes one half second for the object to react, it meant the ice particle was sixty-five feet from the shuttle. That meant the exhaust was traveling at 130 feet per second. Kasher's calculations suggested that this, too, was far too slow.

Kasher pointed out that working these various proofs, the final answers should agree. Clearly the five or six feet per second, the 130 feet per second, and the 8300 feet per second did not agree. If the objects were ice particles, the numbers would agree. Since they do not, Kasher concluded that the objects on the tape were not consistent with ice particles. It doesn't prove what they are, only what they are not.

Kasher had another set of calculations that could be considered his fifth proof. What he did was move the ice particles out to a distance where the figures would work out. He determined that the ice particle would have to be just over twenty-two miles from the shuttle for the speed of the object to be "right." By tracing the change of direction back, Kasher determined that the attitude adjuster would have to be fifteen miles behind the nose of the shuttle. It other words, the numbers could not be juggled to fit the facts as known.

Kasher said, "Again, nothing fits. Nothing fits the ice particle theory. There is virtually no evidence."

Kasher summed up the evidence against the ice particle theory, saying, "First, the main object stops at the beginning of the flash and waits a half second before it accelerates. Moreover, the force that stops the main object is directed toward the shuttle from outer space." There was, of course, nothing out there to apply that force.

He continued, saying, "As shown in the diagrams, the lines of motion of the two main objects, when traced back, do not meet at a point, which would be the location of the attitude adjuster rocket."

Expanding on that, he added, "The rocket exhaust velocity, as calculated from the distance and time to reach the main object would be around 130 feet per second. The actual exhaust velocity is about 8450 feet per second."

Again talking about the velocities, he said, "The final velocity of the main object should be about 98 percent of the actual exhaust velocity or about 8300 feet per second. Instead it would be about 5.5 feet per second if its velocity vector is to point back to the venier rocket. These numbers do not fit with the 130 feet per second measured from the film."

Finally, in what he thinks of as another piece of evidence that is almost as good as the proofs, he said, "For the main object to have a velocity of 8300 feet per second it would have to be more than twenty-two miles from the shuttle. In addition, the adjuster rocket would have to be nearly fifteen miles from the shuttle."

Kasher also had a number of other bits of evidence that he thought of as considerations. They didn't deserve the rarefied status of proofs. "The pre-flash [as seen on the tape] lasts about 150 milliseconds and the main flash for about 400 milliseconds. The venier rockets on the shuttle fire in eight millisecond pulses or continuously for one to 125 seconds. Second, the faster object on the right [on the videotape] slows down in the horizontal direction first and then starts to accelerate upward. Finally, the exhaust plume would have to spread considerably to reach the main object." He laughed and said, "It possibly could, but I don't think so."

Kasher seems to have adequately ruled out ice particles as the source for the strange objects. The point that strikes me is that they were not tumbling. That suggests something that is in a stable relationship with the environment around it. While I have no doubt that some ice particles don't tumble, many of them do. What are the odds that all the objects seen on the tape wouldn't tumble? What are the odds that there wouldn't be something on the tape that would identify them as ice particles?

Kasher pointed out that NASA had provided the tape to four of its engineers and asked them for an opinion. Each of them looked at the tape and concluded that ice particles might explain the objects. But none of the four did any detailed analysis of the tape. They reviewed it quickly and said that they saw nothing that would exclude ice particles.

Of course, we just saw the proofs that the objects weren't ice particles. Kasher, addressing this, said, "What I'm going to tell you is the results of my analysis as a physicist and a scientist. . . . The bottom line is I started out assuming they were ice particles and trying to prove that. . . . Once you really start putting the numbers down there really is just no way. . . . If I was a NASA scientist given the job of proving that these were ice particles, I'd have to go to my superiors and say there is just no way. . . . The evidence strongly indicates they can't be ice particles."

There is one other fact to be considered here. After the controversy erupted about the tape, the NASA Select Channel was altered. Rather than broadcast it in real time, it was delayed. Although there is no evidence, at this time, that the shuttle flights are reviewed before the tape is broadcast, it would seem that someone must examine them. If there were no examination of the tapes before broadcast, there would be no reason to delay that broadcast.

I have spoken to one man, not associated with NASA, who doesn't think this change in policy is of particular interest. He could be right. It might just be a coincidence, but there would be no other reason to change the policy. We are told that our space program is open to public scrutiny, but how open is it if we change policy because difficult questions are being asked by those civilians who watch the missions?

Kasher, on the other hand, is the one who told me that he thought it significant that NASA changed the way the system worked after the tape was released in public. And Kasher is a consultant to NASA and would be in a position to understand their changes in policy. He could conceive of no other reason for NASA to make the change.

Kasher said, about the whole STS-48 episode, "When you put it all together, there is no evidence from the film I analyzed, nothing that I can find in here that remotely supports the ice particle theory. . . . So we have to look at other possibilities and the other possibilities are not very abundant. You can try to make a case for tiny particles close to the shuttle. . . . The shuttle [camera] was focused at infinity so any little particles right by the shuttle camera and not dozens of feet away wouldn't be visible. And we can rule out more mundane things out in space like comets and space junk and satellites. They simply don't change direction like that."

Kasher finished his statements by saying, carefully, "That really leaves only one other possibility, once you get beyond the ice particle theory, and that's that the objects were spacecraft."

Light seen over Shag Harbour on October 4, 1967, before the object was seen to fall into the water. This is the first publication of the photograph. Photo copyright by Wilford Isnor.

The primary staff officers at the Roswell Army Air Field in July 1947. Each of those who I interviewed suggested that something extremely strange had happened.

Walter Haut, the PIO at Roswell in 1947, was responsible for the press release that claimed the Army had captured a flying saucer.

Sheridan Cavitt, the counterintelligence officer at Roswell, accompanied Jesse Marcel to the debris field.

Researchers explore the debris field on the Brazel Ranch.

The impact site just north of Roswell where the craft and bodies were found.

Above and below are shots of the impact site where the alien craft was found in 1947.

Author Kevin Randle on the impact site.

The author of the Roswell Declaration, Kent Jeffrey, prepares to explore the debris field with a metal detector.

Kevin Randle, among others, listens as Phil Klass explains his point of view on the Roswell case.

The Hines House on the Brazel Ranch where Jesse A. Marcel spent the night before seeing the debris field.

The front gate of the Roswell Army Air Field as it appears today. The military left Roswell in the mid-1960s.

6 The Air Force Final Report on Roswell

1994

AFTER FORTY-SEVEN YEARS of claiming that the artifacts found at Roswell, New Mexico, were nothing more spectacular than the remains of a neoprene weather balloon with a radar reflector, the United States Air Force finally identified the material. It was a . . . weather balloon. It was not an ordinary weather balloon, but a special one assigned to the then top-secret Project Mogul. In a twenty-three page report issued on September 8, 1994, the Air Force laid out the evidence for their conclusion.

At the beginning of their research, Air Force investigators decided that they were not going to attempt to interview all the various witnesses who have been identified by UFO researchers. Given the numbers, this isn't surprising. What is disturbing, however, is that they only interviewed five people, three retired military officers, and two civilians who were involved with Project Mogul.

One of the most important of those retired officers is Lieutenant Colonel Sheridan Cavitt. According to Major (later Lieutenant Colonel) Jesse A. Marcel, Sr., Cavitt accompanied him out to the debris field reported by W. W. "Mac" Brazel. Of those three, only Cavitt is still alive and he certainly holds one of the keys to the case.

I first interviewed Cavitt in January 1990, while he wintered in Sierra Vista, Arizona. During that visit he told Don Schmitt and me that he had not been in Roswell in July 1947 and that he had participated in no recoveries of a flying saucer, V-2 rocket, or any type of balloon.

In March 1993, Schmitt and I visited Cavitt at his home in Washington state. During that interview he showed us copies of his orders from 1947. According to Special Order No. 121, dated 11 June 1947, Cavitt was assigned to the counterintelligence office at Roswell and had five days to report, meaning he had to be at the base by June 16. Once he arrived, he claims that he was given a leave. He had been assigned to Roswell, but was not physically present in early July 1947. Because of that, Cavitt said that he was not involved in any of the events now known as the Roswell Incident.

We interviewed him one more time, in June 1994. He mentioned that he had been visited by a Pentagon colonel (Richard Weaver), but he wasn't any more candid about the events in Roswell. In fact, when I asked him why both Marcel and Lewis Rickett, the former master sergeant who had served under Cavitt, had identified him as the officer at Roswell, Cavitt said that he didn't know. Although he had told Weaver he was there, had recovered a balloon, and had, in fact, taken Rickett out to one of the sites, Cavitt still insisted to us that he had no role in those events.

Now we learn from the Air Force report and the supporting documentation, including a transcript of Weaver's interview with Cavitt, that things were not as we had been told. Cavitt said to Weaver, "So, I went out and I do not recall whether Marcel went with Rickett and me, I had Rickett with me. We went out to this site. There were no, as I understand, check points or anything like that (going through guards and that sort of garbage) we went out there and we found it. It was a small amount of, as I recall, bamboo sticks, reflective sort of material that would, well at first glance, you would probably think it was aluminum foil, something of that type. And we gathered up some of it. I don't know whether we even tried to get all of it. It wasn't scattered, well, what I call, you know, extensively. Like, it didn't go along the ground and splatter off some here and some there. We gathered some of it and took it back to the base and I remember I had turned it over to Marcel. As I say, I do not remember whether Marcel was there or not on the site. He could have been. We took it back to the intelligence room . . . in the CIC office."

Cavitt told Weaver that he recognized the debris as the remains of a balloon immediately. He didn't explain why he had not bothered to communicate this rather vital piece of intelligence to Marcel, nor did Weaver ask him. Instead, Cavitt kept this secret so that Marcel apparently misidentified the debris as extraterrestrial and Colonel (later General) William Blanchard ordered the announcement that the Army had recovered one of the flying saucers.

Although Cavitt identified Rickett as the man he had taken to the site, the Air Force investigators never tried to learn what Rickett had said. Rickett died before the Air Force officers began their investigation, but he left both an audio and videotaped record of what he had seen and done. Interestingly, Rickett talks of going out to the site with Cavitt, but he doesn't remember if Marcel accompanied them or not.

Rickett provided testimony refuting some of Cavitt's claims. During a recorded interview conducted on October 29, 1989, Don Schmitt asked "The roads were blocked?" Rickett said, "Yeah, they had . . . on the road we drove on . . . MPs standing there."

Rickett also described material that he had seen. He said that he didn't think it was metal but that "It was damn hard." Describing it, he said, "It wasn't bright and shiny on one side like foil is but it wouldn't wrinkle." Clearly Rickett is discussing something tougher than the foil that would have been used on the radar targets attached to the Project Mogul balloons. Had Air Force investigators asked, I would have provided them with copies of both the audio and videotapes of the Rickett interview. They never asked.

In the course of his interview with Cavitt, Weaver asked if he had been sworn to secrecy. Weaver writes, "Lt. Col. Cavitt also stated that he had never taken any oath or signed any agreement not to talk about this incident and had never been threatened by anyone in the government because of it."

The simple response is that Cavitt, because of who he was and the position he held would not normally be told, after an event, that he couldn't talk about it. There is, however, a body of testimony ignored by Weaver and the Air Force investigators that suggest that others were sworn to secrecy.

In July 1947 Major (later Colonel) Edwin Easley was the Provost Marshal at Roswell. On January 11, 1990, I interviewed Easley for the first time. I told him who I was and verified that he was the Provost Marshal at the base in July 1947. When he confirmed it, I asked if he was familiar with the story of the flying saucer crash. He said, "I've heard about it."

I asked, "Do you have any firsthand knowledge of it?" Easley said, "I can't talk about it." I changed my question and asked again, and Easley repeated, "I can't talk about it."

I finally asked, "Can you tell me if you were at the crash site?" Easley repeated, "I can't talk about it. I told you that. . . . I've been sworn to secrecy. I can't tell you that."

Weaver, in his report, mentioned that he had reviewed *The Roswell Events* created by Fred Whiting of the Fund for UFO Research. Included in there is a complete transcript of that interview with Easley, but Weaver never mentioned it. He didn't ask for a copy of the tape, available at the Fund, nor did he ask me for one. Instead he writes that Cavitt had not been sworn to secrecy, suggesting that no one had been. Easley's taped statements suggest that military officers were, in fact, sworn to secrecy about these events.

We can take the idea of secrecy even farther. Colonel (later Brigadier General) Thomas J. DuBose was the Chief of Staff of the Eighth Air Force in July 1947. Interviewed on August 10, 1990, by Don Schmitt and Stanton Friedman and recorded on videotape, DuBose said, "Actually it was a cover story, the balloon part of it. . . . The remnants that were taken from this location and [Colonel] Al Clark [base commander at Eighth Air Force in Fort Worth in 1947] took it to Washington and whatever happened to them then, I have no knowledge. That part of it was in fact a story that we were told to give to the public and the news and that was it. . . . We were told this is the story [balloon explanation] that is to be given to the press and that is it and anything else, forget it." Had Weaver asked, I would have sent him a copy of that videotape.

Not only did government officials attempt to keep military officers from talking, they also shut down radio reports. George "Jud" Roberts was the minority owner of radio station KGFL in 1947. Majority owner Walt Whitmore, Sr., had interviewed Mac Brazel and planned to broadcast that report. Instead, according to Roberts, representatives of the FCC and from New Mexico's congressional delegation called the station ordering them *not* to broadcast the Brazel interview. If they did, Roberts reports that he was told they would lose their license the next day. There was no talk of hearings, just a threat to prevent the broadcast of the Brazel interview. Roberts has been interviewed on both audio and videotape and had Weaver asked, I certainly could have put him in contact with Roberts.

What this demonstrates is that there is a body of firsthand testimony suggesting that both military officers and civilians were sworn to secrecy and that the material recovered was not consistent with that from a Project Mogul balloon array. Weaver had access to all this data but refused to review it. While I certainly understand that he didn't want to interview everyone we had, it would seem that he would be interested in what retired, high ranking Air Force officers would have had to say. He wouldn't have to rely on the interpretations of those interviews as filtered through us, but could review them on tape. Certainly not as satisfactory as meeting them in person, but a way of determining if, as he suggested, those statements had been twisted, misrepresented, or taken out of context. There is no indication that Weaver made any attempt to review this material. He rejected it out of hand because it would show the weakness of the Project Mogul explanation.

In examining the evidence for Project Mogul, it becomes clear that the case is not nearly as strong as the Air Force would have us believe. The links to Mogul are very weak and the Air Force investigators were unable to discover any documents that would prove their point. In the end, it is speculation based on a limited review of the evidence available.

For the Project Mogul explanation to work, we must believe that Major Marcel was unable to identify a common type of balloon and the rawin target (an instrument for measuring wind). We must accept the idea that Cavitt did recognize the balloon but said nothing to either Marcel or Blanchard or anyone else. We must accept the Air Force theory that there was something special about the Mogul balloon arrays that would have prevented easy identification by some, but obvious identification by others, including Mac Brazel's daughter, Bessie.

There are two important facts that impact on these assumptions. One is that Marcel, as the intelligence officer, was involved in Operation Crossroads. This was the atomic testing held at Bikini in 1946. According to Irving Newton, a weather officer stationed at Eighth Air Force Headquarters in 1947, rawin targets were used in atomic testing. Marcel was involved in this atomic test and because he was the intelligence officer, might have had an opportunity to see that particular equipment.

But more important is a discovery made near Circleville, Ohio, at the beginning of July 1947. Sherman Campbell, a farmer, found a balloon and rawin target on his farm. He recognized it immediately, but believed that, because of the shiny foil, it might account for some of the flying disk reports. He took it to the sheriff, who recognized it immediately for what it was. Campbell then took it to the local newspaper office where it was displayed for several weeks. The newspaper actually received another rawin found by another farmer who also recognized it for what it was.

For those who wonder how the military invented the balloon explanation, it seems that it was handed to them. The story was in the newspapers for them to see. It also demonstrates that rawin targets being found are not the rare occurrences that some would have us believe. And, it demonstrates that those unfamiliar with the balloons and rawins were able to identify them as mundane rather than leaping to the conclusion they were extraterrestrial.

Weaver then uses several of the affidavits published in Whiting's report to reinforce his theory, but never uses all the information available. While the Project Mogul material resembles, in a gross sense, that found by Mac Brazel, it is not an exact match. This is demonstrated by a number of statements made by those who saw and handled the debris.

Jesse Marcel, Sr., when he was shown two of the photographs taken in Brigadier General Roger Ramey's office of the alleged debris, said to Johnny Mann, a reporter at TV station WWL in New Orleans, "That's not the stuff I found." He recognized it as a balloon immediately from the photographs. Why then, couldn't he recognize that same material on the Brazel ranch if that was, in fact, what he had seen in 1947?

Marcel told reporters in various interviews, "I was amazed by what I saw. . . . It wasn't anything I was acquainted with . . . I could not identify [it], even tried to burn it. . . . [It] looked like balsa wood but [there was] no scorch an any material we found. . . . Looked like balsa wood but certainly wasn't."

Jesse Marcel, Jr., when he saw the pictures taken in General Ramey's office, said that it did, in fact, resemble what he had seen, in a very gross sense. The pictures were of foil and sticks, but were not of the debris he'd seen in 1947. He described many of the strange properties others had noticed. He also said that the symbols he saw on one of the small I-beams were purple, not pinkish, and that they were about three-eights of an inch high. Professor C. B. Moore, a project engineer on Mogul, said the symbols on the tape used to reinforce the balsa sticks of part of the Mogul array, were pink and as much as three inches high. Again, a very gross resemblance, but not an exact match.

Sallye Tadolini is quoted by Weaver. He writes that in her affidavit dated September 27, 1993, and supplied to the FUND, she said, ". . . What Bill [Brazel] showed us was a piece of what I still think as fabric. It was something like aluminum foil, something like satin, something like well-tanned leather in its toughness, yet was not precisely like any one of those materials. . . . It was about the thickness of very fine kidskin glove leather and a dull metallic grayish silver, one side slightly darker than the other. I do not remember it having any design or embossing on it . . ."

Weaver didn't bother with the next paragraph in the affidavit because it would create too many questions. Tadolini had continued, saying, "Bill passed it around, and we all felt of it. I did a lot of sewing, so the feel made a great impression on me. It felt like no fabric I have touched before or since. It was very silky or satiny, with the same texture on both sides. Yet when I crumpled it in my hands, the feel was like that you notice when you crumble a leather glove in your hand. When it was released, it sprang back into its original shape, quickly flattening out with no wrinkles . . ."

When I interviewed Tadolini, she said that she had spent part of the morning ironing. She was intrigued by the material's ability to resume its original shape without wrinkles. It would mean that she wouldn't have to iron anything again.

Bill Brazel had found some material on the debris field. When he showed it to his father, Mac said that it looked like "part of that contraption I found." Bill said, "The only reason I noticed the tin foil. . . . [I] took it out [of my pocket] and put it in the box and I noticed that when I put the piece of foil in that box . . . the damned thing just started unfolding. Just flattened out."

What all this demonstrates is that the situation in New Mexico in 1947 isn't as Weaver and the other Air Force investigators would have us believe. There were military officers sworn to secrecy as demonstrated by Major Easley's audio-taped statements, there was a cover-up as demonstrated by Colonel DuBose's videotaped statements, and there was a suppression of the news media as demonstrated by Jud Roberts' taped statements and corroborated by what he tells us today. Clearly the debris recovered at the Brazel ranch site was not the remains of a neoprene balloon and rawin target device. All this opens the door for questions but it doesn't completely eliminate Project Mogul as the culprit in the events. It seems to suggest that something other than a Project Mogul balloon array was recovered on the Brazel ranch and there is additional information that underscores that fact, the Air Force opinion to the contrary.

First it must be remembered that the Air Force claims that Launch No. 4, made on June 4, 1947, is responsible for the debris. They imply in their report that these balloons were something special. In fact, polyethylene, a material that was developed for constant level balloons might have fooled some of the less sophisticated witnesses because of its very nature, but the descriptions provided by the eyewitnesses suggests it was not polyethylene. However, the records show that the first of the polyethylene balloons was not launched until July 3, 1947, and therefore couldn't have been responsible for the material found on the Brazel ranch.

Balloon Launch No. 4, according to the diary kept by Dr. Albert Crary, Project Mogul leader, was made of a cluster of regular meteorological balloons made of neoprene. It did contain a "sonobuoy" or microphone, but no array train according to the documentation available. No "official" record was kept because no data of scientific importance was recovered. Charles Moore told me that he believed they had lost track of Launch No. 4. near Arabela, New Mexico, which is twenty or thirty miles south of the Brazel ranch site. Unfortunately there is no documentation to support this claim.

The other important point, though the Air Force doesn't make it clear, is that there was nothing special about the balloons in Launch No. 4. There was nothing on it that would fool anyone. They were standard balloons, about 15 feet in diameter, and made of neoprene. Neoprene that, after exposure to sunlight, would turn from a tan to a black. The color wouldn't be uniform. The portions directly exposed to sunlight would blacken faster than those in shadow. The point is that the rubber reacted to the heat and light from the sun. Attempts to cut it, or to burn it, would have been successful. And surely someone, if not Marcel himself, would have recognized the material as having come from a neoprene weather balloon.

But what is important here is that the only documented record for Flight No. 4 tells us exactly what it was and there were no rawin targets to create the metallic debris. Dr. Crary's diary suggests that the first flight containing an entire array wasn't made until June 5 and that debris was recovered east of Roswell.

The Air Force maintains that the balloon had lain in the field for more than a month. *The Roswell Daily Record* suggests that Brazel found the balloon first on June 14, ten days after the launch, but left it there for another three weeks. Not only do these statements conflict with one another, they conflict with what ranchers have told me.

According to them, this sort of debris is not left on the pastures because the livestock would ingest it. That sort of debris could kill the animals and a rancher wouldn't leave it where the livestock could get at it. If Brazel had found it on June 14, he would have picked it up on June 14. The only reason to report it was left on the field was to provide an explanation for what Marcel and Cavitt found on July 7.

A second problem here is that Bessie Brazel Schrieber reports that she, with her father, collected all the debris, stuffing it into four burlap bags. If that is true, then there was nothing for Marcel or Cavitt to see later. Marcel told reporters, "We picked up what we could but most of it was left behind." There certainly was more material than would be accounted for by a Mogul balloon and array train.

The Air Force also implies that the reason there was a cover-up was to protect Project Mogul. While the project itself was highly classified, the balloons, rawin targets, and other equipment launched as part of the array trains were not classified. There was little of intelligence value to be recovered by Soviet agents if they knew that balloons were being launched from the Alamogordo Army Air Field.

In fact there was so little of importance attached to the balloons that a story about them was published in the *Alamogordo News.* If Soviet agents were interested in Mogul and balloon launches, that article provided more than enough clues for them. There are photos of the balloon clusters, but more importantly, Watson Laboratories and some of the men involved in those launches were mentioned.

Had what Brazel found been nothing more than an experimental balloon, there would have been no reason for the elaborate events that took place around it. Brazel would have recognized it and disposed of it without having to consult the local sheriff or the military at the Roswell base. This is especially true if Bessie is to be believed. She claimed they had picked it all up.

If it was only a balloon, as Sheridan Cavitt now claims, why didn't he mention it to anyone, saving the 509th from the embarrassment of announcing they had a flying saucer, only to have that statement challenged by the officers at the Eighth Air Force?

There is one other piece of evidence. Brigadier General Arthur Exon reported that in 1947 he had the opportunity to fly over the impact site and debris field. He said, "It was probably part of the same accident but there were two distinct sites. One, assuming that the thing, as I understand it, as I remember flying the area later, that the damage to the vehicle seemed to be coming from the southeast to the northwest but it could have been going in the opposite direction, but it doesn't seem likely. So the farther northwest pieces found on the ranch, those were mostly metal."

His testimony corroborates two sites, the orientation of those sites, and effectively eliminates Project Mogul. There is no way for Project Mogul to create two distinct sites that are part of a single event. Nor is there any way for Project Mogul to create the gouges mentioned by General Exon in other conversations. Weaver ignored Exon's testimony because of the damage it does to the Project Mogul theory.

No, Project Mogul, although highly classified, does nothing to explain the events on the Brazel ranch. There is too much testimony from too many firsthand witnesses. In fact, I have used only testimony gathered from firsthand observations. When all the data are examined, it is obvious to all that Project Mogul is inadequate as an explanation.

In fact, the GAO, in their review of the situation for Congressman Steven Schiff, examined the Air Force position and found it inadequate. The GAO report said, "The Air Force report concluded that there was no dispute that something happened near Roswell in July 1947 and that all available official materials indicated the most likely source of the wreckage recovered was one of the project MOGUL balloon trains."

It must be noted that the GAO did not endorse the conclusion, merely reported on it. It other circumstances, when GAO investigations have corroborated information, they have commented on it positively. In this case, there were no such positive comments.

But there is one more fact that must be mentioned. With the release of the 1994 report, the Air Force claimed the report was going to be their last word on Roswell. They had solved the case. However, a number of UFO investigators report that Air Force officers are still gathering data, and that they will suggest that the bodies recovered were the flight crew of a crashed aircraft. This ignores, of course, the Air Force statement in their 1994 report that they found no records of aircraft accidents that could account for the Roswell Incident. The question to be asked is, if the Air Force solved the case with their Project Mogul balloons, why are they still investigating?

None of this leads directly to the extraterrestrial explanation. Other evidence takes us in that direction. But it must be remembered that all terrestrial explanations have been eliminated by searches of military records, private industry's research and development programs, eyewitness testimony, and a failure to find any documentation to support these other answers. When the investigation is over and all the evidence examined there is little room left for speculation and none for Project Mogul.

7 The Alien Autopsy Circus

1995

EARLY IN 1995, rumors began to circulate about a piece of film that proved the UFO crash at Roswell in July 1947 was real. Philip Mantle of the British UFO Research Association (BUFORA) wrote to a number of investigators, telling them that a film existed showing the autopsy of an alien creature. The body had been recovered after the object had been discovered by military officers in the deserts of New Mexico. Mantle hoped to enlist the researchers' aid in authenticating the film.

It was at this time that I learned of the existence of the film. Details were, at first, sketchy. It seemed, at that time, that Reg Presley, a British musician, had appeared on a talk show and mentioned the film's existence. I was interested, but the film was in England, I had never met Mantle and didn't know Presley. There was nothing I could do about it without more information.

However, my first thought was that it had to be a hoax. Having at that time spent six years investigating the crash at Roswell, I knew that motion picture footage had been made. Witnesses who said they were in the impact area made it clear that both movie and still photographers had been there photographing everything in sight. Of course, those pictures, if they existed, were now highly classified.

The problem was that the pictures had surfaced in England. It seemed to me that if any pictures were going to leak into the public arena, the leak would be American and it would be in the United States. Snobbish yes, but it seemed more likely than an English video distribution company owner stumbling over the controversial film footage.

Ray Santilli, the man who had the film, did have an answer for that criticism. He had been in the United States a year or so earlier, searching for footage of an earlier and unknown Elvis Presley. In 1955, Bill Randle (no relation) had produced a show in Cleveland that included Bill Haley and the Comets, Pat Boone, and Elvis. Santilli, apparently in search of this footage, talked to the cameraman who owned the Presley footage and learned of the autopsy film at that time.

The rumors, many of which were endorsed by Santilli, suggested that the American Army cameraman had somehow managed to keep the film, or at least part of it. These were "outtakes" or reels that needed special processing but somehow were never returned to Army control. To me, it seemed to be a fairly cavalier way to handle material that should have been highly classified, but I still knew nothing more.

Several people I know were trying to investigate the film. Kent Jeffrey, the man behind "The Roswell Initiative," a petition calling for the end to the secrecy about the Roswell crash, tried to learn more, but early on seemed to have little luck. In fact, on January 20, 1995, I spoke to Kent who told me that British rock star Reg Presley told him, Kent, that he had seen fifteen minutes of the total film. According to Kent's information, Santilli had paid about a hundred thousand dollars for the film. The story, again as circulated by Santilli at that time, was that the cameraman had made a dupe of the original film so that the Army wouldn't know that some of it was missing.

Paul Davids, the executive producer of the ShowTime original movie, "Roswell," talked to Santilli himself on January 20. He then called Kent to tell him what he had learned. Paul said that he'd been told President Harry Truman could be seen walking the debris field. There were trucks, a heavy-duty crane, and dozens of soldiers in the film. If that was true, Davids felt that the film had to be authentic. I must say that I agreed with him. It seemed unlikely, maybe next to impossible, for someone to fake that scene without the benefit of Hollywood make-up, money, and special effects.

Paul went on to say that he had been told that a number of faces could be seen during the autopsy footage. It meant there were identifiable people in the footage and that meant that independent corroboration was possible. All of this, if true, convinced Paul that the footage had to be authentic.

I received other reports as well. First word was that there were fifteen rolls of film of about ten minutes each. That meant two hours and thirty minutes of film. There was a preliminary autopsy in a tent, more autopsy footage in a hospital operating room, the debris field with Truman, and pictures of the craft as it was lifted onto a flatbed truck. All of the description sounded as if the film was spectacular and authentic. Again, it would be impossible to fake that kind of footage without the assistance of dozens of people, Hollywood-level special effects, and a great deal of ready cash.

It wasn't clear from those earlier reports if those talking about various scenes and footage had had the chance to see it all. Reg Presley, for example, suggested that he had seen some of the autopsy footage, but little else. Santilli was telling some researchers that footage existed of the debris field and Truman, suggesting that he had already seen that part of the film. But those were suggestions and not bold statements. The truth about the film and what was on it hadn't been revealed by anyone.

Still more information and quite a few rumors circulated. In a letter from Philip Mantle in the spring of 1995, I learned that the cameraman's name was probably Jack Barnett. Apparently, and according to some sources, Santilli had slipped up and inadvertently revealed the man's name. Searches began trying to locate any Barnett who had a connection to motion picture photography, whether through the military, old news reel services, or Hollywood.

There were many others who began to chase this lead. Several Jack Barnetts were found, but none seemed to be the right man. Either they were too young, or they had no connection to photography or the military. And Santilli began to hint that the Barnett name wasn't quite right. It was really Barrett, but he allowed the wrong name to circulate as a "cover" for the real man. More would be learned about this aspect of the case about six months later.

Information about the film continued to flow. Santilli arranged for members of the media, representatives from television networks around the world, and UFO researchers to screen the film. Although I thought about attending, it seemed to be too expensive. Sure, if the film was authentic, it would be worth the expense, but there were too many problems with the authenticity by that time. It smacked of a hoax.

Besides, Kent Jeffrey, because of his regular job, could attend at a fraction of what it would have cost me. He would give me a full report on his impressions. That was the next best thing to being there.

In a special bulletin issued by the International Roswell Initiative, dated May 25, 1995, Jeffrey outlined his whole experience at the showing of the film earlier that month. He wrote, "The film in question is presently in the possession of a company in London, Merlin Productions, owned by a Mr. Ray Santilli. On Friday, May 5, 1995, there was a special showing at the Museum of London. There were approximately one hundred people present. . . . Despite the fact that the film is totally unauthenticated, it has received extensive publicity in Europe. . . . Because of the dubious nature of the film and the questionable way in which it is being handled by those in possession of it, there is a tremendous potential for damage to the entire Roswell effort."

He then provided a synopsis of what happened in London. "The actual showing of the film took place just after 1:00 P.M. in a small auditorium that is part of the Museum of London complex. A handout was distributed at the sign-in table consisting of a copy of the alleged MJ-12 briefing papers [see Chapter 3] and a yellow cover sheet referencing the 1947 Roswell crash and the 509th Bomb Group (at Roswell Army Air Field). Merlin Productions was apparently very concerned about pictures being taken because everyone was physically searched (frisked) for cameras upon entering the auditorium. There was no speaker or announcement to formally welcome those present or to introduce the film. This seems somewhat bizarre and discourteous, as people had come from all over the world for this showing. Also conspicuously absent was a person on stage afterward to publicly answer questions pertaining to the film. After having viewed what was presented, however, it was not hard to understand why this was the case."

According to Kent, "At about 1:05 P.M., the lights dimmed and the film started rolling. Before the actual pictures began, a few short statements scrolled by on the screen with reference to the film having been 'acquired from the cameraman who originally shot the footage' and to the copyright being 'exclusively owned by Merlin Communications.' Interestingly, one would think that if the film were genuine, the copyright would be 'exclusively owned' by the United States government."

What followed, according to Kent, were the first real indications that everything we had heard was not as had been reported. He wrote, "Also, contrary to what had been said previously about '10-minute reels,' there was now a statement on the screen that the film was recorded on 'three-minute' reels. I recently learned from a good friend in the film industry that 1947 vintage 16-millimeter film came on reels of 100 feet, which at 16 frames per second would be about three minutes each."

Then, according to Kent, the "film opened abruptly with its single scene of a small operating or autopsy room with plain white walls and a table in the middle containing an unclad body lying face up. Two individuals in white anti-contamination suits, complete with hoods and narrow, rectangular glass face plates, were the only figures visible in the room. A third person, dressed in white hospital-type garb, was visible through a large glass partition, or window. Although he was outside the sealed room standing behind solid glass, he was wearing a surgical mask that covered his entire face. Perhaps there was concern that he might later be recognized?"

Kent then described the procedures that were followed in the autopsy as the two doctors circled the body and cut into it. It is clear that the cameraman was also in the room, circulating and trying to stay out of the way of the doctors. The film was black and white and the focus, at times, was inadequate.

Kent, in his report, wrote, "I would like to state up front and unequivocally that there is no (zero!!!) doubt in my mind that this film is a fraud." When interviewed on my radio show on El Paso's KTSM-AM just a few weeks after he saw the film, he again said that it was an obvious fake.

That, of course, was Kent's opinion. There were others who seemed equally convinced that the film was the find of the century.

With it, the whole Roswell case would be broken wide open. Finally, according to these people, the evidence of alien visitation had been found.

Because I was working with a number of people on a documentary on the events at Roswell, and because it was alleged that the footage involved the autopsy of an alien being recovered at Roswell, I had the opportunity to see photos from the film in June 1995. There were four of them, from different angles, showing the body on an autopsy table. There was a tray of tools near it. And, of course, there were the items hanging on the wall, or on another small table, inside the room.

I was intrigued by the photographs, only because the shape and size of the head, and the location of the ears, low on the head, seemed to corroborate some testimony that I had heard from men who claimed to have been on the impact site where the bodies were found. The big, dark eyes; the shape of the body including the large, protruding stomach; and the stockiness of the limbs seemed to argue against the body being from the Roswell crash. Still, it was intriguing.

Others who saw the photographs looked at them and found some flaws. First, Russ Estes pointed out that the instruments in the tray did not seem to be strictly for autopsy. He pointed to a clearly visible palpation hammer which is used to check reflexes in the living. A doctor conducting an autopsy would have no need for a palpation hammer.

On the other table was a Bunsen burner. I was told this was not standard equipment, but some have argued that Bunsen burners were used to burn fatty tissue from scalpels. However, the shadows indicated that there was a flask above the Bunsen burner. Russ Estes commented that it looked more like a dressed set than an actual autopsy room. He meant that it had been staged rather than filmed as it happened in real life.

It was also noted that the table was not a standard autopsy table. There were no channels on it to drain body fluids. It seemed to be a standard table, not one used in autopsies.

These were all interesting points, but still didn't lead to a positive conclusion. At this point, the only person I knew who had seen the film was Kent Jeffrey. His opinion was the one that counted here.

In July 1995, I was again in Roswell to speak, and John Purdie, a British documentary maker, was there with some of the autopsy footage. I was given to understand that it was only a small portion of it, but I would have a chance to see, for myself, what the film looked like. This was just about two months after the big premiere in London.

These segments, according to Purdie, were all that Santilli was going to release at the time. They were for the express purpose of aiding John Purdie, of British television's Channel Four, in making his documentary about the Roswell case. I wasn't supposed to tell anyone that I had even seen any of the film at that time.

Just as Kent had described, the film took place in a brightly lighted "operating room." There were two doctors moving around a body on a table. The stomach of the creature was distended. There was a large, gross wound on the thigh. The feet had six toes and the hands had six fingers. The head was large, and the eyes, which were opened, seemed to be the black orbs mentioned frequently by those who claim abduction by aliens.

What I noticed first, and what I looked for first, was the placement of the ears. The eyewitnesses that I have interviewed had said that the ears of the aliens were low on the head. Lower than they would be on a human head. The alien on the table had those ears and it was an interesting fact.

Those of us who had the chance tried to see if there were things in the film that were out of place. Some skeptics seized on the phone cord, suggesting that the coiled version, hooked to the wall phone, had not been available in 1947.

There were also a few scenes of metallic debris. Not a field filled with it in which President Truman strolled, but a tent or building with two tables covered with it. The debris showed controls that could be manipulated by hands with six digits. The body to be autopsied had six digits.

But the debris didn't seem to have the look of something from a craft built on another planet. Instead, it reminded me of the late 1950s visions of what a spaceship would look like in the future. By today's standards, it was horribly out of date. The only interesting items were tiny knobs or buttons at the top of each finger hole that could have been trackballs not unlike those in labtop computers.

About the same time, more of the cameraman's story began to leak into the public arena. Obviously, the leaks were through Santilli and his organization, but it did provide us with clues. The cameraman, whether under the name of Barnett or anything else, now claimed to have photographed the first atomic test at Trinity Site. Here was something that could be independently verified. It was the first such clue that we had.

It wasn't long before a list of names of those associated with the Manhattan Project, as photographers, was found and circulated. Of course there was no Jack Barnett on the short list. Santilli's cameraman seemed to indicate he had been in charge, and the name of the man who, according to the documentation, was in charge was Berlyn Brixner.

John Kirby, a fellow researcher living in Portland, Oregon, wanted to pursue that lead. Using a CD-ROM telephone directory, I found Brixner's phone number and gave it to Kirby. The search for the man, which might have taken days not long ago, was accomplished in a matter of minutes.

Kirby was apparently the first researcher to call Brixner, a friendly 84-year-old man, who wanted to help. He provided Kirby with a list of the men he had worked with as photographers during the Manhattan Project in the late stages of the Second World War. Again, Barnett, or Barrett, failed to appear on the list.

Brixner told Kirby he knew of a couple of other photographers who were working with Bell and Howell 16-millimeter hand camera or with a Cine camera. George W. Thompson had died but John P. Wahlen was still alive.

There was one man, however, who seemed to fit the description of Santilli's cameraman. Jack Snow had been crippled by polio early in life. He managed to get around without the use of a wheel chair, and had been involved in the Manhattan Project as a photographer. The lead, however, did not pan out.

Others who checked with Brixner learned the same things that Kirby had. It didn't seem that Santilli's cameraman could have been one of those on the Manhattan Project. Santilli, of course, had an answer for that. He'd been an Army cameraman who had been on one of the aircraft flying near Trinity Site to photograph the detonation from the air. He never had the opportunity to meet Brixner, according to Santilli, so it made sense that Brixner didn't know who he was.

All this was just one more area in which what Santilli had said didn't seem to fit in with what could be established. There were Army cameraman involved, but the story told by Santilli's cameraman seemed to be at odds with historical fact. This, of course, caused many to believe that the cameraman didn't exist.

FOX-TV was the national network that won the right to broadcast the footage. I was asked to participate in the program and to provide some of the background of the whole Roswell case. Before the interview, I was given another opportunity to see the footage. This time I saw some of the "tent" autopsy, but the film was so dark and poorly reproduced that I could see little else but the two shapes of the doctors, a shape on the table, and what looked to be a lantern hanging from the tent pole.

Again, I also saw the brightly lit autopsy taken in the hospital-like setting, but by now so many had seen it, I knew what to look for, or at. Instead of studying the body, I tried to see the background. There was a clock that could have been from the era, that is, 1947. A curled telephone cord that had generated great interest until it was established that such cords had been available as early as 1938. And the Bunsen burner that was clearly lighted with a flask above it. Maybe the doctors were boiling some coffee.

If what I was seeing was accurate, it was the autopsy of an alien being. The doctors involved would not have had the opportunity to dissect an alien before now, with a single possible exception. If there were other alien creatures killed in the crash, they might have seen one of them. However, this is something unique. American scientists had a chance to autopsy the body of an intelligent being from another world.

But, for all intents and purposes, they completed their work in about two hours. They were joined by a motion picture cameraman who failed to get good shots of the body. They cut into it and removed organs, in what I think of as a fairly cavalier attitude for dealing with a biological sample that would have been unique. They lifted the organs clear and dropped them into steel bowls. There was no still photographer to record each step precisely, or any attempt by the doctors to map the internal structure of the alien being. They poked and prodded and literally ripped the organs out, making few notes and repeatedly getting in the way of the cameraman.

Here is a procedure that should have taken days, if not weeks, to complete. There are a limited number of alien bodies available for autopsy and there isn't much chance that others are going to be found. This is all there will ever be, and yet, according to the clock visible in the background, the whole procedure is completed in about two or three hours.

The entire film of the autopsy lasted just over twenty minutes. There were then scenes of the metallic debris. A single figure is seen moving through it, lifting some of it, but he is photographed from the back. We see, at most, a shoulder, his back and the rear of his pants. I will say that the pants looked as if they were Army issue from the proper time, but that, in the grand scheme of things, means little.

There had been talk, from some who had seen the debris sections of the video that an English word appeared embossed on one of the I-beams. I expected it to be something difficult to make out. But, as the soldier lifted the I-beam and turned it to the camera, the word "video" was quite clear. No, the symbols weren't exact matches, but then you would expect them to be disguised in some fashion. However, the word was clear and easy to read.

Having now had a chance to study the autopsy film at length, to have it stopped and backed up at my whim, at having an opportunity to examine the autopsy room rather than the men in it, I was less than impressed. I had to agree with Russ Estes. It looked like a dressed set. In fact, I noticed, even with the cameraman moving around the table to film at various angles, I only saw two walls. Had this been done in a real room, I would have expected to see a hint of the third and fourth walls.

Before any of the specials could be aired, the *Sunday Times* in London published an article with the headline, "Film that 'proves' aliens visited earth is a hoax." The article, written by Maurice Chittenden, reported that "experts called in by Channel 4 [a British television network], which is due to screen the film as part of a documentary on August 28 have declared it bogus. A source close to the documentary said: 'We have had special effects guys look at it and they say it's a fake.' "

Chittenden continued in the article, writing, "Among the flaws found by the *Sunday Times* are: 'Security coding' on one film disappeared when its accuracy was challenged. A 'letter of authentication' from Kodak was signed by a salesman. President Truman, supposedly visible on the film, was not in New Mexico at the time. Symbols seen on particles of wreckage are totally different from those remembered by an eyewitness. 'Doctors'—performing a supposedly unique autopsy on an alien—remove black lenses from his eyes in a matter of seconds, as if they knew what to expect."

These points were, for the most part, the same that had been raised by UFO researchers during their attempts to verify the authenticity of the film. What was most troubling was not that there were problems, but that the revelation of those problems resulted in an alteration of the story. When evidence was presented that suggested the security markings were more appropriate to Hollywood, those markings disappeared. That, in and of itself, suggested the film was a hoax.

But none of the negative publicity dampened the interest in the film. For weeks there had been speculation about it. The Internet and various news groups were filled with messages about the autopsy footage. Everyone was trying to figure out if we finally had the smoking gun, proving not only the Roswell case but also that flying saucers were extraterrestrial.

Santilli, however, maintained that the film was authentic. To prove it, he was going to allow some of the documentary producers an opportunity to meet with the cameraman. John Purdie called me and asked if I would be willing to accompany him if the meeting were arranged. I couldn't say anything, couldn't ask questions of the cameraman, but would be there as a "sort of assistant" to Purdie. Of course I agreed.

But the meeting never came off. Purdie did receive a phone call from a man who claimed to be the cameraman. They spoke for two minutes and that was it. Clearly Purdie was unable to learn anything important during the short call, no questions were answered. It could easily have been a set up. As of late January 1997, the cameraman still hasn't made a real appearance.

(I say a real appearance, because, apparently, there is a home video of the cameraman answering some of the questions people have asked. Apparently Bob Kiviat, who produced the FOX-TV special, was given the opportunity to submit written questions. The cameraman then answered some of them, but not all in front of a home video camera. It is my understanding that the video is of very poor quality.

Michael Hesemann, a German UFO researcher, told others that this proved that there was a film and a cameraman. In reality, it proved that there was someone who claimed to be the cameraman and it certainly didn't prove a thing about the film.

These details, although interesting, are not particularly persuasive, given what we have learned in the past year. I've included this late information so that we are all aware of it, but realize, until the cameraman is identified and his background can be verified, we still have nothing. A man sitting in front of a home video camera does nothing to verify the story, especially when the weight of the contradictions are amassed against it.)

The last week in August 1995, more than a year ago, was when we could expect some of those answers about the film to surface. The Channel 4 documentary aired on August 28, but there was nothing in it that hadn't been discussed by everyone on the Internet or in various UFO organizations. The most dramatic moments were those of Frank Kaufmann, a former military man who was assigned to the base at Roswell in July 1947 as a civilian employee. He provided his insights to the crash, told how he had participated in the retrieval, and gave an eyewitness account of what the bodies he saw looked like. According to Kaufmann, the alien in the film didn't match those he claimed to have seen.

The FOX special aired a couple of days later. What was appalling was the way they had edited their tape. While I spoke at length about the authenticity of the Roswell case, based on the witnesses I have interviewed and the research I had done, I was less impressed with the autopsy film. I pointed out that many of things that could have been done to authenticate it had not been done. I suggested that we did not have to prove it a fake, Santilli had to prove it authentic but had failed to do so.

Kodak came up again. It seemed to me that if Santilli was truly interested in learning the truth, if he truly knew nothing about UFOs and the origin of the film, he would want to validate it if possible.

Kodak officials, both in England and New York, said that they could learn a great deal if they could have a small segment of the film. They could make a detailed analysis that would be able to suggest when the film was made. While that wouldn't prove it authentic, if the film was made in the late 1940s, it would certainly suggest authenticity. Santilli provided many excuses as to why this couldn't be, or wouldn't be, done.

In fact, in the September 1996 issue, *Fortean Times* reported, "The hint of conspiracy is underlined by Ray Santilli. . . . Asked whether he still plans to accept Kodak's offer to analyze the film, he answers: 'With all due respect to Kodak, I simply do not trust an American corporation with lucrative defence contracts.' Way to go, Ray."

The saga of the investigation of the film is, in and of itself, interesting. It shows to what lengths UFO investigators will go to learn the truth, and it points out one of the major flaws in UFO investigation. Police authorities have the weight of the government behind them. If a witness is reluctant to answer questions, pressure can be brought to bear. In UFO investigation, if a witness refuses to answer questions, there is nothing more that can be done. A good investigator will try to learn the answers in other ways, but that is not always satisfactory.

Small bits of film began to circulate in the spring, as the story began to leak. A small bit of leader, that is, the opaque strip at the beginning of a movie, was provided for analysis. Kodak confirmed that a coding on it—a square and a triangle—suggested the film was from 1947. The problem was that Kodak recycled the codes, so the film could have been manufactured in 1927 or 1967. Besides, there were no images on the leader, so it could have been a piece of film from anything or anywhere, not necessarily from the autopsy footage.

Santilli did provide a few people with small sections of film. Philip Mantle of BUFORA had three or four frames that contained a bright lighted doorway, or what might have been a doorway, that might have been part of the autopsy footage. But Mantle told me, as well as others, that he had no footage with the alien or the interior of the autopsy room visible. Just that brightly lit door that might have been part of the original autopsy footage, or might just have been a few frames of another film used because the film was from the right era. Tests would be needed to determine the age.

Bob Kiviat, producer of the Fox special, was also given a small section of film, again with nothing that would identify it as having come from the autopsy footage. His original section of film was even smaller than that provided to Mantle.

Kodak insisted that they could provide fairly accurate dating, but they required several feet of film. They suggested that, over the years, film would shrink, and by measuring the distance between the sprockets, they could estimate the age. Chemical analysis, especially since the basic composition of film had changed after 1947, could provide additional clues. Kodak insisted they receive, at a minimum, one frame with the alien visible on it. That way they would know that their analysis was not being wasted. Of course, as of late January 1997, that hasn't happened. And, because of the recent statements of Santilli, we know that it will never happen.

After the British and American specials were aired, there was renewed interest, and Santilli's company was selling raw videotapes of the autopsy footage for about fifty dollars each. It was claimed that additional footage, not seen in the specials was on the video, but that was of the tent autopsy, more of the debris, and little else.

It should be noted here that originally Santilli had been talking about over two hours of film showing the autopsy and related material. But, as of late July or early August 1995, I had seen everything available and it added up to little more than twenty minutes. As far as I could tell then, or now, there is no additional footage awaiting release. All footage available has been aired somewhere in the world. All that we have are those twenty minutes with some of it so poor as to be virtually useless.

In September 1995, after both the American and British documentaries had aired, Philip Mantle sent out another letter. According to this one, Mantle was going to take the opportunity to "put the facts straight." Given the changing story and shifting facts, that would be a welcome relief.

According to Mantle, "I was first contacted by Ray Santilli almost two years ago [that would be September 1993] when he discussed with me the possibility of putting together a UFO documentary video. . . . They never made a UFO documentary. . . . For a variety of reasons the planned documentary with Merlin never came off but it was during this time that Ray Santilli told me the story of the Roswell film footage and how he obtained it."

As we had all been told, and again according to Mantle, "Santilli claimed that at some point previously (I do not know the date) he had flown to the USA to research a documentary on the late Elvis Presley. In order to do this he had traced a veteran cameraman who was one of if not the first person ever to film Elvis live on stage. Santilli purchased some archive film of Elvis from the man in question and returned to his hotel happy with the film he had obtained. Before flying back to England he was telephoned at his hotel by the cameraman in question who asked him to go and see him before he left as he had something even more interesting to show him. Santilli agreed but this time it was not film of Elvis but of the UFO crash at Roswell in 1947." [Let's mark this statement because it will become important later. Note that it is of the UFO crash at Roswell.]

Mantle then explains that Santilli had yet to show him the film. He told John Spencer, chairman of BUFORA and Walt Andrus, the international director of MUFON. He also writes, "I also contacted various Roswell researchers whose response was lukewarm to say the least."

I don't know what he expected any of us to do. He was in contact with Santilli, had yet to see the film, and he expected something out of the rest of us. Personally, I filed it away, hoping to learn something more about it later, if the film was ever shown. But the mere knowledge that it existed, frankly, did little for me.

Mantle continued to pursue this, according to his letter, and on March 17, 1995, he met Santilli in his office in London. Although he didn't see any of the film at the time, Santilli did provide Mantle with a copy described as "on-site examination footage." Mantle writes, "I have viewed this section of film over and over again and although it is quite poor quality a number of things can be seen." This is the tent footage in which little of importance is viewed.

Mantle invited Santilli to speak at the BUFORA conference to be held on August 19–20, 1995. A small notice appeared in one newspaper and from there, others learned about the existence of the film. Mantle, when he received inquiries about it, passed them along to Santilli.

On April 28, according to Mantle, he met with Santilli again. This time he saw the footage taken in the autopsy room. Mantle wrote, "Unlike the previous film this was very clear. . . . The alien is laid on a slab inside what looks like a morgue or should I say a hospital."

Mantle, in his letter, provided his take on the May 5 screening. He wrote, ". . . I along with 200 others were invited to attend another screening of the film. . . . We did attend as did Kent Jeffrey of the USA, Roberto Pinotti from Italy, Michael Hesemann from Germany. . . . Also in attendance were representatives from a variety of TV companies from around the world."

He finished the letter with a number of statements about rumors concerning the film. None of them are important or relevant to our discussion. They merely confirm, for example, that Jacques Vallee, a UFO researcher living in San Francisco was not approached by a company from Brazil a couple of years ago. He had not heard about the film until Santilli began to leak its existence.

Other problems began to surface. For example, it had been suggested early on that the film showed the autopsy of the body of a being recovered after the Roswell crash. Other information, including the alleged date of the autopsy and the date of the crash did not follow the conventional wisdom of the Roswell case. Santilli and his friends, and the cameraman communicating through Santilli, were now suggesting the crash had taken place more than a month earlier, that is, in late May 1947.

Almost universally, UFO researchers, television producers and reporters, and anyone else interested in the film were demanding the cameraman come forward. Without him to complete the chain of custody, the film was nearly useless. Couple this to the fact that Santilli, to that point, had refused to provide anything that would be of value in authenticating the film, and we were all arguing over nothing. The film was an interesting aberration and nothing more.

Santilli, through his various contacts, including the editor of *Shutterbug* magazine, Bob Shell, finally offered the cameraman's audio taped statement. Here, as if it will come as a surprise, is more controversy. Shell, appearing on Cable Radio Network's September 2, 1995 edition of "UFOs Tonight!" hosted by Don Ecker, said that the transcript being circulated was an exact transcript. Under close questioning by Ecker, Shell said that he had heard the original tape and read, or typed, the transcript himself. At any rate, the transcript was an exact copy of what the cameraman had said. This discussion, recorded as a matter of course by Ecker, would become important to understanding more about the case.

During the conversation, Ecker said, ". . . Somebody in the United Kingdom sent me allegedly the cameraman's statement, along with some facsimiles that were allegedly the film labels. Now, a number of weeks ago I read this entire statement verbatim on the air. And I think this is somewhat telling in itself. Now, this is purportedly this gentleman's actual statement. And I think it's very safe to say in this statement may be information he originally gave Ray Santilli, this is not the way an American former service man would ever describe himself. Have you . . ."

Shell broke in and said, "What you have is probably the first version of that."

"Yeah," said Ecker. "And what I'm saying [is] this was passed off as his actual statement by Santilli, originally. And I think it's very safe to say that just ain't so, okay? It was passed off deceptively. Do you know what I'm saying?"

Shell responded by saying, "Well, yeah, but I think you have to understand what exactly happened. The cameraman made a taped statement. The tape was mailed to Santilli. . . . Santilli had one of his secretaries to transcribe it. The secretary is British."

"Okay."

Shell continued. "So quite a bit of British [terminology] got into the transcript. . . . I have gone over and retranscribed it and posted it this week on CompuServe's library."

Ecker asked, "From the actual tape?"

"Yes."

"You have a copy of the tape?"

"Yes."

Later, Shell would deny that he had heard the actual tape or that he had ever spoken to the cameraman. In other words, Shell, if he repaired the "transcript" did so without having heard the tape himself. It would mean that he was altering the transcript for no reason, other than to remove the incriminating British colloquialisms from it. That information itself is important.

The statement was filled with things that made no sense, at least to Americans. For example, the cameraman said, "I joined the forces . . ." meaning the military, "in 1942." Americans do not use that British terminology. We say we joined the Army, or the Air Force, or the military, or even the service, but not the forces.

As we have seen, when similar problems about the statement were pointed out, Santilli and his apologists said that the tape had been transcribed by Santilli's British secretary and she had changed the wording. This makes no sense whatsoever. It was a clumsy attempt to explain why common British terms were sprinkled through a statement made by an American. It also means, if we believe the explanation, that Shell's claim of an exact transcript were false. He had been mistaken when he said otherwise.

The cameraman claimed that he remembered very clearly that he had received a call to go to White Sands. On the statement, parenthetically, it says Roswell. But Roswell is not the same as White Sands. The missile range at White Sands was, and is, an Army facility, and it is nearly 150 miles from Roswell. If the cameraman was going to White Sands, why not fly him to the Alamogordo Army Air Field, now Holloman Air Force Base, less than twenty miles away? That part of the statement makes no sense, unless you are trying to keep Roswell attached to the story for the commercial value of the name.

The statement continued, naming a few names, such as George C. McDonnel, the first Air Force assistant chief of staff for intelligence. It also mentions Major General Clements McMullen, at the time, the deputy commander for the Strategic Air Command. The names of both officers had appeared in numerous publications, along with their positions in 1947. If the cameraman had mentioned a captain or major who was his immediate superior in 1947, then we could check it out. Mentioning two general officers who were already well known both inside and outside the UFO community did nothing to validate the statement.

The cameraman then, apparently casually, makes a change in the scenario that is quite significant. He said, "I was ordered to a crash site just southwest of Socorro."

What is this? The cameraman wasn't at a site near Roswell? He was at a site about 200 miles from Roswell. The event that he was talking about, if we consider the date and the location, apparently had nothing at all to do with the events near Roswell.

He was not content to drop that single bomb. He added others, explaining that he had been in St. Louis a few days earlier where he claimed he had been filming tests of a new ramjet helicopter. He returned to Washington, D.C., where he was given his orders and then flew out of Andrews Army Air Field, on to Wright Field, and then on to the Roswell Army Air Field. From Roswell, they drove overland to the crash site.

To anyone who has studied a map or the Roswell case, this makes absolutely no sense. Why fly a cameraman from Washington to Dayton, Ohio and then on to Roswell? Even if they felt the need to land first in Ohio, the trip on to Roswell makes no sense. Why not fly into Kirtland in Albuquerque or Alamogordo? In 1947 there was no interstate highway, but there was U.S. Highway 85. A trip from either base to Socorro was easy and quick. And even today a trip from Roswell to Socorro is long and difficult.

There is another but subtle point to be made here. The base at Roswell was under the Strategic Air Command at the time, and it would make sense that McMullen, as the deputy commander would be involved. The other bases, Wright Field, Kirtland, and Alamogordo, were all part of the Air Materiel Command in 1947. In other words, a different chain of command. Yet we have the cameraman flying out of SAC bases and into AMC bases and then into SAC bases. There is no real reason for this, unless it is a thinly veiled attempt to tie the Roswell case into the quickly unraveling story told by the cameraman.

Frankly, the statement by the cameraman did little to increase our knowledge. Once again we had nothing that could be verified properly because we had no names attached to it. There were some researchers who did try to learn who would have been at both the Trinity Test in 1945 and at the "Little Henry" helicopter ramjet tests in St. Louis. No single name surfaced. And, there were those who were convinced that the film was a fake and therefore deserved no further research.

In October 1995, Television France One (TF1), had finished with their documentary about the autopsy film. They'd had access to material that had been unavailable to others as they put together their specials. For example, Nicolas Maillard of TF1 faxed a letter to the public relations department of McDonnell-Douglas (the corporate entity of the former McDonnell Aircraft Company) which confirmed that McDonnell had used their own employees for the photographic work concerning the Little Henry. Chester Turk shot the motion pictures and Bill Schmitt took the stills. No military personnel were used, though Santilli's cameraman had claimed to have been there, and his own statement suggested he was in the Army until 1952, or about five years after those tests had been made.

Although Santilli's promises to others such as John Purdie of Channel 4 in the United Kingdom and Bob Kiviat of FOX that they would be able to speak to the cameraman had not happened, he made a similar promise to those at TF1. The call, promised in early September 1995, never came. Santilli did agree to submit a list of questions to the cameraman. (Is this beginning to sound familiar?) TF1 drew up the list, and on September 14, about three days after the list was submitted, TF1 received a fax from Santilli with the answers.

Two of the answers were of interest to researchers. TF1 asked, "What tests of the ramjet 'Little Henry' did you film in St. Louis in May 1947?" The answer from the cameraman was, "The initial tests." This was a claim that was known to be false given the information provided by McDonnell Aircraft several weeks earlier.

A second question that must have seemed somewhat irrelevant when asked and would become important later was, "Why didn't the Army use color film for such an event?"

The answer was, "I was given instructions to leave immediately to film an aviation crash of a Russian spy plane. I did not have time to order either colour [please note the British spelling here] film stock or special camera equipment. I used standard issue film stock and a standard Bell and Howell."

Kent Jeffrey, in the *MUFON Journal*, wrote, "Hypothetically, such an answer could explain why the cameraman didn't use color film at the initial crash scene. However, such an answer in no way explains why he didn't use color film for the autopsies—which he claims took place a month later in July in Fort Worth, Texas."

TF1, however, wasn't finished with their work. At the end of September 1995, Nicolas Maillard located Cleveland, Ohio, disc jockey Bill Randle (still no relation), who was the real source of the early Elvis footage that supposedly started this whole episode. This is the footage that Santilli claimed had been sold to him by the cameraman who had also filmed the alien autopsy. According to Randle, the purchase of the Elvis film took place in his office on July 4, 1992, in the presence of Gary Shoefield.

Kent confirmed this in November 1995 when he spoke to Randle. According to Kent, Santilli purchased the film after hours of negotiation and then turned around and sold it to Shoefield, who was representing Polygram. That transaction took place in Randle's office as well.

That wasn't the end of it. According to Randle, the footage Santilli bought was two short segments from two concerts held in Cleveland on July 20, 1955. The afternoon concert was at a Cleveland high school and the second at a Cleveland auditorium. The program featured the Four Lads, Bill Haley, Pat Boone, and the then unknown Elvis Presley. Randle hired a freelance photographer to film the concerts. His named was Jack Barnett.

This provided the information needed to check out Jack Barnett and suggested that Santilli's first statement about the name was accurate. He was born of Russian parents on January 1, 1906, and died in 1967. He had been a newsreel cameraman during the Second World War, had been in on the Italian campaign, but had not been in the Army.

TF1 planned to confront Santilli during a live interview on October 23, 1995, on the Jacques Pradel special with this information to gauge his reaction. Once the interview with Bill Randle was played for Santilli, he said, "Well, firstly, I'm very pleased that you have found Bill Randle . . ."

Santilli then provided a new scenario for the discovery of the autopsy footage. Kent Jeffrey wrote in the *MUFON Journal*, ". . . the person from whom he had purchased the Elvis footage was not really a military cameraman after all. He now claimed that he had met the real cameraman after he purchased the rights to the Elvis film from Bill Randle in Cleveland during the summer of 1992 (previously Santilli had given the year as 1993). Everyone, including the host, Jacques Pradel, seemed incredulous . . ."

Jeffrey, however, pursued the military cameraman angle further. It seems that those on the inside, who were actual military cameramen, could provide some clues about the film. He wrote, "During the course of investigating this film, I was fortunate to be put in touch with three such men, Joe Longo, Bill Gibson, and Dan McGovern, all former WWII combat cameramen, and all of whom have remained active in professional photography business to this day."

Kent then provides a brief background of each man that is no less than impressive. One of them filmed the B-25s as they took off from the *Hornet* on the Doolittle Raid on Japan. Another served with the Eighth Air Force, flying missions over Germany, and was the first American cameraman to film the devastation of Hiroshima and Nagasaki. All worked on classified military projects. As a group of experts, Kent couldn't have found a better collection of men.

Kent wrote, "Part of the modus operandi of the military is regimentation, discipline and strict adherence to prescribed procedures. . . . The mission of the military demands it. Military photographers are no exception. . . . Dan McGovern, Bill Gibson, and Joe Longo all viewed the alien autopsy footage, as well as photocopies of film box labels furnished by Santilli to TF1, supposedly supplied by his cameraman. The three former military cameramen all noted a number of significant discrepancies . . ."

According to Kent, "From the standpoint of appropriate military procedures applicable at the time and which would have definitely been followed, the scenario recounted by Santilli's alleged cameraman makes no sense."

Specifically, they objected to the handling of the film. "According to Santilli, his cameraman claims that he processed the film himself and that authorities in Washington did not bother to collect all the reels. Our three cameramen consider this claim total nonsense. On top-secret projects, a cameraman never, under any circumstances, processed the film himself. Additionally, military regulations required that all film, developed or undeveloped, had to be accounted for—not just every reel, but every frame of every reel. To ensure compliance, either the length of the film on a reel was physically measured (e.g., 99 feet, 10 frames) or a machine called a 'frame counter' was used. Furthermore, according to Santilli's cameraman, there were only three autopsies. The footage he allegedly kept covered a major part of one of those autopsies. On that basis alone, it is inconceivable that the authorities overseeing the operation would have overlooked so much missing film."

A comment is necessary here. The military, according to Herman

Wouk in *The Caine Mutiny*, was designed by geniuses for execution by morons. Established procedures for everything are laid out in great detail. When highly classified material is involved, those regulations have even more force because people could go to jail. We are now presented with a situation, if we are to believe Santilli and his cameraman, where those regulations were repeatedly violated. The tale smacks of someone who was not in the military and had no idea how these sorts of things worked. When compared to the real security operations and other top secret projects, there is a single conclusion to be drawn. If there was nothing else wrong with the cameraman's story, this should be enough to sink it.

But there is more. According to Kent's article, "Three basic types of film were used by the military in 1947, 16 mm color, 35 mm black and white, and 16mm black and white. For very special or important projects (as the autopsy of an alien would have been) 16mm color film was used. Furthermore, McGovern, who filmed a number of autopsies, was very positive that all medical procedures were shot in color. He also stated that for important medical procedures, two cameras were used, both in fixed positions. The first camera was mounted on a tripod sitting on a 'riser' (for extra elevation) adjacent to the operating or autopsy table. The second camera was overhead, mounted on the ceiling."

Here we have what would have been the most important autopsy this cameraman ever filmed and again he violated all the regulations. It would not have violated security for him to have used two cameras, nor would there have been a time crunch that would have called for a modification of normal procedures. Again, what this establishes is that Santilli's cameraman was unaware of the procedures in operation at the time. This points strongly toward the conclusion that no such cameraman exists.

But there is still more that Kent learned in his discussions with actual military cameramen. "Our three cameramen pointed out that a 'motion' picture cameraman would almost always be accompanied by a 'still' photographer. The two would work together as a team. During an autopsy, every step of the procedure would be carefully photographed by the 'still' photographer, who would invariably be visible in the 'motion' picture. (Medical people have also stated that still pictures definitely would have been taken.) In the

Santilli alien autopsy film, there is no evidence whatsoever that stills were taken."

Kent continued, writing, "Even the technique of Santilli's cameraman, according to our three cameramen, was inconsistent with the highly standardized procedures and methods used by military cameramen at that time. McGovern, Gibson, and Longo are in a position to know—all three trained other military cameramen. All three consider the quality of the camera work in the Santilli film appalling and, for a myriad of reasons, not even close to meeting military standards. As Joe Longo put it, 'If anybody in my unit shot the film in that manner, he'd be back scrubbing pots in the kitchen.'

"According to the box label submitted by Santilli, the film used was Kodak 'High Speed Super-XX Panchromatic Safety Film.' According to McGovern, Gibson, and Longo, with a Bell and Howell Model 70 (the camera used by the alleged cameraman), the depth of field should have been very good. . . . Consequently, even with the apparent mediocre lighting conditions in the Santilli autopsy film, the picture quality should have been excellent. Our cameramen all agreed that using the Bell and Howell Model 70 and Super-XX film, with the focus set at 25 feet and the aperture at F-8, under normal indoor lighting, everything from about a foot and a half to infinity would be in focus. This should have been the case with the Santilli film, but obviously was not. McGovern concluded that the Santilli film was 'deliberately blurred so that no subject is visible in detail.'"

There are other problems with this aspect of the film. It is important to note that we are dealing with testimony of three men who were in the military at the proper time and can comment, as experts, on the procedures used. They say nothing that would help underscore the validity of the film, but find a great deal of fault with it. Even the labeling on the film boxes was something they had never seen. ". . . the seal with the eagle—probably placed there to give it an official look—was something none of them had ever seen."

Kent, continued that thought, writing, "In their experience, of the thousands of boxes of film ordered by the military from Kodak, none were stamped with seals."

There are additional problems for Santilli and his cameraman. Again, according to Kent, "One of the Santilli labels reads 'Reel # 52: Truman: 85 Filter 2/3 stop: Force X 2 stop - Possible.' All three cameramen noted that an '85 filter' was used only with color film. The '2/3 stop' indicates the amount of light that would be blocked by the filter and 'Force X 2 stop' indicates the amount of additional exposure time required to compensate for the resultant loss of light. In effect, it is a prescription for underexposing and then compensating by overdeveloping the film—a procedure that would unnecessarily increase the graininess and lower the resolution of the picture."

All of this research on the part of Kent Jeffrey, along with the help of the three professional military cameramen to whom he spoke, suggests that the autopsy film is a fraud. Couple that to the Santilli cameraman's ever changing statements, the obvious British "accent" in the cameraman's statement, and the fact that no one has been able to verify any aspect of the cameraman's incredible story, and the only conclusion possible is that the film is a fake.

But, because these stories have a habit of refusing to die, regardless of the time and effort made to dispose of them, of the wealth of data marshaled against them, let's add a few more details.

In the August 28, 1995, Channel 4 documentary, Santilli referred to the collector who had paid for the autopsy footage. He had said, repeatedly, that he, Santilli, did not have access to the film itself because the collector had it in a vault. It would be up to the collector to offer samples of the film for analysis. Santilli could do nothing to help researchers.

Through the efforts of the investigative team of TF1, however, the name of the collector was learned. Volker Spielberg was the man who supposedly owned the film. Coincidentally, Spielberg, like Santilli, is in the video distribution business.

During a live interview on TF1, Santilli, when pressed about providing the original film, said that it was out of his hands. TF1 then showed taped clips of Spielberg's business office, and the reporter said that TF1 had learned that Spielberg was not a film collector. Contrary to what Santilli had said about not knowing Spielberg personally, TF1 learned of a confidential meeting in Hamburg, Germany among Spielberg, Santilli, and one or two others. It was revealed that Santilli and Spielberg are friends and business partners and have worked together before.

But remember, Santilli had provided a few people with short clips of film that he claimed came from the autopsy footage. From the small sample, just a few frames, that Philip Mantle had received, he offered a frame for analysis. I won't complain that the testing was not done by Kodak, who would be the ultimate experts here, because a sample had been donated for research.

On August 1, 1996, Bob Shell, in a statement that he copyrighted, trumpeted the results of those tests. In those results, Shell talks about various Kodak products and seems to imply that these products were all available prior to 1947, but nowhere actually makes that claim. Instead he said that more testing was necessary.

But the point is that we don't know where those frames of film came from. Mantle's sample, as he told me in early July 1996, contains nothing that links it directly to the autopsy film. It doesn't matter if the tests prove the film was exposed and developed in 1947 because there are no links to the autopsy film. And yet we are told that the test results are in. No, they are not.

There are many other problems with the story as it is now being told. The date of the crash that produced the "Santilli" body shifted to late May or early June 1947. The location has shifted around the southwest and has been given a number of locations near Socorro.

Michael Hesemann, the German researcher, who is working with, if not for, Santilli, has told many that the alien autopsy footage is from nearby Socorro, New Mexico. Hesemann has claimed that he has located the "real" crash site and is the only researcher to have done so. He has also claimed that the real date of this crash is May 31, 1947. Because this is not the Roswell case, Hesemann believes it explains the discrepancies between what researchers have learned about Roswell and the facts that have surfaced around the Santilli autopsy film.

Shell reappeared again. He said that he had gone to Socorro and searched the newspaper files there. Papers for late May and early June 1947 were missing. He found this highly significant, though he had been told that a fire in the newspaper office might be the reason rather than Shell's implied suggestion that this was all part of the cover-up.

To check all this out, I called the offices of the *Socorro Defensor-Chieftain* to learn the truth. One of the reporters checked the files and learned that the newspapers were, in fact, missing from the

May 15 issue, through early June. I also called the library at the New Mexico School of Mining and Technology, and learned that they had some gaps in their files as well.

Is there anything significant here? I doubt it. The story of the fire in the newspaper office seems to cover the point. In twenty years of UFO research, I have heard a dozen stories of newspapers that were confiscated. Never is there any evidence that such a confiscation took place. That these particular newspapers, and remember it was a weekly in 1947, are missing may be nothing more nefarious than a coincidence. Without more evidence, we can't translate this into some kind of support for the rapidly collapsing tale of an alien autopsy.

The date offered by Hesemann and others for the Socorro crash, earlier than the events outside of Roswell, also bothers me. It seems, from a strictly logical point of view, that the earlier date can't be correct. The military reaction at Roswell is not logical, if there had been an event five or six weeks earlier.

In fact, if we look at the newspaper coverage, we can see the problem. On June 24, 1947, Kenneth Arnold reported seeing nine objects in fast flight near Mt. Rainier in Washington state. Within days newspapers around the country were filled with reports of flying saucers. On July 8, it was reported that the Army had captured one near Roswell and within hours, the Army and the Navy, according to the associated press, moved to stop the spread of the rumors about flying saucers.

This suggests that no one in the government, either military or civilian, had any information about the flying saucers until one crashed near Roswell. Handed the information, military officials moved to stop all talk about them.

If, however, something had happened in late May, providing the same sort of information that the crash near Roswell did, we would expect the news to be suppressed after that event. Arnold's story would have never have made it into the newspapers throughout the country. The government would have suppressed it immediately. That didn't happen. In fact, no one seemed to know what was going on, based on what was published in the newspapers during the last of June and the first week of July 1947. Not until after the July 4 weekend.

It would seem that this suggests there was no definitive event before the crash at Roswell. If that is true, then the Santilli film and the story around it is faked.

But even if we ignore the logic of the situation, or the illogic for that matter, we still have all the evidence marshaled against the Santilli film. He has done everything in his power to prevent researchers and investigators from learning the truth. He has misrepresented, from the beginning, exactly what was on the film. When caught in a misstatement, he changed it to make it consistent. When evidence he submitted was challenged, he withdrew it and never mentioned it again. When evidence was presented that challenged him, he changed the evidence or blamed someone else. And when people asked for film to analyze, and when Kodak volunteered to analyze the film for free, Santilli decided he couldn't trust them.

What we have is a story that smacked of hoax from the very beginning. We are left with a story that has no support for it. We have nothing, other than an unidentified source and a piece of videotape that is of poor quality. Clearly, the only conclusion to be drawn is that the alien autopsy tape is just another of the hoaxes that have dotted the UFO landscape.

8 The Chupacabras

1995

THE UFO PHENOMENON IN THE 1990s is not like it was in the 1950s and 1960s. Then UFOs "behaved" themselves, staying in the sky. Reports of landings, or the occupants of the craft, were few. The Aerial Phenomena Research Organization, headquartered in Tucson, Arizona, collected occupant sightings. The National Investigations Committee on Aerial Phenomena did not. It was more of a matter of internal and organizational policy and mission than anything else.

In the 1990s, the major UFO organizations accept occupant reports, and, in fact, study the cases of alleged alien abduction. Seeing the craft on the ground is no longer the sensational claim it once was. And there are related fields that require their own study. Subsets of UFOs include the crop circles and the cattle mutilations. In 1994, a new subset, which has been linked to UFOs by some researchers, appeared first in Puerto Rico, and then throughout the Spanish communities in the United States and in Mexico. These are the reports of the blood-sucking beasts known as the Chupacabras.

But the story of the Chupacabras might have begun even earlier than 1994. In 1989, reports circulated throughout Puerto Rico of a "vampire" bird. Officials, according to some reports, claimed the birds were native to the island, but had been altered by rooster spurs grafted to their beaks. The improbable explanation seemed to satisfy the public. Reports of the vampire birds faded from the public arena.

But reports of UFOs didn't. Puerto Rica has long been a hotbed of UFO activity. In 1990 and 1991, the Laguna Cartagena near Boqueron and Caba Rojo was the scene of many UFO sightings. Some researchers believed that the laguna was an entry or exit point for a subterranean base that exists deep below the surface of the water.

Other areas of Puerto Rico were also visited by alien spacecraft. On May 19, 1995, Moises Picart claimed that a brilliantly lighted UFO flew over the town, illuminating the landscape. It disappeared in minutes, but Picart said that the object was like no commercial, private, or military aircraft he had ever seen.

On November 18, 1995, a huge, glowing disc, about forty feet in diameter, with a row of dark windows was seen hovering over the transmitter of Radio Procer in Barranquites, in the center of Puerto Rico. Apparently the UFO affected the radio station's electronics, causing dials to jump wildly, and even activating obsolete and stored equipment.

There were many witnesses who saw the UFO as it hovered over the radio transmitter tower. Jorge Martin, who investigated the case, reported that Puerto Rican television broadcast reports over their station, but failed to mention that some witnesses saw a number of small, unidentified creatures during the sighting. That information would later become important as various and mundane explanations for the Chupacabras were offered by governmental officials.

Throughout 1994, there were many UFO sightings of a triangular-shaped craft. There were so many of these sightings that the mayor of one of the small towns demanded that President Clinton order an investigation. There is no indication that the request ever reached the White House and certainly no investigation was undertaken by official agencies.

The widely reported sightings, however, created an unhappy situation for many of the interior towns and villages. Sightseers, UFO researchers, and the curious flocked into the area, hoping to see one of the flying saucers. Although the sightings were not well known outside of Puerto Rico, those living on the island were well aware of what was happening.

There were many other sightings, but these few seem to be fairly representative of them. There is no need to list dozens of similar reports simply because they are similar to other reports provided by the eyewitnesses and UFO investigators. The fact remains that many residents of Puerto Rico saw UFOs, including the triangular-shaped craft, on hundreds of occasions during 1993 and 1994.

The first of the mysterious animal deaths was reported publicly on March 11, 1995, when eight sheep were found with strange puncture marks in their chests. They were all drained of blood. No one saw or heard anything unusual in the area, neither strange animals or UFOs.

The first of the Chupacabras sightings came on March 26, 1995, when Jaime Torres noticed a creature of some kind perched in a tree. Torres described the creature as having a rounded, hairless head, large slanted black eyes, thin clawed hands, and a tail. It hissed at Torres, leaped from the tree, and ran into the tropical vegetation. Torres said the hissing made him feel sleepy and faint.

Not long after that, on April 2, 1995, a large group of people saw a three-foot tall greyish creature close at hand. Rather than making the witnesses sleepy, it made them sick. One of the children was reported to have passed out.

Through the rest of spring and into the summer, there were more reports of strange animal deaths. By August 1995, about a hundred fifty animal deaths had been blamed on the Chupacabras. It wasn't until late in the fall that stories began to circulate widely and that reports began to appear in the big daily newspapers.

By the beginning of November, reports of the Chupacabras were coming in at a rapid pace. On the first of November, police officer Abraham Baez reported that a goat, missing an eye, had been found with a strange wound on the neck. According to the police report, it didn't appear that the animal had been attacked by dogs, and there was no evidence of blood in the body.

On the same day, Carlos De Jesus, owner of a junkyard, had just opened but was puzzled when his animals; sheep and geese, didn't appear immediately, demanding to be fed. All were found dead.

De Jesus told reporter Ruben Dario Rodriguez, "The Chupacabras is a serious matter, not a cause for levity. The government should pay greater attention to this weird situation."

The next day Angela Lajes told reporters that her dog had been killed during the night. She found her pet in the morning, apparently drained of blood. When she alerted her neighbor, Angela Santiago, she was told that two cats had also been found, drained of blood, and looked as if there was nothing left inside them. She said that she had heard sounds of a fight during the night, but refused to go out to investigate. She was too frightened to leave her house.

Examination of the bodies of the animals suggested they had all been killed by the same kind of beast. When the wounds were compared to those associated with the Chupacabras, authorities concluded they had an exact match.

On November 6, 1995, two men who had been fishing in the early evening claimed they had heard noise in the jungle behind them. Luis Guadalupe said that he saw a horrible, devil-like creature that had large ears, large luminous eyes, and large claws and wings.

The men fled, running along the shore as the Chupacabras chased them, flying above the trees. They reached a house and one of the men grabbed a machete. The Chupacabras landed on a nearby hutch, ready to pounce. Instead, the creature jumped to the ground and fled into the woods leaving deep footprints in its wake.

The next day, Victor Ortiz, owner of a junkyard, reported that the Chupacabras had killed a cat, nearly killed two sheep, and apparently ate all of a lamb. Although the ground was muddy, there were no footprints. Instead there were signs of a fierce fight.

Similar tales were told all though November and December of 1995. By that point, the slaughter of the animals was being reported almost daily by the newspapers, as well as by television and radio reporters. The Chupacabras, in those reports, was described as having the body of a bi-pedal dinosaur but with no apparent tail. The head is oval shaped, with two large eyes that are sometimes reported as glowing in the dark. The eyes have been described as both black and red. There are two holes for the nostrils and a small mouth with long fangs protruding upwards and downwards. There are reports of small, pointed ears, but most witnesses have not seen them. Although witnesses have reported coarse black hair all over the body, some claim that it can change color to blend in with the environment. There is a row of spines from the front of the head down to the middle of the back. The creature is usually described as small, no more than three feet tall.

The beast has two small arms with three-fingered, clawed hands. The feet also have long claws. It has been reported that the Chupacabras is fast and that it can leap about twenty feet. The quills, or spines down the back, seem to flap and some people believe this is how the beast is able to fly.

By the end of the year, the Chupacabras had migrated from Puerto Rico. On December 21, 1995, near Klamath Falls, Oregon, a pregnant heifer was found with her right ear gone, hide cut from her face, the tongue cut lengthwise along the teeth and all four teats were removed leaving black circles on the udder. There was no blood around any of the excisions or on the ground.

On January 4, 1996, eight calves were found frozen in Isabella County, Michigan. Two were skinned from head to hooves but the other six were only skinned from the neck down. All were about a week old.

On January 7, 1996, Klamath Falls was again the scene of a mutilation. A week-old calf was discovered with its right ear cut off and the entire skull removed.

In March, about a year after the events began to circulate in Puerto Rico, it was reported that forty animals in the northwest rural area of Miami had been killed. One woman claimed that she had seen a dog-like creature standing up, holding two short arms in the air.

At the beginning of May, the Chupacabras arrived in the Rio Grande Valley of south Texas. A pet goat was found dead with three puncture wounds on its neck. These were reported as the telltale signs of the beast and as evidence the Chupacabras had migrated into Texas.

On May 2, the Chupacabras appeared in Juarez, Mexico, just across the border from El Paso, Texas. For the first time there were detailed descriptions of the creature outside of Puerto Rico. This creature was described as looking like a kangaroo with a row of spikes from the top of its head to the small of its back. The creature had three-clawed hands and feet. Some of the witnesses observed an organ like a tube that projected from the mouth that was the "sucking device." The description matched, in a general way, that given of the Chupacabras in Puerto Rico. In fact, suggesting it was kangaroo like, was a much more vivid description than had been available in the past.

On the third of May, in Northern Mexico, a giant bat-like creature was reported to be terrorizing a village there. Goats, their bodies drained of blood, were being found daily. Farmers and livestock owners in the area were forming armed squads to patrol the night. People were being warned to stay inside at night because the beast, whatever it was, had attacked one human. At least, it had been reported to have attacked a human.

In other parts of Mexico, during early May 1996, more reports of the Chupacabras were made. In Sinaloa, for example, dead cows and sheep were found. A small creature, a foot to a foot and a half tall was seen and reported to be able to fly. Again, it matched, in general, the Chupacabras, though somewhat smaller.

The news from Sinaloa got even more spectacular. According to the regional newspapers, police were confronted by one of the creatures and opened fire on it. The beast turned to stare at them. They described it as having a human-like face with red eyes. It jumped a fence and disappeared. Apparently the police were unable to wound it.

The same newspapers also reported a number of human victims who had survived attacks. They said that they were engulfed by a shadowy figure and then lost consciousness. The marks on their bodies, which resembled large bulletholes, were videotaped and then broadcast all over Mexico. Is it necessary to point out that these reports were beginning to resemble the tales of the vampire that had circulated in Eastern Europe about a thousand years ago?

Official spokesman, Jose Burria, of the Department of Agriculture in Mexico, said that the attacks were the result of attacks by dogs or coyotes. There has been no other official statement about the attacks and the number of animal deaths continues to climb.

On May 10, more people in Florida reported that the creature had been seen by them or had attacked pets. And two days later, on May 12, another tale came from Mexico. Twenty-eight rams were found dead, all with puncture marks on their bodies.

The stories continued to spread. When the reports from Puerto Rico died down, they flared up in Mexico and the southwestern United States. Reports came from Tucson, Arizona; southern Utah; and California. Additional reports were made among the Hispanic populations around New York and Boston on the east coast.

The tales were taking on the proportions of an urban legend. There were many stories, some of which could be traced to a single source. But the evidence seemed to be slight. Yes, there were the animals that had been killed, but some of those descriptions seemed to fit the pattern of the cattle mutilations that had been reported for more than twenty years in the United States. The cases from Klamath Falls, in fact, seemed to be more closely linked to cattle mutilations than the Chupacabras. For a short period any strange animal death was linked to Chupacabras.

That does bring a second question to mind. Is there any history of similar attacks? The Chupacabras seemed to have developed, or appeared, early in 1995. History, however, seems to be littered with stories of beasts that are similar to the Chupacabras, but I stress the term similar.

Something like the Chupacabras was seen in south Texas in the mid-1970s. Police officer Arturo Padillo of San Benito, Texas, reported that he saw something like a large, winged creature early on the morning of December 28, 1975. Padillo saw the creature flying above the street lights on the foggy morning. He told reporters that the creature was white and had a wingspan between twelve and fifteen feet. It was larger than the current crop of Chupacabras, which have also been reported to fly.

On January 2, 1976, large, three-toed tracks were found in the mud on the outskirts of Harlington, Texas. The tracks, looking as if they had been left by a large bird, were six inches wide and twelve inches long. Two girls had been playing in the field the day before when they saw a large black bird with red eyes and a sharp beak. They watched the creature through binoculars, but when the creature seemed to be getting closer to them, they fled into the house.

Ray Norton, the news director for television station KGBT in Harlington, saw the tracks himself. They formed a trail about eighty feet in length before abruptly ending. Norton filmed them so that he could broadcast them later that evening.

On January 7, 1976, in Brownsville, Texas, along the Rio Grande, Alverico Guajardo was resting in his mobile home when noise and vibration from outside alarmed him. It sounded to Guajardo as if a sack of cement had hit one corner of his home. He ran outside, but when he was unable to find a flashlight, used the headlights of his car, maneuvering it until he saw a creature, about the size of a man, outlined by the lights. Like the Chupacabras, it had blazing red eyes, but it was also covered with feathers and had a pointed beak.

In mid-January 1976, two other Brownsville girls, Libby and Deany Ford, said they had spotted a "big black bird." Interviewed on KGBT, the girls said that the creature had a face like a bat. Later, they identified it as looking most like a pteronodon, a small flying dinosaur.

Although others have suggested that these sightings represent some of the first reports of the Chupacabras, frankly, the descriptions aren't very close. The bat-like bird that was seen in south Texas was larger than the Chupacabras, was seen flying more frequently than the Chupacabras, and didn't seem to have the same taste for blood. And the Chupacabras doesn't look like a pteronodon.

If there is no historical link to any of these reports of the past, where has the Chupacabras come from? There are a number of theories about it, none of which is particularly persuasive, at least to me.

Jorge Martin, who has done a great deal of investigation of the reports in Puerto Rico, has suggested genetic manipulation. He refers to the Chupacabras as Anomalous Biological Entities (ABEs) and draws the conclusion of a possible link to UFOs. Writing in *UFO Universe,* Martin said, ". . . we can't discard the possibility that the ABEs can also be the product of highly sophisticated genetic manipulation by human agencies. Already, a Chinese-Russian scientist, Dr. Tsian Kanchen, has produced genetic manipulations which have created new species of electronically crossed plant organisms and animal organisms. . . . By these means he has created incredible new breeds of ducks/chickens, with the physical characteristics of both species, goats/rabbits. . . . If the Russians have managed to create this technology, without a doubt, the U.S. and other powers have developed it too. Therefore, the creation of such creatures as the 'Chupacabras' or ABEs by means of this method is a *very real* [emphasis in original] possibility."

Martin continues in the same article, writing, "Puerto Rico has been the site of heavy experimentation by the U.S. on the island's population and territory for decades. Examples of this are the experimentation with Thalidomide and anti-contraceptive drugs on our women, which caused the birth of many malformed children . . . the lethal agent orange and other dioxin based chemical agents . . . as well as gamma radiation tests in our forests. . . . Because of this we can't exclude the possibility that 'someone' may have been experimenting with new and advanced genetic manipulation technology in our territory. The ABEs could very well be the product of such an experiment gone awry . . ."

Of course, no evidence is offered for these rather wild speculations. While it is certainly true that genetic manipulation is being carried out in laboratories around the world, there is no evidence that it has progressed to the point of sophistication suggested by Martin. Similarly, his suggestion of U.S. experimentation on the island population, while partially true, certainly does not reach the proportions suggested. While newspaper reports have shown a deplorable lack of ethics on the parts of some scientists who experiment on human subjects without proper consultation with either the subject or the family, it is unlikely that it has reached the staggering magnitude suggested by Martin.

As a theory, the genetic manipulation does make a neat package. It explains, easily, why the Chupacabras have almost no history until their appearance in early 1995. The major problems are a lack of physical evidence to support the theory, and a lack of scientific documentation in the research journals.

Scott Corrales, among others, has suggested the possibility that the Chupacabras are mutations of the "grays," that is, the aliens who are claimed to be responsible for abductions. In *Nemesis: The Chupacabras at Large*, he wrote ". . . [They] appear to indicate that the witnesses had encountered altered or mutated versions of the Grays: drawings made of the creatures sighted depict an almost 'specialized' being of an arboreal nature, and the coarser-skinned reptilian Grays point toward another classic type."

The close association of some of the Chupacabras sightings and UFO reports is another bit of evidence to suggest this. But there seems to be no logic behind such a creation. It is a creature that kills and mutilates small animals, taking very little in the weight of food from them. It is a predator, apparently adapted to a specific function and unable to consume the entire body of its prey.

Others have suggested that the Chupacabras are primates that have escaped from a research center on Puerto Rico. Corrales notes that rhesus monkeys have frequently escaped and could be living in the wild. The rhesus monkey, however, is only about as large as a house cat and is not normally carnivorous.

A Puerto Rican newspaper suggested that the Chupacabras were giant vampire bats that had hitched rides on cargo ships from South America. None of the eyewitness accounts suggest a bat-like creature. In fact, it is very "unbat-like."

Veterinarians believe that this is all explained as dogs and other wild animals. Those opposed to the view say that dogs rip their victims apart to eat them rather than suck the blood from them. Most people reject the idea of dogs completely.

And, finally, it could be some unknown creature, living in the wild on Puerto Rico, that has had its habitat invaded or ruined by civilization. When it remained away from prying eyes, there were no reasons to suspect it existed. Now, forced out of the jungle, people have begun to see it and report it.

Such an idea is certainly not without precedence. Only recently a new species of deer was found living in Asian jungles. Even with the huge presence of American soldiers in Vietnam as well as on other Asian bases during the Vietnam War, even with all the specialized equipment used to attempt to locate enemy soldiers and supply routes, the small deer escaped detection. A small carnivore living in the jungles of Puerto Rico could have easily escaped prior detection.

Those studying the Chupacabras, including Jorge Martin and Scott Corrales, believe that something real is happening in Puerto Rico and other parts of the world. As Corrales wrote, "Real animals belonging to real people are being slaughtered by a being which is not native to the Puerto Rican ecosystem. We should constrain ourselves from passing judgment on its nature until we have a better idea of what we're up against."

Jorge Martin reported that the twelfth Legislative Assembly of the House of Representatives of the Commonwealth of Puerto Rico resolved, "To the order of the House of Representatives Agriculture Commission to do a profound and exhaustive investigation to clarify the unknown phenomenon and account the damages caused by the so named 'Chupacabras' to the farmers of this country."

They also required that the "Agriculture Commission of the House of Representatives must submit to this Legislative Corps a report on its investigation, with its conclusions and recommendations, within forty five (45) days after the approval of this resolution."

But none of this answers the questions about the Chupacabras. What are they and where did they come from? Clearly something is going on here. Something more than imagination. Or is it?

The Chupacabras smack of urban legends. These are tales that circulate throughout society that have little, if any, reality. Some of the more common urban legends are those that tell of cigarette companies who will buy iron lungs for patients with respiratory diseases if enough empty packages are collected. Or a tale of a woman who wanted a cookie recipe and was informed that it cost two-fifty. She ordered it, put it on her charge card and was horrified to find that it was two hundred and fifty dollars rather two dollars and fifty cents.

These tales move from town to town and region to region. Attempts to find a basis for them, some evidence of fact, always fail. Such seems to be the case with the Chupacabras. Yes, there are dead animals. Yes, there are stories told by witnesses. Yes, there is physical evidence in the form of mysterious footprints and hair samples that have been analyzed. And no, there is no real proof that the beast exists.

On October 3, 1995, it was reported that one of the Chupacabras was injured. According to Jorge Martin, "We took samples of alleged blood from one of these creatures, which it had left on a cyclone fence and a plantain tree as it jumped over it and tripped . . . in the Campo Rico community. . . . Two days before that, a policeman shot one of the creatures in Campo Rico, as if fled from the site. The blood could very well have been from the same creature."

Interestingly, the creature was not killed by the bullets, merely injured. It managed to escape, leaving little in its wake. Martin took blood samples to have them analyzed. He wrote of the results in *UFO Universe,* "The original blood sample seemed to indicate similar characteristics to that of human A type blood, with Rh factor. Further analysis was not conclusive on this."

What that seems to indicate is that the blood was human in origin. It means that someone, rather than something, left it there. Because it seems to be human blood, it does nothing to validate the existence of the Chupacabras. And, since it was only speculation that the blood was from one of the beasts, the evidence is of little value.

According to Martin, writing about the second sample, "Other analysis of the blood and matter associated with it in the sample, showed a material content comparable to feces with detritus, E. Coli bacteria, and worms, and other parasites. Vegetal cellular material was also found. This content was comparable with that you'd find in cases in which an animal or human being was injured, with an open wound in the intestines."

Again, there is nothing that confirms the existence of the Chupacabras. The sample seems to indicate that something had been injured, but only that it was a human or animal, but not who or what it was. The evidence, then, was inconclusive.

The third sample proved more interesting. Again, according to Martin, "The genetic analysis so far has revealed that the blood is in no way compatible with human blood nor with any other blood type belonging to any known animal species known to science."

This bit of evidence finally suggests something other than mistakes and carelessness in gathering the samples. However, it doesn't lead to any conclusion other than that something interesting is going on. Martin himself cannot tie the samples to a specific creature or incident. He can only hint of a connection and, unfortunately, in science that simply isn't good enough.

In fact, we have more such physical evidence. Marc Davenport was the director of a recent Beyond Boundaries expedition to Puerto Rico. He was able to collect hair, dung, and tissue samples from an area where a local resident claimed to have seen Chupacabras resting. Some of the samples were provided to Japanese journalists from *Borderline* magazine published in Tokyo.

Dr. Inagaki Haruku, who has been suggested as the top expert in examining mammal hair, was provided samples from the Puerto Rico expedition. He supposedly said that he could tell the hair was "protective hair," and that it wasn't from a small animal. He also suggested, based on his examination of the root, thickness, and tip of the hair that it was neither human or ape. From the thickness, he also deduced that it belonged to a carnivore.

Using an electron microscope, Dr. Haruku said that he believed the hair was from a member of the canine family. Because of the hair's characteristics, he could rule out bats and small rodents. He did say that it "did not exactly match any of the mammal's hairs I have observed in the past . . . I think the creature is of the canine family. . . . One thing I can also say, this is not a hair of a large carnivore such as a jaguar."

The one thing that must be noted here is that no creature was seen in direct association with the location where the samples were taken. A local did suggest he'd seen chupacabras in the area, but neither Davenport or other members of his expedition saw the creature. That is an important point to remember.

That is not to say that Davenport, Martin, or any of the other investigators are mishandling their work. Under the conditions, they have done a fine job. Unfortunately, what they have been able to gather is not adequate to prove their case. That certainly is not their fault.

Corrales argues that there is plenty of eyewitness testimony, and if in court, the testimony would be more than sufficient to convict. Millions of criminals have been sent to prison on eyewitness testimony. But the difference here is that no one can prove the Chupacabras exists. In a criminal case, the crime is already an established fact. And, we could suggest that tens of thousands have been sent to jail on the basis of eyewitnesses that turned out to be wrong.

What it boils down to is that we have a large number of reports that are unsubstantiated. We have hints of evidence that are inconclusive. We have stories of a new creature. These tales have spread through the Hispanic communities and in Latin America, but we have little corroboration from the outside. And, we have a tale of a beast that seems to be immune to bullets as evidenced by the number of reports in which people and police shot at the creature but failed to kill it.

On the other hand, we have many dead animals, some found under unusual circumstances. Evidence gathered from the bodies suggest they were killed by some kind of unknown creature. Again, there is no good evidence to support the belief that this is a new kind of creature and not something that has been killing animals for centuries.

It is not the responsibility of researchers to prove that the creature doesn't exist. Those claiming it exists present the evidence. To this point, the evidence has been less than persuasive. That is not to say that the evidence won't be found soon, but until it does, we must look at the stories of the Chupacabras with a skeptical eye.

9 Did the Brazilians Capture UFO Occupants?

1996

UFO INVESTIGATIONS IN THE 1990s have moved into cyberspace. We no longer rely on the mail and the telephone to communicate with one another. We no longer wait for the magazines, the journals or newsletters of the UFO organizations, or the books to tell us what is happening. Today we are connected by FAX and e-mail and computer modem. Communication is instantaneous, and our questions are answered almost as quickly as we can ask them. The reports are no longer recorded on audiotape, but often on videotape so that we all seem to be participating in the interrogation of the witnesses. The single hang-up is that we sometimes don't have the answers to FAX or e-mail or modem to one another.

The case from Varginha, in Brazil, is a good example of the way things operate in the 1990s. I didn't learn about it on the evening news or read about it in the newspaper, but first heard of it when someone e-mailed me a question about my reaction to it. In those first few moments, I didn't have a clue, but by scanning my other e-mail, checking the news groups on the Internet, and even browsing through many of the on-line magazines and newspapers, I was able to assemble a picture of what happened, or, in this case, what was happening in Brazil.

Varginha, for those of you who don't know, is a fairly large city of about 150,000 people in the interior of Brazil. It is northeast of Sao

Paulo and northwest of Rio de Janeiro across the Serra da Mantiques, about 160 miles from the coast. The city contains many international corporations and is an industrial center.

These facts are important simply because of our attitudes as Americans. Often we think of the Third World nations as little more than slums filled with the uneducated and superstitious. While there are certainly millions in Brazil who fit that description (not to mention millions in this country who also fit it), there are also millions of others who are tapped into modern society with the same tools available to us. In other words, much of what appeared in the news groups on the Internet came from sources inside Brazil who were posting it themselves.

But the city is also described as a place where there is a great deal of UFO activity. There are many reports of sightings and alien abductions. The south of Minas Gerais (somewhat like a state in this country) is "well known in the world for its extraterrestrial phenomena."

There is one other factor to bring up. I have a copy of a videotaped interview with Vitorio Pacaccini that was made in June 1996. John Carpenter, of Springfield, Missouri, who was in Brazil in June, along with other researchers including Dr. John Mack, Graham Birdsall, and Stanton Friedman, interviewed Pacaccini. Carpenter graciously has allowed me to quote from that interview. I have also spoken with A. J. Gevaerd of Brazil who I met at the 1996 MUFON Symposium held in Greensboro, North Carolina, in July. I was at his lecture, which detailed what he knew of the case. In other words, I was able, through modern technology, to put together this report using my computer, videotape player, and personal contact with some of the principals without having to leave the United States.

The first thing that became clear is that this case is as complicated as any other in the UFO field. Gevaerd, among others, has claimed that it rivals the Roswell UFO crash in importance. Even if that isn't true, it does rival Roswell for its complexity.

First, according to Pacaccini the initial contact with the alien creatures on January 20, 1996, wasn't made by the three girls as many have reported, but by members of the Brazilian Fire Department six hours before the girls claimed to have seen anything. On the videotape made by Carpenter, it is clear that Pacaccini, was talking about something other than the three girls who were quoted in the first stories printed in this country.

Pacaccini, a member of the Brazilian UFO group known as CICOANI, which was formed in the mid-1940s, began his work after hearing about the report in the local media. According to him, "I received a call from a source who said that it was time [for] the jaguar to drink the water." This is a Brazilian expression that meant one of the important witnesses was going to talk about what he had seen.

According to Pacaccini, in Brazil, when there is a problem with an animal, a stray dog, bees, anything wild, the Fire Department is called. It is part of the military. Apparently there are no civilian fire departments in Brazil.

Pacaccini said, "According to our source, in the morning of January 20th the phone was ringing over and over. It was people informing [them of] the appearance of a weird animal in a certain region of Varginha and requesting [they] capture it."

Four men were dispatched into the area and once there alerted their superior, Major Maciel, they had arrived. They followed the directions they had received from six civilians in the area. In fact, according to the reports, some of the younger civilians were throwing rocks at the animal.

They continued down a hill, toward some woods, where they saw the creature. It didn't try to evade them, and, in fact, was described as being "dizzy." Using a net, they captured the creature easily. It made no noise, other than a buzzing that sounded like that of angry bees. It was dragged back up the hill and then put into a canvas-covered box on the back of a truck for transport.

Once they had captured the creature, the fire fighters called Major Maciel and told him, "Major, you'd better come here, sir. Even the army is already here." That was about 10:30 in the morning.

According to Pacaccini, the creature had a large head with a number of bumps or protuberances on it. It was a reddish color, with large red eyes on a big head. It had long, thin arms that hung to the knees, and short, thin legs with big feet. The skin was shiny, as if it had been rubbed with oil and it smelled strongly of ammonia. There was no evidence of genitals. The being wore no clothes.

The creature was taken from the area. Although a few people tried to verify the existence of the beast, or the case in general, a

Captain Alvarenga denied all knowledge. UFO researchers in Brazil said that the captain had lied about it.

That same afternoon, January 20, three girls were taking a shortcut home from work when one of them, Liliane Fatima, glanced to the left and screamed. Crouching in the mud was a strange creature with three protuberances on its head. According to one of the girls, it had one hand on the ground between its legs and the other on the ground behind it. The eyes were enormous and red.

The girls, including twenty-two-year-old Andrade Xavier and fourteen-year-old Valquiria Fatima, ran home. Frightened by what they had seen, and partially due to the reddish skin and the bumps on the creature's head, they thought they had seen the devil. When it slowly turned to look at them, they fled.

The two girls told their mother what they had seen, trying to convince her it was a devil. Luiza Helana Silva went to see the creature, but when she arrived, it was gone. She could smell an strong odor of ammonia, and she saw two strange footprints in the soft mud.

Until then, there was nothing to connect the sightings of the strange creatures to flying saucers. There were, however, reports of UFOs in the area. Over several cities in the area including Varginha, Alfenas, Boa Esperance, and Tres Coracoses, the population noticed something going on. Pacaccini reported that many people had come to him, as well as his colleagues, telling of sightings.

In February, Pacaccini said that he had set up an interview and was driving to that interview when he ran into an old friend. This friend, unidentified by Pacaccini, said that he knew the military had been involved in the capture of the strange creature. Pacaccini was able to interview, through the help of his friend, a member of one of the military recovery teams. This military official provided the names of several of the people who were directly involved including Lieutenant Colonel Olimpio Vanderlei, Captain Ramires, an Army police officer named Lieutenant Tiberio, and a sergeant identified only as Pedrosa. Pacaccini believed this was a "guarantee of proof." Of course, the providing of names means nothing until those individuals have been interviewed.

This could easily be a result of the translations into English, but others have reported that the officer in command was Lieutenant Colonel Olimpio Wanderly Santos. He was accompanied by two other officers, Captain Ramirez and Lieutenant Tide. According to one report, Corporal Cirilo, along with an intelligence sergeant (identified as being "S-2"), drove the middle truck with the aliens inside. The other trucks were driven by Private Vassalo and Private de Mello.

Paraccini said that more witnesses were discovered later and that he was able to contact another military witness. This man was reluctant to talk until he realized that the story was already out. He said that, to his surprise, no one in the ESA (Escola de Sargentos das Army or the Army Sergeants School) knew anything about the operation, because there was a disinformation campaign in operation.

Pacaccini said that his new witness confirmed everything that the first man had said, which confirmed the capture of the creatures. The men met the truck with the box and the creature at one of the area hospitals. Pacaccini then said that the "dead creature was put inside the box, which was closed with a plastic cover." The truck, along with others, in convoy, drove on to Tres Caracoes. This, according to the best information, happened on January 22, or about two days after the first of the creatures was captured. It is not clear if the first one captured died or if the body of another was found.

It should be pointed out that there had to be at least two such creatures. One captured by the fire department in the morning, and a second seen by the girls in the middle of the afternoon. And, if there were two such creatures, then there could easily be three or more.

And, as if to underscore that point, Brazilian ufologist Pedro Cunha claimed that witnesses in Varginha now suggest as many as seven alien beings had been captured. That included the one that was dead, two that were badly injured, and five more that had been hiding.

According to the story, the convoy, when it reached Tres Coracoes, found that there were already police waiting and blocking traffic for them. From there, they apparently continued until they reached Campinas. Pacaccini wrote that he believed the creature was taken there so that it could be placed "in the hands of a professional from Unicamp (University of Campinas)."

At this point, Pacaccini presented another anonymous source. According to him, "We have got access to this information through a scientist of Unicamp, whose name must remain anonymous. This scientist even said he went to Varginha, where he picked soil samples and local vegetation from the place where the being was sighted."

The scientist talked to fellow teachers, good friends of his, and told them that the Brazilian government told him he should not reveal a word of what he knew. Even the head of the university had been warned about the need for secrecy. Yet this man, as well as others, began to speak, almost immediately telling all they knew.

They suggested that legist (that is, one who is learned or skilled in the law) physician Badan Palhares did the first work on the creature. In the reports it is called a necropsy, which is another term for autopsy. There are no results of this published, nor are there photographs. The investigators were able to convince many of those involved to speak, but were unable to secure any additional documentation.

As noted, the two creatures sighted, or captured, outside Varginha may not have been the only ones in the area. Pacaccini reported that he had information from a "well-known lady who lives in the city, [a] member of Varginha's 'high society.'" She told of a creature that had been captured, taken to the closest medical station, and from there, to the hospital.

What we learn by examining the information is that this creature might have been taken to the two Varginha hospitals. It went to the regional hospital first, but that was apparently believed to be too open to the public. The creature was then taken to the Humanitas Hospital. This one is better equipped and is located on the outskirts of town. Apparently the authorities believed they could contain the situation better there. It also was reported that the hospital was near a major highway that would allow for quick and discreet transportation.

One of the hospital directors from Varginha, Adilson Husier, was reported to have said that the story was nonsense. He said, "We couldn't keep an extraterrestrial here. We couldn't deal with it."

Yet still another hospital official was interviewed and apparently gave conflicting stories. At one of the hospitals, the story was that a Dr. Rogerio had treated the alien. Rogerio has been reported to have said, "I don't know how you could waste your time with that kind of stuff; it's nonsense. There are no extraterrestrials." But he is also supposed to have told a reporter from Varginha, "I don't know what it is . . . could be a freak, but I have never seen anything like it.

And in a case involving extraterrestrials and UFO sightings, there is a need for intrigue. The Brazilian UFO researchers have suggested that U.S. officials, maybe Air Force officers, were seen entering the Humanitas Hospital, carrying a strange device. No one has explained how the two people were recognized as Americans, what they were doing there, or what their device was.

At the Regional Hospital, there was a story that the staff had been told not to talk about the subject. A member of the catering staff said that he didn't believe the story, but that a friend had said he'd seen the alien at the hospital. More unnamed and uncorroborated stories.

And to complicate things further, if possible, there was another report that the aliens, a male and a female, were taken, first to a hospital, and then onto the Univeridade de Sao Paulo (the University of Sao Paulo). It was reported that two cars from the university were seen with two strange men in them. One reporter suggested that the two strangers were the Americans.

During this time, as the creatures were being transported around the county, another witness surfaced. This man, described as "the cousin of a son of a military man from the NCO school," somehow got access to film showing one of the creatures. He offered it for sale to one of the largest television networks in Brazil for about $68,000.00, but apparently was turned down. The price has since been reduced.

This strikes me as odd, considering the media feeding frenzy that surrounded the Santilli videotape. Here was something that appeared with no sort of provenance, yet television networks around the world jumped at the chance to spend big money to air it.

There were, supposedly, negotiations to show the film, and the owner of the film, described as a young boy, visited with network officials. They were apparently dubious of his credentials, and there seems to be no chance that the film will be aired publicly, if it in fact exists. Now there are claims that his life is in danger.

About the same time, another similar tale emerged. A police official in Varginha took a copy of the film home, showing it to his daughter and a daughter's friend. According to Pacaccini, the father of the friend (do I need to point out that we have many very convoluted relationships here), who has a good reputation, said that his daughter watched the "horrible" film of the captured creature. As the first girl's father realized the danger of the situation, he vanished with the tape. Please note that no names have been attached to this story. Pacaccini, however, claims through the entire interview that they had much evidence for the report and for the existence of the film, but none has been presented.

On June 28, the *Wall Street Journal* reported on the sightings being made in the Varginha region. Officials had called a press conference to debunk all the UFO talk, but an auto mechanic, who claimed to have seen a cylindrical-shaped UFO, grabbed the headlines. And a psychic in the city predicted that Varginha would be the scene of some sort of natural disaster because of all the UFO activity.

It also seems that city officials in Varginha are not as reluctant to attach their city's name to UFOs are as those from Roswell, New Mexico. There is talk of naming one of the local parks "Seite Extreterrestes" or Seven Extraterrestrials.

Once again, there were the official denials. Captain Eduardo Caliz, the public information officer for the NCO academy in Tres Coracoes, said that he had no idea what the three women (actually a fourteen year old, a sixteen year old, and only one who could be considered a woman at twenty-two) saw, but insisted that the base had been involved in nothing like what had been reported.

The *Wall Street Journal* noted that Caliz had no explanation for why the Army trucks had been driven so far. His statements seem to contradict those given in April, when officials said that the convoy had been part of military maneuvers. Of course, if they were on maneuvers, they might have been required to drive the distances noted. It is just one more area where there seems to be confusion.

By late June A. J. Gevaerd said that he had spoken to more than sixty witnesses who related some aspect of the UFO crash story. It was a cigar-shaped UFO that crashed north of the city. He also mentioned the two strangers who were thought to be Americans.

The search for documentation continued. According to the *Wall Street Journal*, "The most tantalizing proofs are videotaped statements by two young men in civilian clothes who claim to be members of the military detail that disposed of the alien visitors. It is impossible to determine the tapes' authenticity, however, since Mr. Pacaccini won't reveal the men's names. He says they fear reprisals."

Also of interest is the fact that two of the three original witnesses are demanding $200 for each interview. Interest in the case is so high that, apparently, they can earn that much. And, a two-hour documentary broadcast on a Brazilian television network about the case was so highly rated that it was repeated the following weekend.

Now, remember, there was the young man trying to sell his film of the alien, but unable to do so. To me, this suggests the quality of the film was so poor that reporters were able to see it as a hoax easily. With interest running that high, that is, a network repeating a special inside a week, I doubt any television network would turn down the film unless it was an obvious hoax.

So where are we in this case? Those in Brazil are raving about its importance to the world of ufology. Reginaldo de Athayde said, "The Varginha case is one of the most important UFO cases that ever happened in the entire world. I see we have something superior to what happened in Roswell."

Claudeir Covo said, "The seriousness that the researchers are showing when conducting the information and the work itself increases the credibility of ufology. If we consider only the quantity of information already compiled, the richness of details and the several witnesses that have already appeared, we see that this case left Roswell very little."

Eduardo Mondini said, "I'm close to the investigations, helping Ubirajara and Pacaccini with the information from Campinas. . . . We suspect that the legist Badan Palhares has been heading the necropsy [autopsy] studies on the creature. We have no doubts that the E.T. has been brought to Unicamp and then autopsied."

On the other side of this coin, however, the *Wall Street Journal* reported that "Pacaccini's brand of hucksterism is characteristic of the frontier atmosphere in a town where the architecture is of the Quonset-hut school and the newspaper is staffed by a lone reporter. Since the initial sighting, Mr. Pacaccini, a long-time UFO buff, has essentially abandoned his job as a business consultant to provide one-stop shopping for visiting journalists."

Where does this leave us? Brazil has always been a country filled with UFO sightings and reports. They have a national interest in the topic that rivals that in our country. Some of the first UFO pictures were taken in Brazil in 1952. Showing a domed disc as it flew above the jungle, the shots were dramatic. They were reprinted time and again and were among those that the Aerial Phenomena Research Organization used to prove their case. They have been since labeled a hoax by most in the UFO community.

Another set of pictures, taken in 1958, are among the best evidence available, according to many UFO researchers. These have withstood the test of time, to this point. According to the story, there were more than one hundred witnesses as the "saturn-shaped" craft flew over a small island.

The point, however, is that Brazil has always had a fascination with UFOs. They have had their share of hoaxes and frauds. They are not the uneducated. Their researchers, just as those in this country, have the ability and the technical know how to produce a credible hoax. Faked photographs and films have been coming from Brazil since the early 1950s, as we have seen.

In this case, it has been pointed out that there is no physical evidence for corroboration with the exception of a couple of footprints in the mud. There are official denials from military officers named as participants. The names of many other witnesses have been withheld, though they have been heavily quoted in various stories and by various researchers. In fact, we have been unable to verify much of anything. The contradictions pointed out by the *Wall Street Journal* might be no more important than one low-ranking official unaware of what other military units were doing six months earlier.

And we have a number of locals who seem to be doing a credible job of investigation, but we also see that this case is becoming a moneymaking machine for the city. I would be the last to hurl this charge, only because it has been said about me on a number of occasions, and money has not been a motivating factor in my research into Roswell.

That the girls who made the first reports are now demanding money for interviews should not be seen as anything more than a desire for compensation. The reporters, the investigators, and all the others are making money as well. Why shouldn't they also claim a small piece of the pie? The difference is that money doesn't seem to be a motivation for their original account.

The motives of many of the others can be challenged, if not by money, then by personal agendas. This means the reporters, the investigators, the governmental and military officials, and everyone else connected with the story. The investigators, while maybe not rich, have become famous. The reporters, if they have a good story, win the accolades of their editors. The military, if the story is true, would, quite naturally, want to hide the truth from all the outsiders and the curious.

What does this mean? At the moment we have an interesting story that seems not to fit into any UFO category. A number of the researchers have pointed out that the alien described does not match any of the others reported over the last fifty years. That, in and of itself, is not terribly important. It is interesting.

The reaction of the aliens is perplexing. They seemed dazed and dizzy, unable to defend themselves once out in our environment. Couple this to the official denials and the conflicting stories, and we are left with something that is interesting but not terribly important.

If properly documented, this case could become, as those in Brazil have insisted, bigger than Roswell. But we must have more than withheld videotaped interviews with unnamed witnesses. The possibility of the documentation for this case is extremely high, given its current nature, but the documentation has yet to be produced. However, this is a case that requires our continued scrutiny. It could become the case of the decade. Or, it could become just another in a long list of hoaxes that have plagued our research from the beginning.

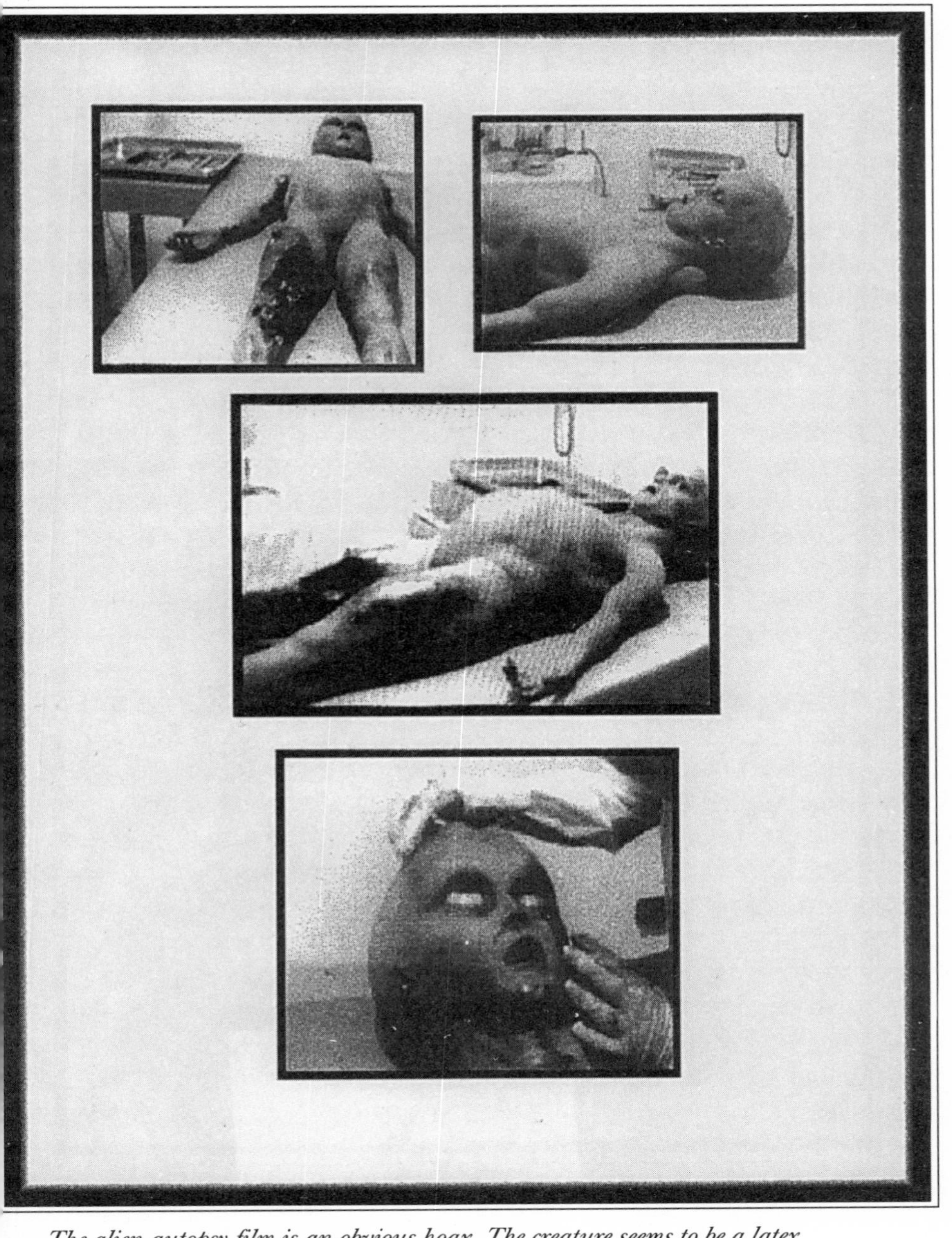

The alien autopsy film is an obvious hoax. The creature seems to be a latex dummy cast in a standing position. Details in the background also suggest a hoax.

The Chupacabras have been seen throughout the Hispanic areas for over a year. The descriptions have varied only slightly from witness to witness. Illustrations by Russ Estes.

One of the clearest photographs ever of a UFO. Unfortunately, computer examination suggests it is a hoax. Brazil has produced hundreds of such pictures.

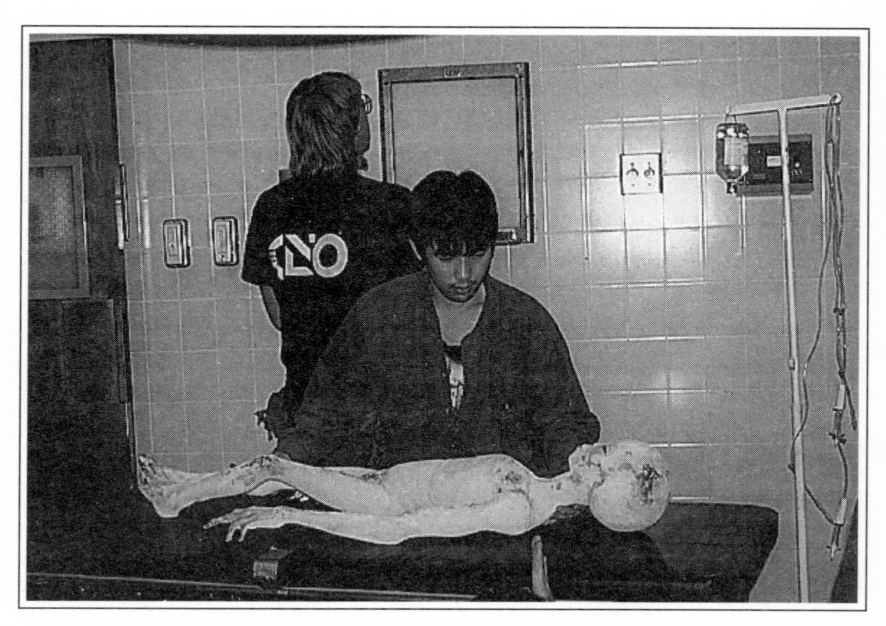

Employees of Steve Johnson's XFX, Inc. prepare one of four alien body props for filming the staged autopsy scene in Roswell, *the ShowTime original movie. It is on display in the "Paul Davids Exhibit" in Roswell, where it is one many items from the film donated by Paul Davids to the International UFO Museum. This is the same creature that was photographed for* Penthouse. *Clearly the* Penthouse *pictures are from this mock-up. Photos copyright by Paul Davids.*

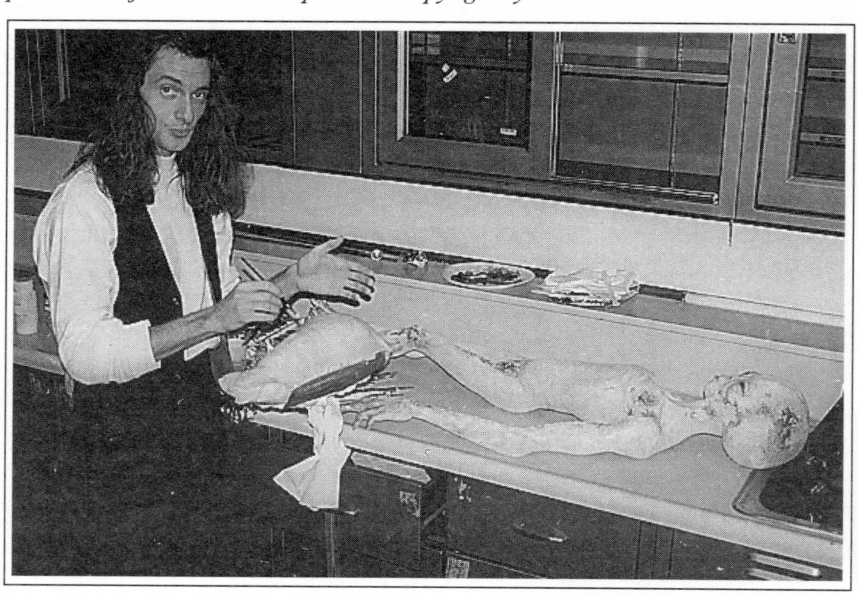

The courthouse in downtown Roswell.

Ballard's Funeral Home in Roswell where Glenn Dennis worked in 1947.

Kevin Randle autographs books at Roswell's UFO Enigma Museum, 6108 South Main Street in Roswell.

Entries in the "Alien competition" in Roswell.

10 The Roswell Alien Photos

1996

ROSWELL HAS BECOME WORLD FAMOUS. It is no longer necessary to say New Mexico when saying Roswell. Dozens of documentaries about the UFO crash have been made, several movies that mention Roswell have been recently produced, several books about the UFO crash near Roswell have been written. Now, once again, photographs claiming to be of the alien beings killed when their ship slammed into the ground are being published in a magazine.

Let's take a few moments and review the Roswell case. According to the best evidence available, the craft, which had been watched on radar off and on for days, crashed north of Roswell late on the evening July 4, 1947. A number of people in the Roswell area, including William Woody, a group of Catholic nuns, and Corporal E. L. Pyles, saw something in the night sky. It seemed to be angling downward. It was at dawn the next day that military officers reached the scene of the crash. There, they saw a craft, described as heel-shaped, impacted into a rocky cliff. Outside the craft were the bodies of two alien creatures. Inside the craft, three more bodies were found.

Those on the impact site, Major Edwin Easley, Frank Kaufmann, and Sergeant Thomas Gonzales, among others, told me about the recovery operation. Each suggested that the bodies were removed first and that the craft was later taken away on a flatbed truck. Although everything was filtered through the base at Roswell, it was all taken, eventually, to Wright Field outside of Dayton, Ohio.

After the impact site, about thirty miles north of Roswell, was located and cleaned, W. W. "Mac" Brazel, a rancher living near Corona, New Mexico, drove into Roswell to speak to the Chaves County Sheriff, George Wilcox. He had found a field filled with mysterious metallic debris. The sheriff called the air base and spoke to Major Jesse A. Marcel, the air intelligence officer. Marcel and Captain Sheridan Cavitt, a counterintelligence agent, followed Brazel back to the ranch to investigate.

Years later Marcel would tell researchers, including Leonard Stringfield, that he didn't know what he had found. A strip of debris, three-quarters of a mile long and two or three hundred feet wide, was visible. There was a gouge down the center. Marcel said that he tried to burn some of the paper-like debris, but it wouldn't burn. To reporter Johnny Mann and others, Marcel said that the debris suggested something extraterrestrial in origin. He said, "I was amazed by what I saw."

Although the Army announced on July 8, 1947, that they had "captured" a flying saucer, within hours, higher ranking officers said it was nothing more spectacular than a weather balloon and a radar target (see Chapter 6, The Air Force Final Report on Roswell). But, Colonel Thomas DuBose told investigators that the balloon explanation was a cover story for the real events.

Frankly, the problem with the Roswell case is the lack of physical evidence. We have been told that it exists. The bits of metal, the craft, or the bodies, if revealed, would certainly prove the case. Documentation, in the form of reports, papers, or photographs would certainly help. It would move the case from the eyewitness testimony category into one that has some good documentation behind it.

I have been told by those eyewitnesses that photographs and movie footage were taken. I have been told that all this documentation exists. As already discussed, I don't think that the alien autopsy film offered by Ray Santilli and shamelessly promoted by Bob Shell and Michael Hesemann is authentic. It is just one more of the many hoaxes that have dotted the UFO landscape since 1947.

Now comes a new assault. This one in the pages of *Penthouse* magazine, which is not one of the pillars of journalistic excellence. Bob

Guccione, publisher of the magazine, claims that he has found, maybe bought, photographs that come from the real autopsy film, and not the fake attributed to Ray Santilli. These, according to *Penthouse's* Guccione, "three extraordinary images published here may well be the most important pictures in the history of photography."

Keith Farrell, one of those who edited the now defunct—though available on-line—*Omni*, wrote "*Penthouse* is publishing these photos in order to focus the light of publicity on the continuing government suppression of its *own* research into the evidence of extraterrestrial visitation to our planet."

To make the event seem even more important, Guccione speculated that had the government or military known about the pictures, they would have prevented the publication of them. The whole thing, Guccione speculates, would have been classified as top secret. The pictures would never have seen the light of day.

Farrell continued in that vein, writing, "As editor of *Omni* for the past six years I had the opportunity to work with Guccione on the development of Project Open Book, *Omni's* attempt to, simply, open the books on the government's investigation of extraterrestrial visitors to our planet. We sought to treat the subject seriously and scientifically, to deal with issues and incidents in the matter that was, above all, rational, that addressed the questions of U.F.O. believers and U.F.O. skeptics."

As Farrell praised himself and the efforts of *Omni*, he also noted that "your favorite magazine doesn't give up." Farrell speculated that the photographs "came into Bob's possession precisely because he doesn't get scared, and won't back off when his convictions are aroused."

According to the story, as published in *Penthouse*, the photographs had been received from a woman who claimed her father was a German scientist working in New Mexico in 1947. He had been part of the team that was assembled to exploit and investigate the crash at Roswell, and had, in the past, worked on the "infamous Philadelphia Experiment." She had been entrusted with a small segment of the film that her father had somehow secured. She was told never to reveal what was on it, or its existence, to anyone. If someone learned of the film's existence, it could mean her death.

This, in and of itself, makes no sense. Why would her father, the unidentified German scientist, give her a few frames of the autopsy footage and then tell her never to reveal she had it? And, more importantly, how would he have come into possession of that footage? We know, from research conducted by Kent Jeffrey (as outlined in Chapter 7), that every frame of film taken on top-secret projects was counted before it was exposed, as well as after, to make sure that no one escaped with classified material. It was developed with two people present. There was no chance for the German scientist to have spirited away a small segment of the film.

Of course, the unidentified woman was told by her father that she would know the right time to reveal the existence of the film. So, he was telling her that the possession of the film could threaten her life, that she must not reveal it, unless the time was right. Guccione and Farrell have no trouble accepting this contradictory information.

The magazine pointed out that the photographs remained in the woman's possession for nearly fifty years. She remembered what her father had said about keeping the secret about alien visitors. But with all the publicity that surrounded the alien autopsy film, with all the interest in UFOs and aliens, she began to consider going public.

The magazine will not publish her name. If the photographs were authentic, the decision makes some sense. After all, I have seen what has happened to men and women who suggest they saw the strange metallic debris, who said they saw the bodies, or, in one case, said that he knew a nurse who saw the bodies. Guccione said, "I respect her privacy and sympathize with her concerns for her safety. . . ." Guccione said that he had little doubt that the government would claim this was simply another hoax.

Not that any of this matters. Guccione was quoted in a wire service story as saying, "I am absolutely 100 percent convinced" of their authenticity. He appeared on cable television's CNBC to show the magazine and the pictures, telling the audience there was no doubt that he had the real thing. Guccione is a hero who found the photographs that we all had wanted to find, and he was publishing them to end the government secrecy.

In fact, to demonstrate the credibility of the photographs, Guccione noted that *Omni* had a team of highly qualified experts who had been studying UFOs. Guccione implied that they had inspected the pictures and that all were impressed with them. In fact, according to the magazine, "It is that unique combination of heart, mind, and irrepressible curiosity that led Bob Guccione to publish this image . . ."

The photographs themselves look very impressive. They show a badly injured being about four feet tall, thin, with a large head, and it seems, large eyes. The creature is clearly not human, though it is humanoid. If the pictures are authentic, as Guccione claims, he has broken the story of the millennium. All that Guccione had said, in the hype to promote the magazine, would be vindicated, if the photographs are of the real thing.

But those of us who have seen the ShowTime original movie, *Roswell*, have already seen this particular alien. It was one of the four or five special-effects models created by Steve Johnson for the movie. There is no doubt about it.

Guccione, during the CNBC program, was asked about that possibility, but said that he believed the filmmakers had access to some of the same pictures that he was now publishing. They modeled their special-effects creation after the real thing. He implied that the models were so accurate because, through other sources, they had seen the same photographs.

As one of those who provided technical assistance for the film, I know this isn't true. I was on the set, spoke to various people involved in the production, and know that the special-effects models, while based on some of the first-hand testimony, were, in fact, the creations of Johnson and his special-effects people. Had they had the real thing, they would have received them from me and I would have published them in my books about Roswell. At the very least, I would be publishing them now.

Paul Davids, the executive producer of the film, has said, repeatedly, that he is 100 percent sure the photographs are of one of the special-effects models. Asked if they could have used the real thing as a model, he told me, "Absolutely not."

In fact, this is not the first time these pictures have surfaced with claims of authenticity. In June 1995, the Internet had pictures that someone posted suggesting they were of the Roswell aliens. I hadn't bothered to look, assuming that they were just other versions of the body from the alien autopsy film. Neal Odom, the producer of "The Randle Report" on KTSM-AM radio in El Paso, Texas, showed me the pictures, saying that he thought they were from the movie. Clearly they were.

And, in Japan, in 1995, these same pictures, or ones that were very similar, were circulated with the same claims. The story coming from Japan might even have included the tales of the German scientist who had somehow gotten his hands on a few frames from an autopsy of the dead alien.

On August 8, 1996, I had an opportunity to speak with Guccione during a live radio "debate" about the authenticity of the pictures. Of course, he insisted that they showed the real thing. He insisted that he had paid nothing for them, but he believed in the authenticity of them. He also said that he had seen the movie *Roswell* and that he didn't believe the creatures in the film looked anything like the alien in his photographs. The neck, according to him, was much longer on the aliens in the movie.

Of course, he was speaking of the model that had been created to give the impression of a living being. When the special-effects bellows and air ducts and tubes and wires were removed, the creature, in its inanimate state, looks remarkably like that in the photographs. Of course, it isn't the same one and that might be what confused Guccione.

On that radio program, he also made the claim that these models were made from the real photographs. I pointed out that they weren't because I was there. But the debate boiled down to Guccione saying he believed the photographs were authentic and me saying that they were photographs of the special-effects model on loan to the museum. He seemed unpersuaded by my suggestion that the wounds on the head matched, exactly, those on the model on display in Roswell.

Linda Moulton Howe and Bob Shell have also entered the debate. According to some of the information posted on the Internet, Howe called Steve Johnson who denied that the alien in the *Penthouse* pictures was one of his creations. That struck me as odd, since it was clear that they were.

Others, however, had a chance to speak to various members of the special-effects team that created the models, and were told that they were the same. The problem, it seems, came about because the FAX copied photographs that Howe sent to Johnson were nearly black and almost impossible to see. He said something to the effect that the alien didn't look like his creation. This was a problem borne of color photographs that had been copied on a xerox machine into black and white and then faxed. The process darkened them to the point it was nearly impossible to see any detail.

Don Ecker, of *UFO* magazine, was able to take the story farther. According to him, he spoke to the man who delivered the pictures to Guccione. He had received them from a woman who had found them on sale at a UFO convention in Mesa, Arizona. According to Ecker, he had the documentation to prove that the man existed and that the woman existed. The story of the German scientist was apparently the same as one that had circulated in Japan in the summer of 1995. It is certainly better than the story of some woman buying them at a UFO convention.

Guccione has been fooled by someone who has misrepresented the pictures, convincing the magazine publisher that they show the real thing. If you wonder how the pictures were taken, how someone outside the film crew, the actors, the director, or anyone else on the set, could have gotten pictures of one of the models, you don't have to go far. From the pictures that Guccione published, it is clear that they were taken in the International UFO Museum, in the small display they have set up. It is clear from the injuries on the head that this is the model that has been photographed.

What is interesting about this whole thing is that Guccione now knows the truth. He had been told by many people who were involved in the creation of the special-effects models, those of us who were on the set of the film, and those of us who have investigated this case. Yet, he maintains that his "crack" team of investigators have found nothing to suggest a hoax.

Well, the creation of the models was not a hoax. The story around the pictures, and how this woman of German ancestry got them is a hoax. There is no doubt about it. This isn't government disinformation, or the government trying to discredit a witness who has the real thing. This is a case of someone taking a picture of a display and then convincing others that he or she photographed the real alien body.

There is no doubt about the identity of these pictures. It is too easy to see for yourself what has happened. I could, if I wanted, produce pictures of the debris field, the alien craft, and the alien being alive. But all of them would be from the movie as well. While on the various sets, I had a chance to take photographs. There was an official still photographer on the set on many days, and Paul Davids, an avid amateur photographer, took hundreds of pictures. But all of them are from the movie and have nothing to do with the events outside of Roswell in 1947, other than the fact that it was a movie about those events.

Somewhere out there, hidden away in a dusty government file, are the real pictures taken during the recovery operation and the autopsies performed on the bodies of the flight crew. Somewhere out there is the evidence necessary to prove that the crash took place. These pictures are not them. It is just more misinformation that muddies the waters and makes it difficult for the rest of us to find the truth.

11 Jim Ragsdale Revisited

1996

IT SEEMS THAT MUCH OF UFO investigation in the 1990s is a reexamination of older cases such as that of a crash of something outside of Roswell, New Mexico, in July 1947. But even with a case that is a half a century old, new information is being learned all the time. Witnesses who had not been interviewed, who had been military officers or enlisted personnel in 1947, have been located and interviewed only in the 1990s. And some of those stories, surfacing in the 1990s, have been reevaluated even later based on additional information.

Such is the case of Jim Ragsdale whose name first came up in the summer of 1992 as Don Schmitt and I were continuing our investigation of the events outside of Roswell, New Mexico. I was in Roswell in November 1992 on a follow-up investigation and had spent the day chasing down leads through the Roswell Fire Department. We were trying to determine how far back the records went, and if we could verify a run, any run, outside the city limits. Records were available back more than seventy years but weren't particularly enlightening.

That evening, in the hotel room, I called the Jim Ragsdale residence to set up an interview with him and the family. The information I had was that Ragsdale had handled, in July 1947, the debris that supposedly came from the flying saucer. Ragsdale had been in a bad traffic accident earlier in 1992 and was still recuperating from his fairly serious injuries. He didn't want to meet that night, but I was told that he had handled metallic debris and seen much more.

In January 1993, Schmitt, Mark Chesney, then a NASA engineer, and I made a trip to Roswell. We planned to meet a number of witnesses, and hoped to interview Jim Ragsdale. The meeting with Ragsdale was arranged for the evening of January 26, 1993. The interview was recorded on audiotape.

It should be pointed out here that the story told by Ragsdale, first to Schmitt and later to me, differs from that now published by the International UFO Museum in Roswell. They, or rather Max Littell, have suggested that I got the story wrong. In truth, I reported accurately what Ragsdale said to me, or what he told Schmitt on tape. While a tape does not mean Ragsdale was telling the truth, it does prove that I reported accurately what he said. There are many disagreements between what he said in January, April, and July 1993 to me and what he told others a year or so later.

But Max Littell, for some reason, doesn't accept this. He wrote in the *Roswell Daily Record*, in an attempt to counter some of the things I had said about the new tale, "The book [*The Truth about the UFO Crash at Roswell*] is now amended to leave out the first chapter that was in their first printing and now starts on page 17."

This is, or course, blatant nonsense. There is little difference between the hardback edition of *The Truth about the UFO Crash at Roswell* published by M. Evans and Company and the paperback published by Avon. There were some additions in the later chapters that provided corroborative detail, but nothing had been removed. Littell, for some reason, was attempting to mislead people with his statement published in the July 3, 1996, edition of *The Roswell Daily Record*.

At the beginning of that first recorded interview with Ragsdale, Schmitt asked him, "Do you remember the name of the ranch it [the crashed saucer] was on?"

Ragsdale said, "It was on . . . [the] Fisher . . ."

"Was it north of here?"

"Yes . . ." He then, with no prompting, changed the name of the ranch, saying, "It was Foster."

What Ragsdale was doing, with the discussion, was establishing a site to the north of Roswell. More importantly, he was doing it with his own words without coaching by Schmitt.

Because we had been to the impact site north of town during the trip, we had photographs of it. Trying to make sure that Ragsdale was describing the same place, Schmitt showed Ragsdale pictures of the terrain. Looking at the photographs of the site north of Roswell, Ragsdale said, "That's the place right there."

He went on to say, in what has become a critical statement, "I was messing around with another man's wife. That's how come I was out in that area."

Schmitt came back to the pictures and, showing Ragsdale the one he had picked, asked, "So you think this looks like..."

Ragsdale interrupted, saying, "That looks like the place."

It must be noted that the photographs of the impact site north of Roswell look nothing like the pictures of the new "Jim Ragsdale" site. It is difficult to believe that Ragsdale could have been so easily fooled by those photographs, thinking they showed the location near Pine Lodge.

He then described the scene, saying that "you couldn't really tell what it was . . . what you could still see, where it hit. I think it was two spaceships flying together and one of them came down and the other one picked up what they could and got out of there."

Schmitt asked about the possibility of lightning hitting the craft and causing it to break up. Ragsdale and Schmitt discussed the role of Mac Brazel in the events.

Ragsdale then said, "But it was either dummies or bodies or something there. They looked like bodies. They weren't very long . . . over four or five foot long at most. We didn't see their faces or nothing like that."

Schmitt asked, "How far from here?"

Ragsdale replied, in what would become an important answer, "Thirty miles. Forty miles."

"In a northwesterly direction?"

Ragsdale, looking at the pictures said, "Right up here."

"Any buildings?"

"No. You couldn't see nothing. You go up on top of the hill. It was a hill," he said, again referring to the pictures, "and you could see the stuff right here."

Ragsdale and his female companion returned to the impact site the next morning. They heard the military arriving on the scene. He said, "Oh . . . it must have been . . . it was two or three six-by-six Army trucks, a wrecker and everything . . . and leading the pack was a '47 Ford car with guys in it . . . MPs and stuff . . ."

Schmitt said, "So you watched for a while."

"Yeah. Sure did. . . . They cleaned everything all up. I mean cleaned it. They raked the ground and everything . . . I would say it was six or eight big trucks besides the pick up, weapons carriers and stuff like that."

Later, in the interview, again all recorded on audiotape, Ragsdale said that he had tried to return later, but the place was guarded. He said, "Me and another fellow went out there and you couldn't get . . . they had the roads sealed off."

Littell, again trying to belittle those early interviews, wrote, "Ragsdale was totally on oxygen with a face mask so was unable to talk plainly and as indicated mostly shook his head either way when answering Schmitt's questions."

This is rank speculation on the part of Littell. In fact, on the tape of that interview, it is clear that Ragsdale was telling his story and not just shaking his head. Littell, wasn't at the interview, nor has he heard the tape. He doesn't know what happened and apparently doesn't care.

On April 24, 1993, I spoke to Ragsdale again. There were some points that I wanted to clarify. For example, if they had witnessed the crash of what Ragsdale thought, at first, was some kind of government experimental craft, why hadn't he reported it to the sheriff or the military that night? Lives could be at stake.

Ragsdale told me that he had been drinking that night, and that he was out in the desert with another man's wife. Neither of them were supposed to be where they were. Besides, they couldn't see much that night. The flashlight he had, according to him, had weak batteries. It wasn't until daylight that he saw the craft and the bodies.

There were, according to Ragsdale, "Small people there. Three or four bodies."

He also told me the name of his companion. According to him, she was killed in a car accident about a month after the event. Although I have tried to verify this, I have been unable to do it. What it means, simply, is that there is more work to be done.

Dr. Mark Rodeghier, scientific director of the J. Allen Hynek Center for UFO Studies in Chicago, IL, in June 1993, had the opportunity to interview one of Ragsdale's sons. The story, as related by him, was essentially the same as that told by his father.

And again in July 1993, Schmitt and I met with Ragsdale with the hope of a videotaped interview. Ragsdale didn't want to sit down for it, but we did discuss the case again. He reinforced what he had told me in the first and third interviews with him, and what he told Schmitt during the second, audio-recorded interview. What this means is that a clear record of what Ragsdale had been saying about the case had been established and it was accurately reported in *The Truth about the UFO Crash at Roswell.*

A year later, in September 1994, I was again in Roswell. At that time I learned that Max Littell had been keeping in close contact with Ragsdale and that things were beginning to shift. In a letter to Ragsdale dated September 10, 1994, Littell wrote, "This letter constitutes a letter of understanding as relates to the International UFO Museum and Research Center and the information prepared by the Museum staff after a series of interviews that have occured [*sic*] during the past few weeks. You have verified the total information being put into print as being totally yours, and not from any secondary source."

What is interesting is the next several sentences. "From this date, any net proceeds realized by the Museum will be divided with you, for your lifetime, on the basis of 25% of any gross amount to Jim Ragsdale, and 75% to the Museum.

"In exchange the Museum will own the rights to do this on a permanent basis and any designation of the impact site, and all material relating thereto will be designated as 'The Jim Ragsdale' incident [which was crossed out] and site. As evidence of good faith of the Museum, an initial check is attached hereto as an advance against proceeds."

Along with that was another document that told Ragsdale's story. But now it had changed radically. According to it, the object passed through the trees to impact less than a hundred yards from where his truck had been parked. Ragsdale and his friend took flashlights and walked over, spending "considerable time looking around."

Now, rather than seeing bodies or dummies in the distance, Ragsdale was close enough to touch them. They were dressed in silver uniforms and wore tight helmets. Ragsdale now claimed that he tried to remove one of the helmets but couldn't. The eyes, according to Ragsdale, were large and oval and didn't resemble anything human. Later still he would suggest that the skin of the dead alien beings was gray.

The craft, according to Ragsdale, was about twenty feet in diameter, and had a dome in the middle. The description given here is not consistent with those provided by other first-hand civilian and military witnesses including Curry Holden and former radio newsman Johnny McBoyle.

In this interview Ragsdale said that it wasn't too long before they heard what they believed were trucks and heavy equipment coming. "We left and were not there when whatever it was arrived." This is, of course, in direct conflict with the detailed descriptions of the convoy offered by Ragsdale in earlier interviews.

Describing how to find the impact site, Ragsdale now said, "A sign post on the Pine Lodge Road indicates '53 miles to Roswell.' Near this sign is a road going south toward Pine Lodge . . . and the turn off to Arabella leads east and south. Two or 3 miles down this road towards Arabella is the site of our pickup that night and nearby is the impact site."

The discrepancies that have appeared are more than the minor changes expected as someone tries to remember events in the distant past. We all expect a story to shift with each telling simply because of the mechanism of memory, but these changes go beyond that. We have moved from Ragsdale seeing the bodies in the distance to trying to pull a helmet off one. We have gone from a vague description of the alien to one that seems to match those given by people claiming to be abducted. We have gone from Ragsdale watching the arrival of the military and describing the convoy to leaving before the trucks were in view. And we have slipped from a site thirty to forty miles north of Roswell to one that is sixty or seventy miles away. Such changes reflect a story that is either being invented with each telling, or someone who has been coached to change his story. This is the difference between an account that was freely given as opposed to one that was purchased.

How do these things happen? How can one man tell what he claims to be the truth and alter it so radically? Is there another factor that might help us understand the changes? The answer is yes, and his name is Max Littell.

Interviewed in *The Jim Ragsdale Story,* Littell tells how he learned of Jim Ragsdale. "In 1993 . . . we did have an investigator/author visiting us, and when his partner took the car on another errand, he needed a ride to his motel. I offered, and the individual said, 'Great, but I need to go by and see a party on the way, if it's all right.' This turned out to be Jim Ragsdale."

While I was in the car, checking on another witness whose husband had seen the craft and bodies, Don Schmitt and Mark Chesney rode to Ragsdale's house with Littell. I confess I don't understand why he fails to mention the names of the investigators. While Littell and Chesney waited in the car, Schmitt was inside for over an hour, talking to Ragsdale. This was the first comprehensive interview conducted.

Littell continues, saying, "Getting into the car, the writer said, 'I hope Ragsdale lives until morning.' . . . The investigator had apparently recorded the interview, or had taken enough notes that he could prepare a statement from Ragsdale. He asked if I could get the statement signed and notarized. . . . I said that this could easily be accomplished."

The rationale was that Ragsdale's health, being as precarious as it was, made it important to get a signed statement as quickly as possible. Mrs. Ragsdale suggested that Jim might not live much longer because of various health problems. Both of them seemed to believe that he would be hospitalized shortly and didn't have long to live.

Littell said, "Within a few days, the instrument arrived, and I met Ragsdale for the first time. The instrument was read to him, he signed it, the document was notarized, and I mailed it back to the investigator. Notaries do not make copies of the instrument, so I do not remember any of the statements made."

This statement by Littell has no basis in fact. Ragsdale was interviewed by Schmitt on January 26, 1993, and the affidavit was signed on January 27. Mark Chesney had listened to the tape, suggested an affidavit be written, and prepared a handwritten version. He discussed it with Littell and the two of them, in Littell's office, made a few changes. Then Littell, because he could type much faster than Chesney, typed it up. In other words, the instrument was not sent to Littell. He had a hand in preparing it, so it is surprising that he remembers nothing about what was in it.

Or maybe it isn't.

The statement made on January 27, 1993, said, "On a night during July, 1947, I, James Ragsdale, was in the company of a woman in an area approximately forty (40) miles northwest of Roswell, New Mexico, during a severe lightning storm. I and my companion observed a bright flash and what appeared to be a bright light source moving to the southeast. Later, at sunrise, driving in that direction, I and my companion came upon a ravine near a bluff that was covered with pieces of unusual wreckage, remains of a damaged craft, and a number of smaller bodied beings outside the craft. While observing the scene, I and my companion watched as a military convoy arrived and secured the scene. As a result of the convoy's appearance we quickly fled the area. I hereby swear the aforementioned account is accurate and true to the best of my knowledge and recollection." Ragsdale signed it and Littell notarized it. He sent the original to me, but kept copies in the files of the International UFO Museum.

After that Littell began talking with Ragsdale frequently. We wanted Ragsdale to show us the exact location and Littell said he would drive him out. In the "Max Littell Meets Jim Ragsdale," chapter of *The Jim Ragsdale Story*, he is quoted as saying, "Believing the alleged impact site to be only 30 miles from Roswell, I offered to take a doctor and nurse, along with oxygen. Since the site was only 30 miles from Roswell, I thought we could be out and back in two hours.

"At this point, Ragsdale told me, 'It is not 30 miles to the site because it is 53 miles to the turn-off.' I replied, 'Fifty-three miles out on Highway 285 to Albuquerque would put you two thirds of the way to Vaughn.' Ragsdale responded, 'It's not 285 but Highway 48, Pine Lodge Road.'" (Do I need to point out here that this dialogue is phony? People don't talk that way. The directions, in the conversation, are provided so that readers will easily understand what is being said, but both Littell and Ragsdale would already know this.)

The question is how did Ragsdale, who had spoken to me four times about the case, and who was recorded by Schmitt, get from a site thirty to forty miles north of town to one where the turn off is more than fifty? When we interviewed him, why did he insist the site was much closer to town? And why did he identify it from photographs which look nothing like the terrain around Pine Lodge that he was now describing to Littell?

This is a major change in the story. Littell has suggested that we made a mistake when talking to Ragsdale originally. He, Littell, was able to iron out the problems, resolving the question with the "true" site now nearly seventy miles away.

But the problem comes back to Ragsdale. Not only had he identified the site from photographs shown to him by Schmitt, but he also used a map. In fact, in an attempt to help us locate the site today, he mentioned that it was close to the El Paso Natural Gas Pipeline, which runs north of town. That is not to suggest that he was working on that line, or that it existed in 1947. It was a landmark used by Ragsdale in 1993 to help us situate the impact site on the map. And now that site has been moved a very long distance.

In *The Jim Ragsdale Story*, it says, "Further substantiating the location of Ragsdale's site, a rancher who has lived and worked all around the alleged impact site said that it would be impossible to reach the site from Pine Lodge Road—in 1947 or now—as any road would lead to a ranch house."

Of course, we are not told who this rancher is. He's just someone who has lived in the area. And it is ignored that the "alleged" impact site has been identified by Major Edwin Easley, the provost marshal of the 509th in 1947; Dr. W. Curry Holden, chairman of the Department of History and Anthropology at Texas Tech; Dr. C. Bertrand Schultz of the University of Nebraska; as well as other first-hand witnesses. (Please note here that there are many witnesses to substantiate the site north of Roswell. This is fact that seems to be overlooked by those criticizing my work.) Other civilians, such as William Woody, a long-time Roswell resident, said that when he and his father drove out Highway 285 on July 5 or 6, 1947, they saw military personnel off to the west, along the roads there. The granddaughter of Sheriff George Wilcox also suggested a site north of Roswell and in Chavez county.

In *The Jim Ragsdale Story*, it says, "An impact site closer to Roswell, just off Highway 285 to Vaughn lacks the verification of a witness pointing to an exact spot . . ." That's almost true. The truth is, there are a number of witnesses who have pointed to the exact spot near Highway 285. Among those mentioned earlier is Frank Kaufmann, and one other, high-ranking military officer who requests I not use his name. Given the number of others who have allowed their names to be linked to that site, the addition of one more seems to be overkill.

Contrast all this to the people who lived in the Pine Lodge area in 1947. Of those interviewed by me or other investigators, not a single one talked about this event. In other words, there is corroborative testimony, some by very credible sources, for the "alleged" site north of town and none for the "Ragsdale site." In fact, Littell suggested in June 1996 that a reporter for *The Roswell Daily Record* should check to see if anyone out in the Pine Lodge area remembered anything. That should have been done *before* the publication of *The Jim Ragsdale Story*.

There is one other aspect that should be discussed. Littell and his cronies insist that there is physical evidence of the crash near the Pine Lodge. They point to a path that seems to be broken through the trees, rocks that seem to have been adversely affected by heat, and other such evidence. Vennie Scott, the former Mrs. Jim Ragsdale, however, tells a slightly different tale.

According to William P. Barrett, a writer interested in the story, "Vennie Scott scoffed at the claim that damaged trees around Site No. 5 [the Ragsdale site]—where her family did in fact camp and hunt deer for decades—was evidence of a UFO crash in 1947. The trees were injured, she insisted, in 1969 or 1970 by a fire she witnessed that was caused by nearby inebriated campers. 'These drunks let their fire get away from them,' she said. 'That fire just burnt a circle and quit. And that's the place he's saying he saw the spaceship land. . . . That burnt spot is not what the spaceship made, because I was about 400 feet from where the drunks set the fire. . . . We helped them put the fire out.'"

But Littell wasn't done. Interviewed by Barrett for a story on the Roswell crash sites—and there are now six of them—Littell "Freely acknowledged that Ragsdale Production, Inc., [headed up by Littell's son-in-law] never tried to find or talk to any of these people. 'As far as we were concerned, this story of Ragsdale is valid,' said Littell. 'What am I trying to prove he's lying for? We're not going to do that. You go ahead and prove he's lying. I'm just telling you what the man said.'"

Littell did secure a second notarized statement from Ragsdale. That would mean that there were two sworn statements available that seemed to contradict one another. But like everything else in the Roswell case, it isn't that simple.

Barrett, in his attempt to be as thorough as possible, checked all of this out. He noticed that the longer, second, first-person statement contained a significant number of different details. Besides changing the site to near the Pine Lodge, Ragsdale was talking of a nocturnal visit to the site where he even tried to pull a helmet off one of the bodies.

But the important point, according to Barrett, is "In addition to the varying detail, Ragsdale's second statement had another problem. The document carried the seal of notary Kathy Weaver of Logan County, Oklahoma—home of Ragsdale's daughter, Judy Lott—along with Weaver's written declaration that the two-page document was 'subscribed and sworn to before me this 15th day of April, 1995.' Weaver admitted to *Crosswinds* [that is, Barrett] last month that Ragsdale didn't actually sign the statement in her presence. 'I swear to God he did not,' she said."

Apparently what happened, according to Barrett's story, is that Weaver added her signature and embossed notarial seal after Judy Lott, a co-employee of the same firm where Weaver worked, brought the document, already signed, to Weaver's office. Because she knew Lott, she notarized the statement. Weaver agreed, again according to Barrett's story, that it's "bad practice for notaries to attest to a signature not written while they're watching but that 'we do it all the time.'"

This procedure, under legal precedent, invalidates the force of the notarization. According to Barrett, "All that remains is an unsworn statement—a mere piece of paper, really—without the added credibility that it has been rendered in the presence of Almighty God subject to the laws of false swearing and even perjury."

Judy Lott denied that Ragsdale had signed the statement without a notary present. In fact, she told Barrett, "We had the notary come to our home because Dad was too ill and couldn't leave the house." But then, confronted with the information that the notary had denied ever meeting her father and hadn't witnessed the signature, Lott acknowledged that her father had not signed it in front of the notary. In fact, according to other information, Ragsdale might not have even been in Oklahoma when the affidavit was signed.

With the second statement invalidated, it meant that the only affidavit left was the one that we had created in early 1994. In an ironic twist it was Max Littell who was the notary on the first statement. It meant that he was the witness to Ragsdale's signature on the only valid affidavit, which is in direct conflict with the new statement that was being pushed as the real statement by Littell.

To make it worse, if possible, Lott insisted that she had typed the statement herself. This, to me, made no sense because, according to a story published in the Lubbock, Texas, *Avalanche-Journal* on June 30, 1996, Ragsdale hadn't told his daughter the tale until November 1994. But I had a copy of the statement created in September 1994. How could Judy Lott type it two months before she learned what her father had to say?

Barrett had an answer for that question, too. Littell said that he had prepared the statement himself. Littell typed it up as part of the agreement made with the International UFO Museum to "tell" the whole Ragsdale story. Lott had been caught once again.

In fact, Barrett followed up on these agreements, learning that the president and registered agent of Jim Ragsdale Production, Inc., was Danny Boswell. The secretary was Lana Boswell. The vice president was Max Littell. Barrett asked a number of Roswell residents what these people had in common and learned that Danny was Littell's son-in-law and Lana was his daughter. Also on the board was Judy Lott. Littell maintains that the profits from the sale of the videotape, book, and the Ragsdale story in general would be split between the UFO Museum and the Ragsdale heirs, after the corporation expenses were paid.

Again, these weren't the only problems with the tale and the surrounding events. Ragsdale told Schmitt and me that he had never gotten close to the craft or the bodies. Now he was talking about a craft with a hole torn in the side. In a tale reminiscent of that told by others, Ragsdale claimed to have looked into the craft. ". . . Inside there was a chair that looked like a throne. It looked like it was made of rubies and diamonds."

Remember, Ragsdale had said in the first interviews that he hadn't gotten close to the ship and the bodies. During the night, on his first trip toward the craft, his flashlight failed, and when he returned in the morning, the military was on the way to cordon off the area. From his hiding point on the ridge, he said that he watched the convoy arrive and the military police scatter to cordon the area. He had no opportunity to get down to the ship and look inside.

To bolster the Ragsdale testimony, Stanton Friedman was interviewed about his opinion of the Ragsdale tale. He said, "I could not imagine any reason for his lying, knowing full well that he was dying. Obviously I would like backup testimony, but the woman is also dead."

How about the financial inducement offered by Littell and the International UFO Museum as a reason for lying? How could they own the Ragsdale story if he had already handed it to Schmitt, Chesney, and me? Of course, it had to change because, if it didn't, it was too late for an exclusive.

Friedman said he would like backup testimony, all of which has been offered for the "alleged" site north of town. In fact, members of Ragsdale's family, interviewed before the divorce and the major changes in the story, all said the same things about the original tale. One or two were surprised by the changes that were being made.

Littell, in his response to these points, wrote, "Even Stanton Friedman who has interviewed hundreds of people said, of the video interview: 'The man was completely lucid, positive in his actions and statements, and I would equate this to a deathbed confession.'"

This is, of course, the same Stanton Friedman who continues to defend the testimony of Gerald Anderson, a man who had admitted to lying about aspects of his claimed involvement in the Roswell case, who has admitted to forging a number of documents about the case, and whose testimony is nearly universally rejected. In other words, Friedman's endorsement does little to bolster the Ragsdale tale.

But there are even problems with the idea the video statement was made about five days before Ragsdale died. Vennie Scott, the ex-Mrs. Ragsdale, told a number of people that she found it difficult to believe that Jim Ragsdale was saying anything to anyone five days before his death. She maintains that Ragsdale was in and out of a coma during the last several weeks of his life so that he wouldn't have been able to provide any statements. The timing of the deathbed statement seems to be a matter of dispute.

And, because of the circumstances of the first audio-recorded interview, it could be suggested that it, too, has the force of a deathbed confession. Both Ragsdale and his former wife believed that he would be hospitalized in the morning. It was one of the reasons that Chesney suggested that an affidavit be obtained as quickly as possible. No one knew if Ragsdale would survive the week. So now the only question is, which version of Ragsdale's tale is more accurate?

What has happened is that a tale, told by a man who was found by Schmitt, Chesney, and me, and which helped establish the crash of an alien craft near Roswell, has become a political football with some monetary strings attached. The truth has taken a backseat to the promotion of the tale. Littell couldn't have an exclusive story if Ragsdale had already been taped by us. That story isn't nearly as dramatic as the one being pushed now, but it is probably more accurate.

So a story that could have helped us understand the Roswell case has been changed. Now, we don't know which set of facts are right. Both have been told on tape. Both have been sworn to in signed and notarized affidavits. Only one has independent corroboration for parts of it and that one doesn't have an impact site near Pine Lodge.

But the sad truth here is that the politics of the Roswell case have taken precedence over the truth. And Ragsdale's story, which once might have been important, has been rendered absolutely useless.

And that gives us another example of what is happening in the 1990s. The truth takes a backseat to the personal agendas of the investigators, to the people promoting a case, and those who see UFOs as a way of gaining fame that might have passed them by.

The Ragsdale story, rejected by one of the first of the Roswell investigators is suddenly endorsed by that man simply because it suggests a flaw in the work that I had done. He didn't bother with attempting to learn more about the changes. He was only interested in the new version because it was at odds with what I had said and reported. Personal agenda over the truth. Flash over substance.

So now, I find myself in the unenviable position of having to expose the new story as untrue, and by doing that, render, through my own work, the original tale useless. I must point out how that original tale disagrees with the new version. I must point out that Littell has his own agenda, that things he has written about the case are wrong, and that he seems to be the influence in the changes. That Judy Lott's own story is riddled with holes, that she has been caught a number of times suggesting things that are inaccurate, and that she has a strong profit motive.

And that's where we are. Money, personal agendas, and politics have muddied the waters around the Roswell case in general and the Ragsdale tale in particular. All we can do is to continue to try to do the best we can, ignore the distractions, and publish what we learn, regardless of how it fits our own agendas. Given that, all I can do is suggest that the Jim Ragsdale story, as it now is told, is a hoax.

12 The Decline and Fall of Roswell

1996

FOR NEARLY TWENTY YEARS NOW, we have been hearing about the UFO crash at Roswell. There have been hundreds of magazine articles written about it; reality-based television programs, as well as the various news magazines, have discussed the case; and movies have been made about it or have mentioned it frequently. Several books have been written. I contributed two of those books. There is no doubt in my mind, based on the evidence I have seen, that there was an alien spacecraft that crashed outside of Roswell.

But, it must also be noted that the spacecraft crash has been turned into a cottage industry in Roswell. There are three UFO museums there, though one is outside the city and hardly qualifies. According to various hotel, motel, and restaurant owners and managers, a solid, steady business is now generated by tourism. It's estimated that five million dollars are brought into the local economy because of interest in the UFO crash.

And when there is money or fame to be found, there are those who will grab onto it whether deserved or not, and others who have it thrust upon them. Walter Haut, for example, as a young lieutenant assigned to the airfield at Roswell, wrote a press release saying that the Army had captured a flying saucer. Because he wrote that release, he has been considered an expert on the Roswell case. He has been interviewed hundreds of times about his knowledge. The fame was thrust upon him, though he would prefer it if some cash was thrust in his direction instead. Haut is an honest man who was in the right place at the right time.

But there are others who seem to have tried to grab, at least some of the glory, if not some of the cash. I've already detailed the story of Jim Ragsdale (see Chapter 11), who during his lifetime received little cash and less glory, and Max Littell, who is now deeply involved in that tale. There are others who have come forward, some with impressive stories that have proven to be less than accurate or are outright hoaxes. Again, I have already written about the Santilli film (see Chapter 7) and the *Penthouse* (see Chapter 10) photographs. Somewhere there is someone making some money on this UFO sighting.

The Air Force has been working very hard to discredit the case. I confess that I'm at a loss to understand why they are concerned with what a bunch of UFO nuts believe. Why do they care enough to spend taxpayer dollars to continue their research? I don't know the answer to that. I just know that more tax money is being spent on something the Air Force claims was a weather balloon and radar reflector (see Chapter 6).

There are others inside the UFO community who are working just as hard as the Air Force to reach the same conclusions. Some of it seems to be personal vendetta. Apparently one or two of them, angry at some perceived slight, believe the best revenge is to destroy the Roswell case. Others, who seem to be quite passionate in their beliefs, suggest that Roswell was nothing extraordinary and believe that it is hype that has made the case rather than solid research. They are as honest in their beliefs about the lack of evidence for the Roswell case as many of us on the other side are in our beliefs that Roswell was the scene of an alien spacecraft crash.

One of those who apparently desired the fame, though had no involvement in the case before 1990, was Gerald Anderson. He appeared telling his tale after the second airing of the *Unsolved Mysteries* segment on Roswell in January 1990. According to him, as a youngster, only five or six years old (he provided both ages), he had been on the scene of the spacecraft accident when the military arrived and chased everyone off. He had seen Barney Barnett there, the only known witness to the Plains of San Agustin aspect of the Roswell case. He had seen the craft and the bodies and even communicated telepathically with the survivor. His was a grand story, important because he was one of the few living witnesses who had seen the alien bodies before the military had taken them away.

I was the first to interview Anderson and I was excited about his tale. I was cautious, but excited. Here was a man who claimed to have seen the bodies, who could speak of them in the first person, and who was willing to go on the record. Here was a man who had been a police officer. He seemed to have a great deal of credibility. It was an exciting find.

But his tale quickly unraveled. As just a single example, he said that the leader of the archaeological expedition whose members also saw the craft and bodies was Dr. Adrian Buskirk. At last, after years of research, we had a name to go with the tale of archaeologists told by Barney Barnett.

Tom Carey, a MUFON member and researcher living in Pennsylvania, undertook the task to find the archaeologists in general and Dr. Buskirk in particular. Within minutes, actually, of beginning a literature search for anything written by any Buskirk, Carey put his hands on a reference to *The Western Apache* written by Dr. Winfred Buskirk. Not the Adrian of Anderson's story, but an archaeologist, or rather an enthnologist, who had been in the southwestern United States at the proper time. Carey couldn't believe his luck. He figured it had to be the wrong man. It wasn't.

Anderson, in his attempts to help researchers identify the archaeologists, provided an "identikit" sketch of the man. When Carey compared it to the photograph on the dust jacket of *The Western Apache* he knew that he had found the right man. Anderson's Dr. Buskirk had been located and was still alive.

But Dr. Buskirk denied that he had been on the scene of an alien spacecraft crash. In fact, in the summer of 1947, he was in Arizona completing work on his Ph.D. and, according to him, "was too busy to be engaged in any archaeological sideshows."

The question was, how could Anderson have named a real man who had an archaeological, or rather, anthropological background, if he hadn't seen him on that desert crash site in 1947? The answer, it turned out, was that Anderson attended high school in Albuquerque, where Buskirk taught history and anthropology. Not only that, but according to Buskirk, Anderson had taken a class in anthropology from him. In other words, Anderson, in attempting to name the archaeologists that Barney Barnett described, had plugged in his high-school teacher. As Jerry Clark described him, he was "The inconveniently alive Dr. Buskirk."

Now, we are hearing that Buskirk didn't remember Anderson as one of his students. To some, it is just an amazing coincidence. But Dr. Buskirk was able to review the high-school transcripts and learned that Anderson had, indeed, taken his anthropology class in the fall of 1957. When that was suggested, Anderson said that he didn't remember what high school he attended, but the documentation exists to prove it.

Interestingly, those who still have a desire to believe Anderson report that five former students remember nothing of Gerald Anderson in the class. Of course this is irrelevant. Who cares what the students can or cannot remember after nearly forty years? Dr. Buskirk, the teacher, confirmed, in writing, that Anderson took his anthropology class.

But let's say, for the sake of argument, that Anderson hadn't. So what? We've put him in the same high school and even though that high school had nearly three thousand students and was scattered among three buildings, Anderson was there as a student and Buskirk was there as a teacher. We found a link and it wasn't on the Plains of San Agustin.

That wasn't the only problem with Anderson's tale. He changed it radically as new information was presented, he lied about his background, and he was caught forging documents in an attempt to bolster his credibility. In the end, Anderson destroyed himself and he hurt the credibility of the entire Roswell case. He should become nothing more than a footnote about those who have attempted to "cash in" on the Roswell case.

The Anderson tale, as it was originally told, seemed to corroborate the second- and third-hand testimony of Barney Barnett. Barnett was the soil conservation engineer who told a number of friends about seeing a crashed flying saucer out on the Plains of San Agustin. He spoke of four little bodies and a wrecked craft but before he could get a long look at them, he was chased off by military authorities. Barnett and the archaeological team were told never to mention what they had seen to anyone.

The problem with the Barnett story, frankly, is that there is no first-hand corroboration for it. Barnett's tale is stand-alone, and although it seems that he did tell friends and family about seeing the saucer and the bodies, he died before anyone could interview him.

Barnett did talk of archaeologists and Tom Carey and I found a group of archaeologists who did talk of seeing a craft and bodies. These people were not on the Plains of San Agustin but over closer to Roswell. Of all those who were working on the Plains, or near the Plains, on that summer of 1947, not one of them remembers anything happening anywhere around there. Some were there prior to the events, some after, and some during, but not a single one had a tale of a UFO crash to tell, with one exception, and that is Robert Drake.

Drake, according to the story, was traveling with three others, completing survey work on the Plains in September 1947. On their way back to Albuquerque, they stopped at a ranch where Drake spoke to a lone cowboy who told him about the UFO crash. Drake told Tom Carey that he, Wesley Hurt, Dan McKnight, and Albert Dittert talked about the crashed saucer all the way back to Albuquerque that night.

Hurt, however, told me that he hadn't heard the tale of the crashed flying saucer until "people started calling me about fifteen years ago [1979 or 1980]." He confirmed that he had worked with the other men on a site survey. That was a matter of public record including articles written for professional journals.

Both McKnight and Dittert told Carey that they remembered nothing of the flying saucer crash tales. Each remembered Drake, and even the trip he was talking about, but nothing about flying saucers or dead alien aliens.

When confronted with this information, Drake said that he had *not* discussed the flying saucer crash with the other men. And, Drake couldn't remember, or never knew, the name of the cowboy who had shared the incredible story with him.

It also turns out that Ruth Barnett kept a diary during all of 1947. It was a daily reminder book that someone had given her and she kept it all through 1947. There is not a hint that Barney Barnett was involved in anything unusual at any time during the summer of 1947. Their lives seem to be very routine and mundane.

To make it worse for the proponents of a Plains UFO crash, if possible, the dates they have always used for that event simply don't work. The argument had been that the crash took place on the evening of July 2, 1947, and that Barnett had stumbled onto the wreckage on the morning of July 3. The diary, however, rules out that possibility. If the crash took place instead on the night of July 1, then Barnett was out of his Socorro office and in "the high country," meaning the Plains. He could have seen the crashed saucer during the day of July 2. But on July 3, the day after the supposed July 2 crash, and in fact, on every other day until July 8, Barnett was in the office or in Socorro, New Mexico. There was no chance for him to get out on the Plains.

So, we are left with a second-hand tale told by friends and family of Barnett that has no first-hand corroboration. There are a number of researchers who have been looking into this report and a few of them have suggested some interesting developments in the last year or so. But when I put the critical question to them, that is, "Are there any first-hand witnesses to an event on the Plains?" each has answered, "No."

But let's move on to the main thrust of the Roswell case, and that is the events that took place near the Roswell Army Air Field. There have been some rather disturbing developments in the last year. First, skeptics and debunkers, as well as the Air Force, have launched various attacks. Some of those have been detailed elsewhere. The Project Mogul idea, while sounding good to those who know little or nothing about the case, or who want to accept any explanation rather than believe an alien spacecraft crashed, is as good as any. But what is happening now is a collapse of some of the best witness testimony available.

Before going into detail on that, let's look at the attacks launched against Major Jesse A. Marcel, Sr., the air intelligence officer of the 509th Bomb Group in July 1947. It was Marcel's tale of picking up pieces of the alien ship that started the whole affair. When he spoke to Stan Friedman and Len Stringfield in 1978, he provided enough detail to start an investigation. Once the base and time frame was established, other witnesses were located.

But recently Marcel's reputation has been called into question. Bob Pratt, a reporter for the *National Enquirer* in 1979, spoke to

Marcel. He graciously provided UFO researchers copies of that interview. In August 1996, he told me that the interview was originally recorded and that he made the transcript from the tape that night. In other words, we can be fairly certain that transcript is an accurate representation of what Marcel said to Pratt during the interview.

Pratt also told me that he was aware of the questions being raised about Marcel's integrity and was surprised by them. He found Marcel to be an intelligent, articulate, and somewhat self-effacing man. The discrepancies between what Marcel said about his educational background and his military career and what is in Marcel's military file surprised him.

I have been looking into that with the help of Jesse Marcel, Jr. The unfortunate thing is that we have almost no records from his father. We know, for example, that Marcel, Sr., during the 1930s, was a topographic draftsman and did topographic mapping from aerial photographs. He seemed to have flown as part of the job, and mentioned that he had several thousand hours of pilot time in the right seat, meaning copilot time. It would seem, from the records available, that Marcel had no pilot's license, but that he would have ridden in the right seat as part of his mapping job. His military record shows nothing of this bootleg time and we know that after he got out of the service he did no private flying.

By the same token, while Marcel was not a "rated" officer, meaning that he did not fly as part of his job in the military, we do know he flew on many occasions. We see from his record that he was awarded a number of air medals, and, by regulation, the only way to be awarded an air medal is to be engaged in aerial flight. In other words, the record does substantiate his claim that he did fly as part of his military job. In fact, he told Pratt that he had more than 400 hours in combat.

So, what we seem to be able to learn is that Marcel did participate in "aerial flight" as part of his job as an intelligence officer. He claimed that he had flown as a pilot, bombardier, or waist gunner at different times. Though unrated in any of those positions, given the nature of aviation units, it seems reasonable to believe that he would have flown in those positions at some point, as long as there was a rated officer or enlisted man near him as he did.

What this means is that the record does not reflect the high number of hours that Marcel claimed, but does reflect some hours as he claimed. Could it be that he had other hours that were not part of the record that came about in his position as a topographer and later with the 509th Bomb Group? Certainly. And even if the number of hours is an exaggeration, it doesn't seem to be much of one.

Marcel also told Pratt that he had received five air medals but the record shows only two. Some feel that Marcel was exaggerating his record by suggesting he had more air medals than he had earned. But this makes no sense. If you are going to exaggerate, why not suggest a higher combat award? Having one air medal or a hundred really doesn't mean much.

In my own case, my record reflects only two air medals, but I have more than forty. The record is inaccurate and I have the documents to prove the additional awards. It was never worth the effort to correct my file to make sure that it was right. The basic award is listed and I just let it go. Maybe Marcel did the same thing.

The fact is that some of the things Marcel told Pratt about his military career are not reflected in his military record, but I'm not sure it is of particular significance. Marcel was just who he said he was in July 1947, that is, the air intelligence officer of the 509th. We have all kinds of documentation to prove it.

The real worry is in his educational background. He told Pratt that he had a "degree in nuclear physics (bachelors) at completed work at GW University in Wash. attended (LSU, Houston, U of Wis, NY Univ, Ohio State, Docotr pool? and GW . . ." (I have reproduced here exactly what the notes from Pratt said. As I said, he told me that he transcribed them from a tape, but the tape no longer exists.)

His record shows that he attended Louisiana State for a year and a half and that he majored in physics. That was in 1931. After that, he was working in various capacities at a variety of private sector jobs. He did attend a number of military schools and that he entered active duty from Houston, Texas. Some of those military schools might have been given at any number of universities, and that could be why he claimed to have gone to those schools.

Notice that I said claimed. The only record we have is that he attended LSU, and that after leaving active duty (and therefore wouldn't be reflected in his record) he attended an extension class for radio and television repair apparently given by LSU. I have found no records to suggest that Marcel had attended any of the schools that he mentioned, and we have found no documentation to suggest that he had a bachelor's degree. If he had one, we haven't found it and his son is as confused as the rest of us.

These things are somewhat worrisome. It creates some conflict in the record, and makes us wonder about Jesse Marcel. On the other hand, he was the air intelligence officer of the 509th in July 1947, he was a major on active duty when many others had been caught in the reduction in force, and he did get a letter of commendation for outstanding performance dated July 26, 1946, and signed by Roger Ramey, commanding general of the 8th Air Force.

There is additional work to be done here, but, at the moment, there is no reason to reject the Marcel testimony out of hand especially when it is remembered that we can corroborate many of the things he said about the events of July 1947. We might want to look a little closer at what he said, but there could be some explanations for why the record does not reflect what he said that would clarify the situation. At the moment, we're looking for that clarification.

On the other hand, some problems have arisen in the story told by former Roswell mortician, Glenn Dennis, that are more than worrisome. The first problem, and one that really means very little, is that Dennis, in July 1947, wasn't a mortician but an embalmer. A mortician is the leader in the mortuary and the embalmer does some of the work in the mortuary. And, Dennis later did become a mortician, so this problem really means very little. No, there are other, larger problems on the horizon.

When I first interviewed Dennis in person, that is, November 1990, he told the same basic story he tells today. He received a number of phone calls from the base mortuary officer asking questions about bodies and coffins. Later, because the mortuary also ran the ambulance service (not an uncommon arrangement, especially in the 1940s) he had to take an injured airman out to the base.

While there, he saw, in the backs of a number of ambulances, strange metallic wreckage. He didn't think much of that because, in aircraft accidents, wreckage was sometimes transported in the ambulances.

Inside the hospital, he noticed there was unusual activity. He thought he would look up a nurse he knew and buy a Coke. She saw him in the hallway and told him to get out before he got himself into deep trouble. But then a nasty officer saw him and asked what he was doing there. He was ordered from the hospital when another, red-haired officer yelled to hold him. He wanted some words with him.

According to the tale told by Dennis, this officer was accompanied by a black NCO and both had bad attitudes. Dennis was told that there had been no aircraft accidents, there had been nothing going on, and he would return to the city. He would tell no one what he saw. If he mentioned it, they would be picking his bones out of the sand.

Dennis left the base puzzled, but a day or so later he spoke to the nurse, who he identified as Naomi Self. He met her at the officers club where she told him the tale of a preliminary autopsy of little creatures from another star system. She told him not to tell a soul about the event, and within days, she was transferred off the base, apparently sent to England. Dennis received a note from her, telling him her address in England. The letter he wrote to her came back marked deceased. She had been killed in an aircraft accident, according to the other nurses at the base.

It is a marvelous tale and certainly makes for good television, not to mention great prose in a nonfiction book. And there were many things that Dennis said that could be checked. Unlike so much of the UFO field, here was a story where we could look for corroboration.

One of the first things I did was check the the yearbook produced in 1947 by the Information Office of the 509th Bomb Group. It contained the names and photographs of the majority of the people assigned to the base that year. Walter Haut, the editor of the book, told me that ten to twenty percent of the people failed to appear in the book, so when there was no picture for a Naomi Self, that wasn't particularly significant.

I next checked the *New York Times Index*. In the pre-computer age, this is a great tool. I could look up aircraft accidents and find them broken down by date, type of aircraft, location, and when and where it appeared in the newspaper. I didn't have to search each individual edition, but could look it up in the index. I searched everything from July 1947 through 1955 and found no aircraft accidents in England, Europe, or the United States that had claimed the lives of five nurses as Dennis had said.

Don Berliner, who was working with Stan Friedman, made a similar search using the *Stars and Stripes.* That is a newspaper printed for the military overseas. It contains military news, and if a group of Army nurses had been killed in an aircraft accident, it should have been reported there. It was not.

This was worrisome, but not overly so. It might be that Dennis had been given some disinformation. If the nurse had been killed, it explained why she had not written to him since she arrived in England. If, on the other hand, the story was not true, it didn't explain why he never heard from her.

There is a secondary problem here as well. There was talk, some of it from investigators, some of it from Dennis himself, that suggested his interest in the nurse might have been more than just friendship. After all, if they weren't more than friends, why, on a short stop before going overseas, did she drop him a note with her address in it? That implies a somewhat stronger relationship, and that, too, is worrisome. In 1947, Glenn Dennis was already married and had a young daughter. He shouldn't have been writing to the nurse, especially since he has described her as very religious.

During my research in Roswell, I noticed that in 1947, the *Roswell Daily Record* contained a listing at the bottom of the front page welcoming the newcomers to the city. There would be two or three names each day. I searched from January 1, 1947 through the end of July 1947, but Naomi Self never appeared there. Is that significant? Probably not. They might not list the name of a young, single woman who had been recently assigned to the base, though there were some listings of single women arriving in the city.

I also searched the various available records of the 509th Bomb Group including the very detailed Unit History for the spring and summer of 1947 but found no references to a nurse named Self. The base telephone directory, published in August of 1947, listed numbers for many of the officers including some of the nurses, but had no listing for Naomi Self. Every document I checked failed to produce any corroboration for her existence. None of this was significant in and of itself because not everyone at the base had been listed in those sources. In the aggregate, however, it was becoming quite worrisome.

Don Schmitt claimed that he had found a family named Self

living in a large, midwestern city. With a colleague, he went to that city, called the home of the family and asked for Naomi. Told that she was out shopping, he asked if Naomi had been an Army nurse at anytime. When he was told that she was, Schmitt was convinced he had located Dennis' nurse. A visit to the house, according to Schmitt, resulted in his meeting a large black lady who spoke with a Caribbean accent. She denied any knowledge of Naomi Self, Army nurses, or even recent telephone conversations with Schmitt. Schmitt said that the woman he talked to had no Caribbean accent.

I mention this only because I now have good reason to doubt that the episode took place. Although the tale has been used to suggest some kind of skullduggery on the part of the military and the Self family, it is a story that should be eliminated from the file. There is no evidence that it is true, and it is just another dead end.

With the help of a police officer, I was able to identify five women named Naomi Self and spoke to four of them. Dennis had also said she had a brother named William and I located more than 250 men with that name. Other researchers have done much the same. We've duplicated the work simply because none of us have had any luck and these efforts were no more effective than any of the others.

At one point, in a conversation with Dennis, he asked me why we hadn't found his nurse yet. I pointed out that it wasn't easy tracing a name from nearly fifty years ago but I hoped to find something. Of course, in today's environment, with CD-ROM telephone directories containing seventy or eighty million residential phone numbers, the task is much easier, but it is still somewhat time consuming, especially when it is a woman who might have married and changed her last name.

A number of the former members of the medical team at Roswell in 1947 have been located. A nurse, Rosemary Brown, for example, said that she had no memory of a nurse who had been with the unit for a short period, as described by Dennis, or of a nurse named Naomi. A doctor said that he remembered very little of the staff at Roswell because it was so long ago.

The single exception is a man named David Wagnon, whose record does place him in Roswell at the proper time. He seems to remember the nurse, but that is based more on a description since he was unable to remember the name himself. He recognized it from a list of alphabetically arranged names read to him by Stan Friedman. That lead is being pursued, but I have little hope it will bear any fruit. Besides, it would be a single verbal account with no corroborative documentation to back it up, and, at this time, we need to have that corroborative documentation.

In fact, there is no documentation for the existence of a nurse at Roswell named Naomi Self. A researcher in Arizona, V. G. Golubic, undertook the search for the nurse in much the same fashion that Tom Carey undertook the search for the archaeologists. Golubic has become, you might say, the expert on the medical staff at Roswell in July 1947. And, his search has paid off. He has identified about eighteen women who were assigned to the base as nurses, both military and civilian, in the correct time frame. Nurses who were not part of the yearbook or the base telephone directory but whose names did surface in various documents recovered through Freedom of Information Act requests, interviews, and other sources. Additional research by Golubic included an intensive genealogical search of Minnesota families with related last name spellings. Also identified and located were the Cadet Nurse Corps Identification Cards from a government-sponsored training program of the mid-1940s, containing 124,064 names. Ultimately, a Naomi M. Self, couldn't be vectored in from the multiple sources available.

Golubic first located and then spoke with two other nurses, V. Helmbold and C. Walker, who were both at Roswell, one prior to and the other soon after July 1947. Neither has memories of Naomi Self, but both remember the five nurses pictured in the yearbook. According to Golubic, he has found no trace of her, except for the confirmation provided by David Wagnon. He is pursuing the situation with a mixed photographic line-up of all the nurses who were assigned to the base from 1947 through 1948. Golubic has spoken to Wagnon a number of times about it. He also points out that he has spoken to twenty to twenty-five members of the medical team at Roswell, and Naomi just doesn't surface.

From the above group, Golubic found and interviewed two other significant individuals. J. Comstock, the hospital commander in 1947, could recall neither Naomi Self nor the events relating to the crash. Mrs. W. White, a nurse by training, was also the wife of the chief of surgery, and part of the only family of high-ranking members of the medical staff who lived on base. She had nothing to contribute to the search for Naomi Self. Curiously, the Air Force had not tried to locate the medical staff or its commander until Golubic began to investigate.

Further, I had tried to get the morning reports, that is, an official document created each day by every unit in the military and submitted to higher headquarters, for the medical staff, or Squadron M, at Roswell. Included in the morning reports are the names of personnel on leave, who have returned from leave, who are on special orders for any of a variety of reasons, who are reporting in or have been detached from, the unit. It provides the name and service number of the individual. It is a valuable tool in the search for the Roswell personnel. My requests failed. I was told the specific morning reports had been destroyed. I attached no significance to that because there had to be, literally, millions of those documents which would be of little historical significance.

Golubic, however, refused to take that as a serious answer and repeatedly asked for the morning reports. He was able, after four or five attempts, to learn that they did exist. He put his hands on the morning reports from October 1, 1946, through December 31, 1947, for Squadron M of the 427th AAFBU (Army Air Force Base Unit) and the 509th Bomb Group. Naomi Self did not appear on those documents anywhere. This has now moved from worrisome to outright concern for the truth.

But there were new problems. In December 1995, I learned that Dennis was telling some people that he didn't really care for any of the "Roswell researchers" and had not provided them with the real name of his nurse. He had given us information that was close, but her real name was Naomi Maria Selff. Had that been right, I think we would have turned up something in one of the documents. I mean, if I had found a Naomi Selff, I would have noticed that because it is so close. Even with the new name, there was no documentation.

Dennis was not finished with the name game. He told another researcher that her real name was Naomi Sipes. Of course, had the name Naomi Sipes appeared anywhere, I would have noticed it, as would any of the others searching for the nurse. With the unusual first name and a last name that began with an "S" it is certainly close enough. But again, even with the new name, there was no documentation.

But the tale doesn't end there. When it was pointed out that no documentation, no corroboration, that nothing verified the existence of the nurse, Dennis changed the tale again. He had not supplied anyone with the right name. In fact, the last name didn't even begin with an "S." He was changing the tale as he was confronted with the evidence, and such changes do not bode well for the credibility of the story.

He also said that Naomi Self was born in Twin Falls, Minnesota, and that she took all her schooling in Minnesota. Well, not according to various authorities in Minnesota. We've been unable to find a single document or record to confirm this. Naomi Self didn't go to school anywhere in Minnesota. And remember, given her age and occupation, we can limit the search to a few specific years. We don't have to search decade after decade because, according to Dennis, she was in her early twenties in 1947.

What we've seen in the last year to eighteen months, is an erosion in the credibility of the Roswell case. We have seen those who have no interest in the case, other than as a means of making money, come forward with what they claim to be proof. The Santilli film is nothing more than an attempt to cash in on the Roswell case.

These attacks on the credibility of the case must be seen as worrisome by the serious researcher. Some of them are of little importance such as the revelations about Jesse Marcel, Sr. They are points of trivia that could easily have simple explanations if we could ask Marcel about them. And, as I have said, he was exactly who he said he was in 1947, respected by his superiors, and serving in the Army Air Force.

But others, such as Glenn Dennis, who has been considered one of the important witnesses, have begun to collapse. There is little that can be said except that we have found nothing to confirm that his nurse exists or existed. And when challenged on these points, he begins to change the tale. In a police investigation, such changes signal the end of the story. It suggests the witness has been less than honest.

When we look at it in the proper light, we realize that most of the testimonies that we're now rejecting come from the civilian population. These are Gerald Anderson, Barney Barnett, Robert Drake, Jim Ragsdale, and now Glenn Dennis. Of the military, only Marcel is being attacked (at the moment) and those attacks revolve around what he said more than forty years after the event about his record but not about what he said concerning the UFO crash or who he was in 1947.

Of course, it should be pointed out that those maintaining nothing happened at Roswell, such as Sheridan Cavitt, have also had their testimonies called into question. The evidence, detailed in a different chapter, suggests that Cavitt has been less than honest in his accounts of the events he was involved in. And Charles Moore, the graduate student on Project Mogul seems to have been honest, but was also sorely mistaken. He has become a leading debunker in the Roswell case merely because he said that he launched the balloon that caused the debris. Interestingly, he has no evidence of this, but is believed anyway.

This is not to say that I am rejecting now the idea that an alien ship crashed outside of Roswell. I am as convinced as ever, simply because of the number of military sources with whom I have spoken. And, there are some solid civilian witnesses including two members of the archaeological team who were on the site, Johnny McBoyle, the radio newsman who saw the craft, and Jud Roberts, the KGFL owner who reported that governmental officials threatened to shut down his station if they reported on the find or broadcast their recorded interview with Mac Brazel.

What it does demonstrate is that we must be more resourceful in our search of information and the corroboration of it. We must not accept stories told by seemingly credible sources because it is what we want to hear. We should accept only those tales that can be substantiated by additional testimony and documentation. Without that, we are going to be fooled by those who have spun a convincing tale.

The Roswell case is so complex, with so many investigators, researchers, witnesses, and interested parties, each with his or her own agenda, that we might never sort it out. That is, unless we finally gain access to the records about the crash. With those historic documents in hand, we will learn exactly what the truth is and what it is not. To do that, we will need to convince a disbelieving media that the story deserves proper media attention, but that won't happen until we clean our own house. I hope this is a first step in that direction.

13 The Roswell Phoenix

IT MIGHT BE THOUGHT, given the previous chapter, that I have lost my fascination with the Roswell case and am willing to write it off. Nothing could be further from the truth. In fact, I have to ask, if Roswell is not the scene of a flying saucer crash in 1947, why is the Air Force working so hard to convince us that it isn't? Why should they care? What is hidden at Roswell that causes them to want to divert our attention?

We, in the UFO community, have found in the last year a number of statements by high-ranking military officers, that suggest there have been *no* flying saucer crashes. Lieutenant General Nathan F. Twining, the commanding officer of the Air Materiel Command in 1947, in a letter dated September 23, 1947, wrote, ". . . Due consideration must be given the following: . . . (2) The lack of physical evidence in the shape of crash recovered exhibits which would undeniably prove the existence of these objects."

During a meeting of the Scientific Advisory Board held at the Pentagon on March 17 and 18, 1948, Colonel Howard McCoy, while discussing the "Utilization of Technical Intelligence," said, "We have a new project—Project Sign—which may surprise you as a development from the so-called mass hysteria of the past summer when we had all the unidentified objects or discs. This can't be laughed off. We have over 300 reports which haven't been publicized in the papers . . . I can't even tell you *how much we would give to have one of those crash in an area so that we could recover whatever they are* [emphasis added]."

And several months later, the same Colonel McCoy wrote, in a document dated November 3, 1948, "There remains a certain number of reports for which no reasonable everyday explanation is available. So far, no physical evidence of the existence of the unidentified sightings has been obtained. . . . Although it is obvious that some types of flying objects have been sighted, the exact nature of those objects cannot be established *until physical evidence, such as that which would result from a crash, has been obtained* [emphasis added]."

Do these statements, from legitimate government documents and made by high-ranking military officers, prove that there was no UFO crash at Roswell? Have we finally found an answer that eliminates that case completely? Or are there other conclusions that can be drawn?

First, it must be pointed out that each of the quoted documents were classified only as secret. Had the Roswell crash taken place, everyone agrees that the information would have been classified as top secret. Because of that, it couldn't be mentioned in a document with a lower classification. If the Roswell case was mentioned, then the whole document would have been classified as top secret and we wouldn't be trying to answer these questions about them.

That doesn't, of course, explain the references in the documents to a lack of crash recovered debris. And these arguments are really a matter of semantics and aren't particularly persuasive. If we're going to accept a UFO crash at Roswell, then we have to have better explanations for these statements by high-ranking military officers than to simply suggest that the classification on the documents is in error. Or that the classification of the document required that no mention be made of the allegedly top secret Roswell crash.

The statement by Twining, however, is explained easily. To understand it, we must understand the context in which it was made. In July 1947, Brigadier General George Schgulen, the assistant chief of staff for air intelligence, forwarded to Twining at the AMC Headquarters a number of UFO sighting reports for analysis. Schgulen supplied all the data, and Twining's team analyzed it. From the documentation recovered by various researchers, there is no indication that Twining's men added anything to the mix. In other words, they merely analyzed the data forwarded to them, reporting back, exactly what they could deduce from that particular data. Since there was nothing about crash recovered exhibits in the material sent to them, they made mention of the lack of such exhibits.

In fact, it might be that those conducting the analysis for Schgulen were not privy to the Roswell material and therefore were unaware of it. They wrote their report for review by General Twining and he signed it. That does not translate into Twining lying about the crash recovered debris, nor does it translate into the men working under Twining lying to their superiors as has been suggested by some. It merely means that the men who wrote the report for Twining's signature were unaware of the crash recovered debris so they could make no reference to it.

I probably should also note that Twining, when he learned about the Roswell case, would have communicated that information to his superiors if they didn't know about it already. In other words, the men who needed to know about the crash already did know. Twining gained nothing by making reference in the "secret" document by suggesting the crash, but gained a great deal by letting the reference to a lack of debris go forward. If you already know the answer to a question, you rarely ask it. That document prevented those who might have heard rumors from asking questions about those rumors because they knew of Twining's report to Schgulen. The Twining letter, then, provides little in the way of a persuasive argument in either direction.

McCoy's statements made in other arenas, however, are more difficult to explain. To suggest that he wouldn't have known about the Roswell crash, had it taken place, is ridiculous. McCoy, in 1948, was the head of Air Force intelligence at Wright-Patterson Air Force Base. If there was a Roswell crash, he would have learned of it. That makes his comments more puzzling, unless we conclude that there was no crash.

Or does it?

Let's think about this for a moment. Again, if the Roswell crash happened, it would be highly classified. Nearly everyone agrees with this premise. If it is highly classified, the number of those privy to the information is going to be small. They certainly aren't going to mention it outside the small group cleared to hear about. To do otherwise is to compromise the secret and these men, at that time, were skilled at keeping secrets.

Therefore, if there was a Roswell UFO crash, the explanation for McCoy's statement must lie elsewhere. It seems to me that McCoy might have been actively attempting to divert attention. Let's assume for the moment that all the men at the briefing were cleared to learn about the Roswell crash, if it had taken place. Let's also assume that at that meeting, nothing of a top secret nature could be discussed. Suddenly we find ourselves in a situation that is not unlike that in many courts. Evidence has been found but because of the rules in effect at the trial that specific evidence is not admissible. In other words, everyone pretends that it does not exist.

Now, in this situation we have evidence that the Air Force wants to pretend doesn't exist. If they can convince people that there has been no crashes of flying saucers, they won't have to answer embarrassing questions about them. Add to the fact that the minutes of the meeting were only classified secret, and we have a situation where no one could mention there had been a crash without violating security.

So they couldn't mention anything about it, but there was no reason for them not to suggest there hadn't been a crash. Anyone seeing the minutes would see McCoy's comment and believe, given the circumstances, that no such crash had taken place. It would keep people from asking the embarrassing questions because those people would believe they already knew the correct answer. The big secret was kept by suggesting there was no big secret to keep.

I find this scenario somewhat displeasing because it presumes that someone is clever enough to make it work. It means that someone understands human nature well enough to attempt to prevent people from beginning a search. You don't look for something that you already know doesn't exist.

But I find it strange that McCoy would keep making that same statement. He told one group that he wished one would crash in March and then, months later, he told another group the same thing. Now, the scenario isn't quite as strange because we see a pattern to the denials. It is, as was characterized during the Watergate investigations, "a nondenial denial." McCoy didn't say that one hadn't crashed, only that he wished one would so that they could learn what they were. The crash recovered debris would provide the answers to their questions.

I confess that in studying the UFO phenomenon, I have always been left somewhat cold by the arguments of logic designed to prove why the obvious isn't obvious, and why people said what they said. If we argue long enough, and loud enough, we can twist everything around to prove our point of view no matter how convoluted the logic might become. I can see McCoy, doing his duty as an intelligence officer, making a comment to lead those searching for answers in a different direction, but such proof is in the "negative." I prefer the positive.

And there are positive signs that something unusual happened outside of Roswell. In the last few weeks, I have learned of more of them. Take, for example, the tale of Cactus Jack told by Iris Foster. After seeing the *Unsolved Mysteries* program detailing the Roswell crash story, she wrote to me, telling me about Cactus Jack. He was an old-time prospector, pot hunter, and frankly, grave robber, who made a marginal living in the desert southwest. According to Foster, he told her in 1971 that he had been down there when the spaceship had crashed. The story intrigued me because he was apparently telling it nearly twenty years before anything was published about the Roswell case.

According to Foster, Cactus Jack told her that he had seen the "object which was round, but not real big." He said he saw four bodies and said that they were small. Their blood, according to Jack, was like tar, thick and black, and it stained their silvery uniforms.

Foster was sure of the date because it had been when she had owned her cafe and Cactus Jack had come in frequently. According to Foster, he had been injured in a fire in the mid-1980s but she wasn't sure what happened to him after that. She thought he was dead but just didn't know.

Tom Carey, a researcher living in Pennsylvania, and fascinated by any of the stories that touched on archaeology or anthropology, wanted to find Cactus Jack. He knew that I had been to Taos, the last known home of Cactus Jack, had searched the newspaper files for a mention of the story about the fire, and had failed. To me the search for Cactus Jack was a side issue, but Carey wanted to learn more about it.

Although he didn't have much luck at first, he finally was able to learn that Cactus Jack had died and even managed to obtain a copy of his last driver's license. He also found the article in the Taos newspaper confirming that Cactus Jack had been injured in a fire just as Foster had said. There was a picture of Jack in the hospital with his head wrapped in bandages.

But more importantly, Carey was able to locate some of Jack's old friends. They too, had heard the story of the crashed UFO. Although it doesn't prove that Cactus Jack had seen what he claimed, it did prove that he had been telling the tale for quite a number of years, certainly before there had been any publicity about the Roswell case.

Tied into this is the story of the anonymous archaeologist who called me in February 1990. He claimed to have been on the scene in July 1947 and described what he had witnessed, telling me that he had seen a crashed object that to him looked more like a fat fuselage with no wings that had been badly damaged. He had seen three bodies that had large heads and large eyes. Before he had a chance to see anything more, the military had arrived and rounded up him and the other archaeologists.

At the time of the original call, I wasn't sure who I had talked to. He had refused to give his name, but did say that he thought I should have the information. Anonymous information, provided over the telephone, isn't worth much in and of itself. The tale told did tend to corroborate some things that I had been hearing that contradicted the conventional wisdom, which I found somewhat interesting. But, it was anonymous and there was no way to verify anything said.

But that wasn't the end of it. Carey, as he continued his search, talked to Dr. George Agogino who said that he, too, had talked to the man who told of the fat fuselage. Carey read my notes of the conversation to Agogino who told Carey, "That's what he told me."

What Agogino did was corroborate the tale told by the anonymous archaeologist. Suddenly it was no longer a tale told to me by an unidentified caller, but a tale told to others as well. More importantly, we had a name to go with the source. The anonymous archaeologist had been identified, and I spoke to him again when I saw him at his place of business. The tale gained a great deal of importance now that I know who he is.

There are a couple of other points to be made here. Edwin Easley, in July 1947, was the provost marshal at the Roswell Army Air Field. I spoke to him on a number of occasions. I asked during that first conversation if I had the right man, if he had been the provost marshal in July 1947 at Roswell, and he said he was. When I asked about the UFO crash, he told me, "I can't talk about it."

There are those in the UFO community today, and there are skeptics, who insist that Easley suggested the topic was classified because he didn't want to talk to me at all. The quickest way to get me off the telephone was to say that the events were classified and he couldn't talk about them. In reality, the quickest way would have been to suggest that he knew nothing about the crash. After he said that he knew nothing, what would be the follow-up question?

But Easley told me, repeatedly during that telephone conversation, that he had been sworn to secrecy. He couldn't talk about the events. Not that they didn't happen, not that it was all invention, delusion, and imagination, but that he was sworn to secrecy. He couldn't talk about it.

I asked him at the end of our short conversation if I had additional questions, would he mind if I called back? He said, "No." In other words, if he had wanted to get rid of me, he would have said not to bother him again, not that he didn't mind if I called again.

In February 1991 I spoke to him on the telephone while I was at a briefing about the Roswell case at the Center for UFO Studies. During that conversation, Easley provided the details of the case that he thought he could. For example, he told me that Mac Brazel, the New Mexican rancher who found the metallic debris, had been held at the guest house on the base. Mac Brazel had told friends and family that he had been in jail, put there by the military. Easley's statement seemed to corroborate that story, though being held in the guest house is not the same as being in jail. However, if you're not allowed to leave, if the door is locked, and there are armed MPs standing around to prevent your escape, it's not much different than being in jail.

The question that springs to mind, of course, is why Mac Brazel would be held by military authorities if there wasn't some truth to the story? And, as I say, Easley's statement did corroborate part of the tale and that was important.

But the most important aspect of that conversation with Easley was the end of it. Here was a man who clearly knew something about the details of the Roswell case. He had been sworn to secrecy according to what he had said himself. He didn't want to talk about it and his answers were often short and sometimes cryptic. For example, I asked him if he thought we were following the right path. He asked what I meant by that and I said that we believed the craft found had been extraterrestrial.

He said, "Let me put it this way. That's not the wrong path."

Let's look at that again. Here is a man who retired from the military as a full colonel. In 1947 he was a major and in charge of the military police at the Roswell Army Air Field. He went from Roswell to a career in the Air Force. He certainly wasn't the type of individual to invent such a tale. In fact, had I not spoken to him a number of times, his role in the Roswell events would never have been known. He didn't come forward, I searched for him. His testimony about the craft being extraterrestrial is extremely important because I heard him say it.

But there is additional corroborative testimony for Easley. Joe Stefula, a researcher living in New Jersey tracked down another of the officers who had been assigned to the MP company at Roswell in July 1947. The man told Stefula that Major Easley had told him to go out to the crash site. He said, "The military police had guards there."

Stefula also learned from the former military officer that he had been told he was not to talk about what he had seen. According to Stefula, Easley reminded the officer that they were not to discuss anything about the crash incident. He remained quiet, not even telling his wife about it, until Stefula called him.

So Easley's testimony, especially that I had received in February 1991, is extremely important to understanding the nature of the Roswell case. Had the object found been of mundane configuration, had it merely been an aircraft of some new design, or even a weather balloon that had been launched as part of a top secret project, Easley would have known. He wouldn't have been sworn to secrecy, and he certainly wouldn't have told me that it was something extraterrestrial in origin.

The testimony of those who were there, at Roswell, in 1947 is something I find important. We can look at the problems that develop because of those trying to exploit the case. We examined some of those problems in the last chapter. But when we get down to it, the testimony of Edwin Easley is extremely important in understanding the Roswell events. Colonel McCoy might have wished that one would crash, but according to Colonel Easley, one did.

There is something more to add to this discussion. In reviewing the material including the yearbook created for the 509th Bomb Group in 1947, I could see who the important officers were. Colonel William Blanchard, as the commanding officer was, of course, very important, as were both his deputy commander and his executive officer. The main staff officers were also very important and those included Major (later Colonel) Patrick Saunders. I first spoke to him on June 14, 1989, learning that his health was not as good as it could have been. He had already had a number of heart attacks.

Almost the first comment he made was that he knew nothing about the little green bodies and said that the whole thing was a big joke. He did confirm that he had been the 509th adjutant for only a few weeks when the events of July 1947 transpired.

I asked him if he could remember any of the rumors and which of those might have some truth to them. He told me, simply, "I can't specify anything." Saunders, it seemed, was not a witness to the story.

Patrick Saunders died in November 1995, after a fall that put him into the hospital. He had been a career officer, had flown a number of combat missions, and had been decorated with a number of medals including the Legion of Merit and the Distinguished Flying Cross. Of course, he had he been the adjutant at Roswell in 1947 and had a flying saucer crashed, he would have known about it.

And, apparently he did.

Of course, he told me almost nothing during our telephone conversation. But later, when both *UFO Crash at Roswell* and *The Truth about the UFO Crash at Roswell* were published, he bought copies. In fact, he bought lots of copies, because, according to what he wrote on the first page of *The Truth about the UFO Crash at Roswell*, that was the truth.

The quotation, in his own handwriting, on the first page of that book is, "Here's the truth and I still haven't told anybody anything!"

This is Saunder's gift to us from the grave. He obeyed his orders in life, keeping the faith by not revealing what he knew. But what he left us was a clue.

In fact, in the months before he died, he confided in a number of close and lifelong friends. He told one that suddenly, they were confronted with a capability greater than ours. They, meaning the creatures in the flying saucers, had control of the sky. The Air Force was powerless against them. And we, as a country, had just seen the power of control of the sky. It was one of the factors that defeated the enemies in the Second World War.

Saunders went on, telling people that we had no idea about what their, the pilots of the craft, intentions might be. Their technology was more advanced than ours. Since we didn't know if they were a threat, the governmentwas reluctant to release anything about them. Losing the control made them all look bad.

What's important here is that Saunders did not share this information with UFO researchers or outsiders. He kept it to himself, telling close friends and family. It can't be said that he was seeking fame or fortune by creating a tale to put himself in the limelight. He told only his closest friends and family. And, I do have a copy of his handwritten note about the book containing the truth.

So, when we look at the Roswell case, it isn't as black and white as the skeptics would have us believe. The statements made by Twining and McCoy, while persuasive, are not the last word. I would be willing to accept them as the last word, if it hadn't been for the conversations that I held with Edwin Easley and Patrick Saunders and many others. I would accept them if I hadn't spoken to others who were on the impact site where the alien ship crashed. I have interviewed a number of people who told me they were there and related what they had seen. Sure, the testimony of some of them is suspect. The testimony of others has been rejected for, what I believe to be, good reason.

But there is that small core of solid testimony from individuals who were telling me about the alien ship with no expectation of any sort of reward.

If it wasn't for those conversations that I had held with those people, if it wasn't for the testimony from a number of sources, I could easily accept that there was no crash of an alien ship at Roswell. When I look at the statements made by high-ranking military officers who should have known but who say the event didn't happen, I have to wonder what was going on. Is there something else that would give us the proper answer? Is there some clue that we have missed?

But it all comes back to Easley's suggestion that the craft was extraterrestrial.

And it all comes back to Patrick Saunder's handwritten statement in *The Truth about the UFO Crash at Roswell* that says, "Here's the truth. . . ." If not for that, I think I could forget about Roswell

14 Conclusions

1996

Having researched this volume carefully, there are a few conclusions that can be drawn. These are the results of the work that I have done in the last six years as I have worked to uncover what happened near Roswell in 1947, and as I explored some of the other UFO cases that have reached the UFO spotlight. They came about as I assembled the information for this report. There are no earth-shattering revelations here, but there are a few truths that must be reinforced.

First, it doesn't seem as if the Earth has been visited by alien creatures frequently. Please note the word, "frequently." Carl Sagan, in one of his many writings, suggested we could expect one visit every ten thousand years. I don't think it is that infrequent, but I wouldn't be surprised to learn that the number of actual sightings is less than one percent of those reported. Even with that, there are still dozens of good sightings that have been made over the last fifty years.

And, I believe that once our civilization was found, the frequency of the visitation would go up. Prior to Columbus voyaging to the New World, the number of visits by Europeans was extremely rare. The Vikings, maybe, and an occasional sailor who survived shipwrecks and Atlantic weather. But once Columbus made it and returned to Europe, the number of visits grew steadily until there were thousands of them. Now, hundreds of thousands cross the Atlantic each year.

So the evidence for alien visitation is rare, but it is out there. Some of the cases we have just examined in this report lead to that conclusion. Even with all the negatives that have come out about the Roswell case in the last twelve months, the evidence still suggests that an alien spacecraft crashed there. And even with all the hoaxes that have been perpetrated on us in the last fifty years, there is still a solid core of good evidence and solid research.

The second important point to be made is that the quality of the investigations by the UFO community has improved immeasurably. In the 1960s and 1970s, the investigators were amateurs who believed in UFOs and stopped short of asking all the questions. They believed what they were being told and didn't bother with corroboration. Today, the majority of the investigations are being conducted by amateurs who believe in UFOs, but they ask all the questions they can think of. They don't stop short, but continue to search for corroboration. This is borne out by the research conducted by Jerry Black, Rex and Carol Salisberry, Dr. Jack Kasher, Tom Carey, V. G. Golubic, Kent Jeffrey, Chris Styles, Doug Ledger, and a hundred others that probably should be named here.

More importantly, when the data break against them, they don't reject the data, but lay it out for all to see. Many of these people I named would have preferred to underscore the reality of the UFO phenomenon rather than to expose hoaxes when a case seemed to be solid. The Salisberrys, for example, believed that Ed Walters was seeing and photographing a real flying saucer. Their research proved otherwise and it is to their credit that they learned the truth and published it.

Third, we have seen an improvement in the technical expertise used in our research. We have learned that we can't know everything and that experts are important in understanding the technical aspects of evidence. In the past, when experts offered their opinions, we, inside the UFO community, would reject those opinions if they didn't support our points of view. Today, we know that many experts are disinterested in the cases and more concerned with maintaining the standards of their professions and producing solid research. The discussion of typefaces on the MJ-12 documents is a case in point. My discussions with one questioned document examiner revealed his passion for his work and his disinterest in the content of the documents. He was more interested in solid research than in supporting a single point of view.

Fourth, we are no longer fooled by the misdirection offered as alternatives to explanations. We have learned how to read between the lines of those who have an agenda. One of the best examples of this is the quote from Dr. Wescott in the MJ-12 chapter, in which it seems that he is endorsing the idea that the document is authentic. But by reading his quote carefully, we understand that all he is saying that he found nothing, from his point of view as a linguist, that would prove that Rear Admiral Hillenkoetter didn't author the Eisenhower Briefing. He is not suggesting that the briefing is authentic, only that there is nothing in it to exclude Hillenkoetter as the author.

These sorts of expert opinions have been used in the past to bolster a point of view. We now understand what they mean. And we are learning more about them.

And finally, we are learning that there are times when we must cut loose our favorite cases or witnesses. Jim Ragsdale, for example, a witness I spoke to first in November 1992, is another case in point. He told, as I have pointed out, a nice little tale. It was fun to tell audiences that the Roswell case began like every science fiction movie about alien invasions ever made. A couple in the woods, where they weren't supposed to be, seeing the craft slam into the ground. It always brought a laugh. But now, I begin in a newer and drier fashion. I have cut the Jim Ragsdale case loose because there are too many contradictions in the various stories he told to the various researchers at various times.

Why? Well, the personal agendas, as mentioned earlier, have gotten in the way of the truth. A quest for minor fame and promotion of one of the Roswell museums has put the truth in the backseat. I think Max Littell's line about the case, as reported by William Barret, demonstrates this better than anything else. "As far as we were concerned, this story of Ragsdale was valid. What I am I trying to prove he's lying for? We're not going to do that."

Of course, they should have tried to verify the report, but they couldn't be bothered with it. Instead, they, or rather Littell, produced a little book about Ragsdale and a videotape that featured

Ragsdale's daughter, and they continue to promote the tale, all for sale at a nice price. The truth seemed never to hit them.

But, they have managed to destroy the Ragsdale story. Although the first version was probably closer to the truth, under the influences, that is, of the money offered, he radically altered what he was saying. Now, the question to be asked is which version is accurate and how do we know? The only intelligent thing to do is to eliminate the tale, regardless of what we can prove about Ragsdale.

So I have cut Ragsdale loose. I hate to lose a first-hand witness to the craft and the bodies, and who did, originally, corroborate the crash site north of town. But there is really no choice. Rather than provide fodder for the skeptics and the debunkers, I'll rely on other, less contradictory testimony.

UFO investigations in the 1990s are now made up of intelligent people doing the best they can using their own resources and expertise. But we have learned what we're doing and the quality is improving all the time. The debunkers still misrepresent the facts, as do some of those in our own ranks, but we're thinning them out. We're getting rid of them, eliminating the hoaxes and the tricks, and the weak cases. What we're left with, as I have reported in this work, is a solid core of good cases showing that UFOs are real, extraterrestrial, and here.

Bibliography

Air Defense Command Briefing, Jan 1953. Project Blue Book Files.

ANDERSON, Ted. Alleged diary for July 1947.

ASIMOV, Issac. *Is Anyone There?* New York: Ace Books, 1967.

BARKER, Gray. "America's Captured Flying Saucers—The Cover-up of the Century." *UFO Report* (May 1977).

———. "Archives Reveal More Crashed Saucers." *Gray Barker's Newsletter* 14 (March 1982).

———. "Von Poppen Update." *Gray Barker's Newsletter* (December 1982): 8.

BARNETT, Ruth. Personal diary, 1947.

BECKLEY, Timothy Green. *MJ-12 and the Riddle of Hangar 18.* New Brunswick, NJ: Inner Light, 1989.

BERLITZ, Charles, and MOORE, William L. *The Roswell Incident.* New York: Berkley, 1988.

BINDER, Otto. *What We Really Know About Flying Saucers.* Greenwich, Conn.: Fawcett Gold Medal, 1967.

———. *Flying Saucers Are Watching Us.* New York: Tower, 1968.

———. "The Secret Warehouse of UFO Proof." *UFO Report.*

BLOECHER, Ted. *Report on the UFO Wave of 1947.* Washington, D.C.: The author, 1967.

BLUM, Howard. *Out There: The Government's Secret Quest for Extraterrestials.* New York: Simon and Schuster, 1991.

BLUM, Ralph, with BLUM, Judy. *Beyond Earth: Man's Contact with UFOs.* New York: Bantam Books, 1974.

BONTEMPTO, Pat. "Incident at Heligoland." *UFO Universe* (Spring 1989): 18–22.

BOWEN, Charles (ed). *The Humanoids.* Chicago: Henry Regency, 1969.

Briefing Document: Operation Majestic 12, November 18, 1952.

BROWN, Eunice H. *White Sands History.* White Sands, N.M.: Public Affairs Office, 1959.

BRYAN, C. D. B. *Alien Abduction, UFOs, and The Conference at M.I.T.* New York: Alfred A. Knoff, 1995.

BUSKIRK, Winfred. *The Western Apache: Living in the Land Before 1950.* Norman, University of Oklahoma, 1986.

CANADEO, Anne. *UFO's The Fact or Fiction Files.* New York: Walker 1990.

CANNON, Martin. "The Amazing Story of John Lear." *UFO Universe* (March 1990): 8.

CAREY, Thomas J. "The Search for the Archaeologists." *International UFO Reporter* (November/December 1991): 4–9, 21.

CARPENTER, John S. "Gerald Anderson: Truth vs. Fiction." *MUFON Journal,* No. 281 (September 1991): 3–7, 12.

———. "Gerald Anderson: Disturbing Revelations." *MUFON Journal,* No. 299 (March 1993): 6–9.

CAMERON, Grant, and CRAIN, T. Scott, Jr. *UFOs, MJ-12 and the Government.* Seguin, TX: MUFON, 1991.

CATOE, Lynn E. *UFOs and Related Subjects: An Annotated Bibliography.* Washington, D.C.: Government Printing Office, 1969.

CHAVARRIA, Hector. "*El Caso Puebla.*" OVNI: 10–14.

CITIZENS AGAINST UFO SECRECY. "MJ-12: Myth or Reality?" *Just Cause* (December 1985).

———. "Confirmation of MJ-12?" *Just Cause* (June 1987).

———. "The MJ-12 Fiasco." *Just Cause* (September 1987).

———. "More On MJ-12." *Just Cause* (March 1989).

———. "MJ-12 Update." *Just Cause* (June 1989).

———. "Conversation with Dr. Sarbacher." *Just Cause* (September 1985).

CLARK, Jerome. "The Great Crashed Saucer Debate." *UFO Report* (October 1980): 16–19, 74, 76.

———. "Crashed Saucers—Another View." *Saga's UFO Annual 1981* (1981).

———. *UFO's in the 1980s.* Detroit: Apogee, 1990.

———. "Crash Landings." *Omni* (December 1990): 92–91.

———. "UFO Reporters. (MJ-12)." *Fate* (December 1990). Committee on Science and Astronautics, report, 1961.

COHEN, Daniel. *Encyclopedia of the Strange.* New York: Avon, 1987.

———. *UFOs—The Third Wave.* New York: Evans, 1988.

COOPER, Vicki. "Crashed Saucer Stories." *UFO,* 6, No. 1 (1991): 15.

———. "The Roswell Case Revived: Was It An Alien Saucer." *UFO* (January/February 1991): 25–29.

CORRALES, Scott. "How Many Goats Can a Goatsucker Suck?" *Forteantimes* (August 1996): 34–38.

CRARY, Dr. Albert. Personal diary, June–July 1947.

CREIGHTON, Gordon. "Close Encounters of an Unthinkable and Inadmissible Kind." *Flying Saucer Review* (July/August 1979).

———. "Further Evidence of 'Retrievals," *Flying Saucer Review* (Jan 1980).

———. "Continuing Evidence of Retrievals of the Third Kind." *Flying Saucer Review* (January/February 1982).

———. "Top U.S. Scientist Admits Crashed UFOs." *Flying Saucer Review* (October 1985).

DAVIDSON, Leon, ed. *Flying Saucers: An Analysis of Air Force Project Blue Book Special Report No. 14.* Clarksburg, Va.: Saucerian Press, 1971.

DAVIES, John K. *Cosmic Impact.* New York: St. Martin's, 1986.

DAVIS, Richard. "Results of a Search for Records Concerning the 1947 Crash Near Roswell, New Mexico." Washington, D.C.: GAO, 1995.

DENNETT, Preston. "Project Redlight: Are We Flying The Saucers Too?" *UFO Universe* (May 1990): 39.

DOBBS, D. L. "Crashed Saucers—The Mystery Continues." *UFO Report* (September 1979).

"DoD News Releases And Fact Sheets." 1952–1968.

EBERHART, George. *The Roswell Report: A Historical Perspective.* Chicago: CUFOS, 1991.

ECKER, Don. "MJ-12 'Suspected Forgery,' Air Force Says." *UFO,* 8, No. 3 (1993): 5.

EDITORS OF LOOK. "Flying Saucers." *Look* (1966).

EDWARDS, Frank. *Flying Saucers—Here and Now!* New York: Bantam, 1968.

———. *Flying Saucers—Serious Business.* New York: Bantam, 1966.

———. *Strange World.* New York: Bantam, 1964.

Eighth Air Force Staff Directory. Texas, June 1947.

ENDRES, Terry, and PACKARD, Pat. "The Pflock Report in Perspective." *UFO Update Newsletter,* Vol.1: No.5 (Fall 1994). 1–6.

ESTES, Russ (producer). "Quality of the Messenger." *Crystal Sky Productions,* 1993.

Fact Sheet. "Office of Naval Research 1952 Greenland Cosmic Ray Scientific Expedition." October 16, 1952.

FAWCETT, Lawrence, and GREENWOOD, Barry J. *Clear Intent: The Government Cover-up of the UFO Experience.* Englewood Cliffs, NJ: Prentice-Hall, 1984.

FERRELL, Keith. "The Alien." *Penthouse* (September 1996): 150–153.

Final Report. "Project Twinkle." Project Blue Book Files, Nov. 1951.

Flint (Michigan) City Directories 1945–1950.

"Flying Saucers Again." *Newsweek,* April 17, 1950, p. 29.

"Flying Saucers Are Real." *Flying Saucer Review* (January/February 1956): 2–5.

FOSTER, Tad. Unpublished articles for Condon Committee Casebook. 1969.

FOWLER, Raymond E. *Casebook of a UFO Investigator.* Englewood Cliffs, NJ: Prentice-Hall, 1981.

———. "What about Crashed UFOs?" *Official UFO* (April 1976): 55–57.

———. *The Watchers.* New York: Bantam Books 1990.

FRIEDMAN, Stanton. *Top Secret/Majic.* New York: Marlowe & Company, 1996.

FULLER, John G. *The Interrupted Journey.* New York: Dial, 1966.

———. *Incident at Exeter.* New York: G.P. Putnam's Sons, 1966.

———. *Aliens in the Sky.* New York: Berkley Books, 1969.

GILLMOR, Daniel S., ed. *Scientific Study of Unidentified Flying Objects.* New York: Bantam Books, 1969.

GOOD, Timothy. *Above Top Secret.* New York: Morrow, 1988.

———. *The UFO Report.* New York: Avon Books, 1989.

———. *Alien Contact.* New York: Morrow, 1993.

"Guidance for Dealing with Space Objects Which Have Returned to Earth," Department of State Airgram, July 26, 1973.

HALL, Richard. "Crashed Discs—Maybe." *International UFO Reporter,* 10, No. 4 (July/August 1985).

———. *Uninvited Guests.* Santa Fe, N.M.: Aurora Press, 1988.

———. "MJ-12: Still Holding Its Own Through Thickets of Debate."

———. ed. *The UFO Evidence.* Washington, D.C.: NICAP, 1964. *UFO* (January/February 1991) 30–32.

HANRAHAN, James Stephen. *History of Research in Space Biology and Biodynamics at the Air Force Missile Development Center 1946–1958.* Alamogordo, N.M.: Office of Information Services, 1959.

———. *Contributions of Balloon Operations to Research and Development at the Air Force Missile Development Center 1947–1958.* Alamogordo, N.M.: Office of Information Services, 1959.

HAUGLAND, Vern. "AF Denies Recovering Portions of 'Saucers.'" *Albuquerque New Mexican,* March 23, 1954.

HAZARD, Catherine. "Did the Air Force Hush Up a Flying Saucer Crash?" *Woman's World* (February 27, 1990): 10.

"History of the Eighth Air Force, Fort Worth, Texas" (Microfilm). Air Force Archives, Maxwell Air Force Base, Ala.

"History of the 509th Bomb Group, Roswell, New Mexico" (Microfilm). Air Force Archives, Maxwell Air Force Base, Ala.

HUNEEUS, J. Antonio. "Roswell UFO Crash Update." *UFO Universe* (Winter 1991): 8–13, 52, 57.

———. "A Full Report on the 1978 UFO Crash in Bolivia." *UFO Universe* (Winter 1993).

HURT, Wesley R., and MCKNIGHT, Daniel. "Archaeology of the San Augustine Plains: A Preliminary Report." *American Antiquity* (January 1949): 172–194.

HYNEK, J. Allen. *The UFO Experience: A Scientific Inquiry.* Chicago: Henry Regency, 1975.

HYNEK, J. Allen, and VALLEE, Jacques. *The Edge of Reality.* Chicago: Henry Regency, 1972.

"Internation Reports: Tale of Captured UFO." *UFO,* 8, No. 3 (1993): 10–11.

IRVING, Robert. "SFX, Lies and Videotape." *Fortean Times* (August 1996): 40–41.

JACOBS, David M. *The UFO Controversy in America.* New York: Signet, 1975.

JOHNSON, J. Bond. "'Disk-overy' Near Roswell Identified As Weather Balloon by FWAAF Officer." *Fort Worth Star-Telegram,* July 9, 1947.

JONES, William E., and MINSHALL, Rebecca D. "Aztec, New Mexico—A Crash Story Reexamined." *International UFO Reporter,* 16, No. 5 (September/October 1991): 11.

JUNG, Carl G. *Flying Saucers: A Modern Myth of Things Seen in the Sky.* New York: Harcourt, Brace, 1959.

KEEL, John. "Now It's No Secret: The Japanese 'Fugo Balloon.'" *UFO* (January/February 1991): 33–35.

———. *UFOs: Operation Trojan Horse.* New York: G.P. Putnam's Sons, 1970.

———. *Strange Creatures from Space and Time.* New York: Fawcett, 1970.

KEYHOE, Donald E. *Aliens From Space.* New York: Signet, 1974.

KLASS, Philip J. *UFOs Explained.* New York: Random House, 1974.

———. "Crash of the Crashed Saucer Claim," *Skeptical Enquirer,* 10, No. 3 (Spring 1986).

———. *The Public Deceived.* Buffalo, NY: Prometheus Books, 1983.

———. "Roswell UFO: Coverups and Credulity." *Skeptical Enquirer,* 16 No. 1 (Fall 1991).

LAPAZ, Lincoln, and ROSENFELD, Albert. "Japan's Balloon Invasion of America." *Collier's,* January 17, 1953, p. 9.

Library of Congress Legislative Reference Service. "Facts about UFOs." May 1966.

LORE, Gordon, and DENEAULT, Harold H. *Mysteries of the Skies: UFOs in Perspective.* Englewood Cliffs, N.J.: Prentice-Hall, 1968.

LORENZEN, Coral and Jim. *Flying Saucers: The Startling Evidence of the Invasion from Outer Space.* New York: Signet, 1966.

———. *Flying Saucer Occupants.* New York: Signet, 1967.

———. *Encounters with UFO Occupants.* New York: Berkley Medallion Books, 1976.

———. *Abducted!* New York: Berkley Medallion Books, 1977.

MACCABEE, Bruce. "Hiding the Hardware." *International UFO Reporter* (September/October 1991): 4.

———. "What the Admiral Knew." *International UFO Reporter* (November/ December 1986).

MACK, John E. *Abduction.* New York: Charles Scribner's Sons, 1994.

MANTLE, Philip. "The Roswell Film Footage." *MUFON Symposium Proceedings* (July 1996): 87–109.

MCCLELLAN, Mike. "The Flying Saucer Crash of 1948 is a Hoax." *Offical UFO* (October 1975): 36–37, 60, 62–64.

"McClellan Sub-Committee Hearings." March 1958.

"McCormack Sub-Committee Briefing." August 1958.

MCDONALD, Bill. "Comparing Descriptions, An Illustrated Roswell." *UFO,* 8, No. 3 (1993): 31–36.

MCDONOUGH, Thomas R. *The Search for Extraterrestrial Intelligence.* New York: Wiley & Sons, 1987.

MENZEL, Donald H., and BOYD, Lyle G. *The World of Flying Saucers.* Garden City, NY: Doubleday, 1963.

MENZEL, Donald H., and TAVES, Ernest H. *The UFO Enigma.* Garden City, New York: Doubleday, 1977.

MICHEL, Aime. *The Truth about Flying Saucers.* New York: Pyramid 1967.

MOORE, Charles B. "The New York University Balloon Flights During Early June, 1947." The author, 1995.

MOORE, William L., and SHANDERA, Jaime H. *The MJ-12 Documents: An Analytical Report.* Burbank, Calif.: Fair Witness Project, 1991.

National Security Agency. Presidential Documents. Washington, D.C.: Executive Order 12356, 1982.

NEILSON, James. "'Secret U.S./UFO Structure." *UFO,* 4, No. 1, (1989): 4–6.

"New explanation for 1908 Siberian blast." *Cedar Rapids Gazette,* January 25, 1993.

NICAP. *The UFO Evidence.* Washington, D.C.: NICAP, 1964.

NICKELL, Joe. "The Hangar 18 Tales." *Common Ground* (June 1984).

NICKELL, Joe, and FISCHER, John F. "The Crashed-Saucer Forgeries." *International UFO Reporter,* 15 No. 2 (March/April 1990): 4–12.

———. "Further Deception: Moore and Shandera." Unpublished paper, The authors (1993).

OBERG, James. "UFO Update: UFO Buffs May Be Unwitting Pawns in an Elaborate Government Charade." *Omni,* 15, No. 11 (September 1993): 75.

O'BRIEN, Mike. "New Witness to San Agustin Crash." *MUFON Journal,* No. 275 (March 1991): 3–9.

PACKARD, Pat and ENDRES, Terry. "Riding the Roswell-go-round." *A.S.K. UFO Report,* Vol. 2, No. 1, pp. 1–8.

PALMER, Raymond and ARNOLD, Kenneth. *The Coming of the Saucers.* Amherst, 1952.

PEEBLES, Curtis. *The Moby Dick Project.* Washington, D.C.: Smithsonian Institution Press, 1991.

———. *Watch the Skies!* New York: Berkley Books, 1995.

PFLOCK, Karl. *Roswell in Perspective.* Mt. Rainier, MD: FUFOR, 1994.

———. "In Defense of Roswell Reality." *MUFON Report* (Feb. 1995): 5–7.

———. "Roswell, A Cautionary Tale: Facts and Fantasies, Lessons and Legacies." In Walter H. Andrus, Jr., ed. *MUFON 1995 International UFO Symposium Proceedings.* Seguin, TX: MUFON, 1990: 154–68.

———. "Roswell, The Air Force, and Us." *International UFO Reporter* (November/December 1994): 3–5, 24.

Press Conference—General Samford, Project Blue Book Files, 1952.

"Project Blue Book" (microfilm). National Archives, Washington, D.C.

PRYTZ, John M. "UFO Crashes." *Flying Saucers* (October 1969): 24–25.

RAAF Base Phone Book. Roswell, N.M., August 1947.

RAAF Yearbook. Roswell, N. M., 1947.

RANDLE, Kevin D. *The October Scenario.* Iowa City, Iowa: Middle Coast Publishing, 1988.

———. *The UFO Casebook.* New York: Warner, 1989.

———. *A History of UFO Crashes.* New York: Avon, 1995

RANDLE, Kevin D., and CORNETT, Robert Charles. "Project Blue Book Cover-up: Pentagon Suppressed UFO Data." *UFO Report,* 2 No. 5 (Fall 1975).

RANDLE, Kevin D. and SCHMITT, Donald R. *UFO Crash at Roswell.* New York: Avon, 1991.

RANDLES, Jenny. *The UFO Conspiracy.* New York: Javelin, 1987.

"Report of Air Force Research Regarding the 'Roswell Incident.'" July 1994.

"Rocket and Missile Firings." White Sands Proving Grounds, Jan–Jul 1947.

RODEGHIER, Mark. "Roswell, 1989." *International UFO Reporter* (September/October 1989): 4.

RODEGHIER, Mark, and CHESNEY, Mark. "The Air Force Report on Roswell: An Absence of Evidence." *International UFO Reporter* (September/October 1994).

RUPPELT, Edward J. *The Report on Unidentified Flying Objects.* New York: Ace, 1956.

RUSSELL, Eric. "Phantom Balloons Over North America." *Modern Aviation* (February 1953).

SAGAN, Carl, and PAGE, Thornton, eds. *UFO's: Scientific Debate.* New York: Norton, 1974.

SANDRESON, Ivan T. "Meteorite-like Object Made a Turn in Cleveland, O. Area." *Omaha World-Herald* (December 15, 1965).

———. "Something Landed in Pennsylvania." *Fate* (March 1966).

———. *Uninvited Visitors.* New York: Cowles, 1967.

———. *Invisible Residents.* New York: World Publishing, 1970.

SAUNDERS, David, and HARKINS, R. Roger. *UFOs? Yes!* New York: New American Library, 1968.

SCHAFFNER, Ron. "Roswell: A Federal Case?" *UFO Brigantia* (Summer 1989).

SCHMITT, Donald R. "New Revelations from Roswell." In Walter H. Andrus, Jr., ed. *MUFON 1990 International UFO Symposium Proceedings.* Seguin, TX: MUFON, 1990: 154–68.

SCHMITT, Donald R., and RANDLE, Kevin D. "Second Thoughts on the Barney Barnett Story." *International UFO Reporter* (May/June 1992): 4–5, 22.

SCULLY, Frank. "Scully's Scrapbook." *Variety* (October 12, 1949): 61.

———. *Behind the Flying Saucers.* New York: Henry Holt, 1950.

SHANDERA, Jaime. "New Revelation about the Roswell Wreckage: A General Speaks Up." *MUFON Journal* (January 1991): 4–8.

SHEAFFER, Robert. *The UFO Verdict.* Buffalo, NY: Prometheus, 1981.

SLATE, B. Ann. "The Case of the Crippled Flying Saucer." *Saga* (April 1972): 22–25, 64, 66–68, 71, 72.

SMITH, Scott. "Q & A: Len Stringfield." *UFO,* 6, No. 1 (1991): 20–24.

"The Space Men at Wright-Patterson." *UFO Update.*

Special Report No. 14 (Project Blue Book), 1955.

SPENCER, John. *The UFO Encyclopedia.* New York: Avon, 1993.

SPENCER, John, and EVANS, Hilary. *Phenomenon.* New York: Avon, 1988.

Status Reports. "Grudge—Blue Book, Nos. 1–12."

STEIGER, Brad. *Strangers from the Skies.* New York: Award, 1966.

———. *Project Blue Book.* New York: Ballantine, 1976.

STEIGER, Brad, and STEIGER, Sherry Hanson. *The Rainbow Conspiracy.* New York: Pinnacle, 1994.

STEINMAN, William S., and STEVENS, Wendelle C. *UFO Crash at Aztec.* Boulder, Colo.: The author, 1986.

STONE, Clifford E. *UFO's: Let the Evidence Speak for Itself.* Calif.: The author, 1991.

———. "The U.S. Air Force's Real, Official Investigation of UFO's." Private report: The author, 1993.

STORY, Ronald D. *The Encyclopedia of UFOs.* Garden City, New York: Doubleday, 1980.

STRINGFIELD, Leonard H. *Situation Red: The UFO Siege!* Garden City, New York: Doubleday, 1977.

———. *UFO Crash/Retrieval Syndrome: Status Report II.* Seguin, TX: MUFON, 1980.

———. *UFO Crash/Retrieval: Amassing the Evidence: Status Report III,* Cincinnati, Ohio: The author, 1982.

———. *UFO Crash/Retrievals: The Inner Sanctum Status Report VI.* Cincinnati, Ohio: The author, 1991.

———. "Roswell & the X-15: UFO Basics." *MUFON UFO Journal,* No. 259 (November 1989): 3–7.

STURROCK, P. A. "UFOs—A Scientific Debate," *Science,* 180 (1973): 593.

SUTHERLY, Curt. *Strange Encounters.* St. Paul, MN: Llewellyn Publications, 1996.

STYLES, Chris. "Shag Harbour in Perspective." *MUFON Symposium Proceedings* (July 1996): 26–51.

SWORDS, Michael D., ed. *Journal of UFO Studies, New Series,* Vol. 4. Chicago: CUFOS, 1993.

Tech Bulletin. "Army Ordnance Department Guided Missile Program." Jan 1948.

Technical Report. "Unidentified Aerial Objects, Project SIGN." Feb. 1949.

Technical Report. "Unidentified Flying Objects, Project GRUDGE." August 1949.

TODD, Robert G. "MJ-12 Rebuttal." *MUFON Journal* (January 1990): 17.

TODD, Robert G., RODEGHIER, Mark, GREENWOOD, Barry, and MACCABEE, Bruce. "A Forum on MJ-12." *International UFO Reporter* (May/June 1990): 15.

U.S. Congress, House Committee on Armed Forces. *Unidentified Flying Objects.* Hearings, 89th Congress, 2nd Session, April 5, 1966. Washington, D.C.: U.S. Government Printing Office, 1968.

U.S. Congress Committee on Science and Astronautics. *Symposium on Unidentified Flying Objects.* Hearings, July 29, 1968. Washington, D.C.: U.S. Government Printing Office, 1968.

VALLEE, Jacques. *Anatomy of a Phenomenon.* New York: Ace, 1966.

———. *Challenge to Science.* New York: Ace, 1966.

———. *Dimensions.* New York: Ballantine, 1989.

———. *Revelations.* New York: Ballantine, 1991.

"Visitors From Venus," *Time* (January 9, 1950): 49.

WALTERS, Ed, and WALTERS, Frances. *The Gulf Breeze Sightings.* New York: Avon Books, 1991.

———. *UFO Abductions in Gulf Breeze.* New York: Avon Books, 1994.

WALTON, Travis. *Fire in the Sky.* New York: Marlowe & Company, 1996.

War Department. *Meteorological Balloons* (Army Technical Manual). Washington, D.C.: Government Printing Office, 1944.

WEBBER, Bert. *Retaliation: Japanese Attacks and Allied Countermeasures on the Pacific Coast in World War II.* Corvallis: Oregon State University Press, 1975.

WHITING, Fred. *The Roswell Events.* Mt. Rainier, MD: FUFOR, 1993.

WILCOX, Inez. Personal writings, 1947–1952.

WILKINS, Harold T. *Flying Saucers on the Attack.* New York: Citadel, 1954.

———. *Flying Saucers Uncensored.* New York: Pyramid, 1967.

WISE, David, and ROSS, Thomas B. *The Invisible Government.* New York: 1964.

ZEIDMAN, Jennie. "I Remember Blue Book." *International UFO Reporter* (March/April 1991): 7.

Index